Principles of Social Research

Understanding Public Health series

Series editors: Nicki Thorogood and Rosalind Plowman, London School of Hygiene & Tropical Medicine (previous edition edited by Nick Black and Rosalind Raine)

Throughout the world, there is growing recognition of the importance of public health to sustainable, safe and healthy societies. The achievements of public health in nineteenth-century Europe were for much of the twentieth century overshadowed by advances in personal care, in particular in hospital care. Now, with the dawning of a new century, there is increasing understanding of the inevitable limits of individual health care and of the need to complement such services with effective public health strategies. Major improvements in people's health will come from controlling communicable diseases, eradicating environmental hazards, improving people's diets and enhancing the availability and quality of effective health care. To achieve this, every country needs a cadre of knowledgeable public health practitioners with social, political and organizational skills to lead and bring about changes at international, national and local levels.

This is one of a series of books that provides a foundation for those wishing to join in and contribute to the twenty-first-century regeneration of public health, helping to put the concerns and perspectives of public health at the heart of policy-making and service provision. While each book stands alone, together they provide a comprehensive account of the three main aims of public health: protecting the public from environmental hazards, improving the health of the public and ensuring high-quality health services are available to all. Some of the books focus on methods, others on key topics. They have been written by staff at the London School of Hygiene & Tropical Medicine with considerable experience of teaching public health to students from low-, middle- and high-income countries. Much of the material has been developed and tested with postgraduate students both in face-to-face teaching and through distance learning.

The books are designed for self-directed learning. Each chapter has explicit learning objectives, key terms are highlighted and the text contains many activities to enable the reader to test their own understanding of the ideas and material covered. Written in a clear and accessible style, the series will be essential reading for students taking postgraduate courses in public health and will also be of interest to public health practitioners and policy-makers.

Titles in the series

Analytical models for decision making: Colin Sanderson and Reinhold Gruen
Controlling communicable disease: Norman Noah
Conflict and health: Natasha Howard, Egbert Sondorp and Annemarie ter Veen (eds)
Economic analysis for management and policy: Stephen Jan, Lilani Kumaranayake, Jenny Roberts, Kara Hanson and Kate Archibald
Economic evaluation: Julia Fox-Rushby and John Cairns (eds)
Environmental epidemiology: Paul Wilkinson (ed.)
Environmental health policy: Megan Landon and Tony Fletcher
Financial management in health services: Reinhold Gruen and Anne Howarth
Global change and health: Kelley Lee and Jeff Collin (eds)
Health care evaluation: Sarah Smith, Don Sinclair, Rosalind Raine and Barnaby Reeves
Health promotion practice: Maggie Davies, Wendy Macdowall and Chris Bonell (eds)
Health promotion theory, second edition: Liza Cragg, Maggie Davies and Wendy Macdowall (eds)
Introduction to epidemiology, second edition: Ilona Carneiro and Natasha Howard
Introduction to health economics, second edition: Lorna Guinness and Virginia Wiseman (eds)
Issues in public health, second edition: Fiona Sim and Martin McKee (eds)
Making health policy, second edition: Kent Buse, Nicholas Mays and Gill Walt
Managing health services: Nick Goodwin, Reinhold Gruen and Valerie Iles
Medical anthropology: Robert Pool and Wenzel Geissler
Public health in history: Virginia Berridge, Martin Gorsky and Alex Mold
Sexual health: A public health perspective: Kaye Wellings, Kirstin Mitchell and Martine Collumbien
Understanding health services: Nick Black and Reinhold Gruen

Forthcoming title

Environment, health and sustainable development, Second Edition: Sari Kovats and Emma Hutchinson (eds.)

Principles of Social Research

Second edition

Edited by Mary Alison Durand
and Tracey Chantler

 Open University Press

Open University Press
McGraw-Hill Education
McGraw-Hill House
Shoppenhangers Road
Maidenhead
Berkshire
England
SL6 2QL

email: enquiries@openup.co.uk
world wide web: www.openup.co.uk

and Two Penn Plaza, New York, NY 10121-2289, USA

First published 2014

Copyright © Mary Alison Durand and Tracey Chantler, 2014

A catalogue record of this book is available from the British Library

ISBN-13: 978-0-33-526330-5 (pb)
ISBN-10: 0-33-526330-1 (pb)
eISBN: 978-0-33-526331-8

Library of Congress Cataloging-in-Publication Data
CIP data applied for

Typesetting and e-book compilations by
RefineCatch Limited, Bungay, Suffolk

Praise for this book

"Public health is basically shaped and determined by human actions. The editors and contributors to this book provide clear, authoritative guidance to those who will use social research to understand human actions and promote public health. The book is very evidently grounded in the expertise of authors both as teachers as well as researchers."

Ray Fitzpatrick, Professor of Public Health and Primary Care, University of Oxford, UK

"The book offers a comprehensive introduction to the principles and basic practice of social research in health and public health for both professionals and undergraduates new to this field. The use of published public health social research and practical tasks to be completed will enable readers new to the field to understand how to move effectively from turning a real world problem into a research questions and how to design appropriate research to address the questions."

Dr Stephen Clayton, Senior Lecturer in Public Health, University of Central Lancashire, UK

Contents

List of authors

SARAH BERNAYS is a Lecturer in the Department of Social and Environmental Health Research at the London School of Hygiene & Tropical Medicine.

JOHN BROWNE is Professor of Epidemiology and Public Health at University College Cork.

TRACEY CHANTLER is a Health Services and Systems Research Fellow in the George Institute for Global Health in the Nuffield Department of Population Health at the University of Oxford, and a distance learning tutor at the London School of Hygiene & Tropical Medicine.

MARY ALISON DURAND is a Lecturer in the Department of Health Services Research and Policy at the London School of Hygiene & Tropical Medicine.

MARTIN GORSKY is Reader in the History of Public Health in the Department of Social and Environmental Health Research at the London School of Hygiene & Tropical Medicine.

JUDITH GREEN is Professor of Sociology of Health in the Department of Health Services Research and Policy at the London School of Hygiene & Tropical Medicine.

ANDY GUISE is a Research Fellow in the Department of Social and Environmental Health Research at the London School of Hygiene & Tropical Medicine.

TIM RHODES is Professor of Public Health Sociology in the Department of Social and Environmental Health Research at the London School of Hygiene & Tropical Medicine.

SARAH SMITH is a Senior Lecturer in Psychology in the Department of Health Services Research and Policy at the London School of Hygiene & Tropical Medicine.

Acknowledgements

Open University Press and the London School of Hygiene & Tropical Medicine have made every effort to obtain permission from copyright holders to reproduce material in this book and to acknowledge these sources correctly. Any omissions brought to our attention will be remedied in future editions.

Overview of the book

Introduction

The problems facing public health are increasingly those of human behaviour. At an individual level there are problems of developing more effective models of health promotion to encourage healthier lifestyles; at the level of society there are problems of understanding the effects of social change on health, or what the barriers are to effective policy implementation. Increasingly, public health practitioners and managers are turning to social research to help understand human behaviour.

This book introduces some of the principles of social research as applied to public health. It is aimed at those with some understanding of health and health care, but little exposure to social research. It does not, therefore, aim to provide readers with all the skills that they would need to carry out a social research study; rather, it aims to develop their understanding of the key principles involved.

The contribution of social science to public health has not just been to introduce a 'tool box' of research methods such as focus groups or surveys. It has also brought a set of disciplinary perspectives that are in many ways different from those of biomedicine. This book introduces some of the social science disciplines that have turned their attention to health and health care. The main disciplinary areas drawn on here are the sociology of health and illness and medical anthropology (which have informed much qualitative research in health and health services research, particularly in high-income countries) and psychology (which has made a major contribution in particular to more quantitative approaches). The specific theoretical contributions of these disciplines are not discussed in this book; rather we focus primarily on the use of qualitative and quantitative research approaches and methods.

Why study the principles of social research?

Not everyone has to (or wants to!) carry out social research, but most people in public health will at some point have to read the findings of others and assess how useful they are for their own practice. They may also need to commission social research, or collaborate with researchers from the disciplines introduced here. Studying this book will enable readers will develop their understanding of how to assess social research by grasping such issues as the choice of appropriate design and the strengths and weaknesses of particular data collection methods. Readers will also develop their understanding of the various perspectives from which social scientists approach research, aiding their ability to contribute to multidisciplinary public health practice.

Structure of the book and changes to the second edition

This book follows the conceptual outline of the Principles of Social Research module at the London School of Hygiene & Tropical Medicine. It is informed by the materials presented in the lectures and seminars of the taught course which have been adapted for distance learning.

The key principles of social research have not altered since Judith Green and John Browne produced the first edition of this book. The changes in this edition therefore have involved varying degrees of revision of existing chapters (from minor to more substantive) and their updating with relevant examples from the literature. There are also a number of more significant changes. In line with changes to the taught course module in recent years, the 'Introduction to history in health' chapter in the first edition has been replaced with a chapter on documentary research, the focus of which is broader than using documentary sources and data for the purposes of historical research alone. The 'Introduction to applied medical anthropology' chapter has been removed from the second edition in line with a greater emphasis in the module on methods rather than disciplines: however, issues encountered in ethnographic research are covered in Sections 1 and 2. We have also included a new chapter on the principles of research ethics in practice, as ethical principles should guide the conduct of any social or health research.

As with the previous edition, there are four sections in this book, containing a total of 16 chapters. Each chapter includes:

- an overview;
- a list of learning objectives;
- a list of key terms;
- a range of activities;
- feedback on the activities;
- a summary.

The following description of the section and chapter contents will give you an idea of what you will be studying.

Section 1: Planning your social science research

In the first section we introduce the social sciences, the principles of research design and the debate about what 'science' might mean in this context. The chapters in this section aim to orientate the reader to the general problems faced in turning a topic of interest into a question that can be answered through research, and then designing a particular project that can answer it.

Section 2: Qualitative methods of data collection and analysis

This section and Section 3 are about 'methods' and are concerned with different kinds of research design and methods of collecting data. For convenience we have divided them into qualitative methods and quantitative methods, although we recognize that, in practice, this division may not be a very convincing one. The chapters in Section 2 are not an exhaustive discussion but aim to introduce the most common data collection methods used in qualitative research in health, including interviews, focus groups and participant observation. We include an introduction to qualitative analysis to aid understanding of qualitative research outputs.

Section 3: Measurement and quantitative methods

As with the preceding section, the chapters in this section are not an exhaustive discussion but aim to introduce the most common methods and data collection techniques used in quantitative research in health, including questionnaires. We have not covered statistical analysis: many public health practitioners are more familiar with the principles of quantitative analysis, and discussion of statistical methods is outside the scope of this text.

Section 4: Issues in social research

The final section focuses on a number of key issues and approaches which, while alluded to in earlier sections, were not discussed in any detail. Chapter 14 outlines some of the key ethical principles that should govern all research practice. Chapter 15 explores the rationale for, and practicalities involved in, conducting documentary research. Most social and public health research involves the use of documents (e.g. as literature reviews or to set the context). However, documents may also constitute primary research data in their own right. Finally, recognizing that much public health research uses a range of methods, often drawn from more than one discipline, Chapter 16 discusses a number of issues raised by integrating within the same project some of the methods and disciplines covered in the book.

Acknowledgements

We would like to thank, first of all, and most importantly, Judith Green and John Browne, whose comprehensive consideration of the principles of social research in the first edition of this book made revising and updating the book a much easier task than it might have been. We have appreciated their support and generosity in answering our questions and queries. Our thanks also go to Virginia Berridge and Karina Kielmann for their contributions to the first edition: these have informed the current edition. Secondly, major thanks are due to Martin Gorsky who wrote the new chapter on documentary research, to Tim Rhodes and Sarah Bernays who wrote the chapter on ethical principles, and to Andy Guise for significant input into the revision of Chapter 16. Thirdly, we very much appreciate the contribution of Sarah Smith in updating the chapters in Section 3 on measurement and quantitative methods. We thank Judith Green, Bob Erens and Ruth Lewis for their considered and helpful comments in reviewing the second edition.

SECTION 1

Planning your social science research

Second edition revised and updated by Mary Alison Durand

Introduction to social research

1

Overview

For many people trained as health professionals or managers, the terms and concepts used by social scientists are unfamiliar and difficult to apply to the 'real life' practical problems that they need to address in their working lives. The chapters in this first section introduce you to some of the language used by social scientists, and provide an opportunity to reflect on how social research methods could be used to address issues raised by public health practice. These chapters introduce the social sciences, the concept of scientific research and research design. They will explore how the methods of social scientists can be used to study health and health behaviour. The aims of the section are to provide the skills needed to identify when social research methods can contribute to our understanding of health and health care systems, to develop research questions and to identify appropriate research designs for answering them.

This chapter introduces a range of social science disciplines from which the research methods and designs discussed in this book have been drawn, and outlines how they can contribute to research in public health.

Learning objectives

After studying this chapter you will be better able to:

- identify how social science research methods can contribute to our understanding of public health and health management problems
- distinguish between qualitative and quantitative research methods

Key terms

Method: A set of strategies for asking useful questions, designing a study, collecting data and analysing data.

Methodology: The study of the principles of investigation, including the philosophical foundations of choice of methods.

Qualitative: Pertaining to the nature of phenomena: how they are classified.

Quantitative: Pertaining to the measurement of phenomena.

What is social science?

By 'social research methods' we mean methods developed within the social sciences. 'Social science' is a general term for the study of aspects of human behaviour. It includes many disciplines, including sociology, anthropology, psychology and history. The research methods that you will come across in this book are largely drawn from these disciplines.

While these disciplines have different interests, theoretical approaches, origins and favoured methods, they share a rigorous and systematic approach to research, and all have contributed to our understanding of health, health behaviour and health care. Some of the areas of health care that have interested, and currently interest, social scientists include:

- assessing local needs for health care;
- understanding the factors that influence people's decision to seek health care;
- understanding why patients do or do not adhere to treatment regimes;
- evaluating the health and quality of life of patients after treatment;
- exploring how the beliefs and behaviours of health care workers can impact on the implementation of policy;
- evaluating the impact of new public health and social policies on the population or sections of the population;
- evaluating the impact of complex public health interventions.

In this book, you will explore how social research methods can be used to address issues that are relevant to your work in the health sector. As a health professional, manager, or public health practitioner you may not need to carry out your own research. But, in making decisions about health care needs, how to prioritize them and how your practice and services can meet them, you will almost certainly have to evaluate the research findings of others and perhaps commission original research. The first aim of this book is to provide you with some skills in identifying when a 'problem' is one that can be addressed by social science research methods.

People's health status, health behaviour, and how they utilize health services (their health-seeking behaviour) are influenced by a complex range of factors, including inherited biological characteristics, lifestyle, social circumstances and economic factors. Understanding how health care systems can meet health care needs in an efficient, effective and acceptable way relies on an understanding of how these factors affect both health and an individual's use of health services. The first activity asks you to reflect on where social sciences might fit into the range of possible explanations for health and health behaviour.

✎ **Activity 1.1**

The following could be identified as possible causes for differences in rates of heart disease between different groups in the population. Which ones do you think are appropriate subjects for social scientists to study:

(a) genetic factors
(b) stress
(c) lifestyle factors (such as rates of smoking and exercise)

(d) luck

(e) economic circumstances

(f) access to health services?

Feedback

Those that are related to human behaviour are (b), (c), (e) and (f). However, social scientists are also interested in people's attitudes to, for example, luck, and in issues such as how information about genetic risk is communicated to patients. Whether or not a topic is appropriate for social science methods depends more on the kind of question asked than on the area of interest.

Research methods

Having identified that an issue is one that is relevant to the social sciences, the next task is to decide what kind of research method is appropriate. A research method is a particular strategy for answering a research question. It includes:

- The formulation of a research question. This is discussed in Chapter 3.
- The choice of an appropriate research design. This refers to the logic of how our data will be collected so that those data will allow us to answer our research question appropriately and adequately. For instance, our question may require us to use a quantitative design, such as a randomized controlled trial, or a qualitative design such as an ethnographic one. We will also need to consider the design features specific to our individual study, such as the type of people we select for inclusion in our study; the method(s) we use to recruit these people; how many people we need in the study; how people will be randomly allocated to one treatment or another (if we are conducting a randomized controlled trial); whether we contact study participants on a number of occasions or just once. Chapter 4 discusses some of the issues of research design.
- The choice of data collection methods, such as a survey or in-depth interview, along with the development of our data collection tools (e.g., a questionnaire for use in a survey, or a list of prompts to use in an in-depth interview or focus group).

Social science disciplines use a range of research methods, and some methods are associated more with particular disciplines than others. Table 1.1 lists some examples of the kinds of general questions different disciplines ask about health care, and the methods often (although not exclusively, and not always) used to collect data. There is considerable overlap in the approaches of the different social science disciplines, and in practice public health research programmes often draw on more than one discipline. In this book, our focus is more on the appropriate use of research methods to answer a specific research question than on the disciplines from which those methods have been drawn.

The choice of a method is influenced, although not dictated, by the aim of research – by what the researcher is trying to find out. However, there are other factors that influence the choice of method used, which come from the fundamental beliefs of the researcher about what knowledge is and how it can be known. In Chapter 2 you will find out more

Table 1.1 Social science disciplines and the study of health care

Discipline	Examples of research interests	Typical data collection methods used
Sociology	What impact do social factors have on health?	Face-to-face surveys
	How do health professionals understand policy change?	In-depth or semi-structured interviews
Anthropology	How does culture affect health behaviour?	Observation of 'natural' behaviour, either as participant or outsider
	How do people conceptualize 'health'?	Narratives (e.g., illness narratives)
History	How have health policies changed over time?	Analysis of historical documents
	How have people in other times understood health?	Oral history
Psychology	How do patients' attitudes affect their health behaviour?	Questionnaires (for attitudes)/analysis of 'routine' data (e.g., GP attendance) for behaviour
	How do health interventions impact on psychological outcomes such as depression?	Structured interviews, psychometric questionnaires (e.g., quality of life measures).

about different orientations towards knowledge and how they inform methods. This general study of methods is called *methodology*.

Much health research in practice uses a variety of disciplines or methods to address different aspects of the same problem, and as you work through this book it will become apparent that a multidisciplinary and/or multi-methods approach is often the most appropriate way to carry out research on many public health problems, or to investigate the impact of complex public health interventions on health behaviours. There are so many influences on health and health behaviour that, to gain a full understanding, an explanation is needed on a number of levels. In the example in Activity 1.1, the possible influences on heart disease are of course related – the amount of stress people experience may be influenced by their economic position, and their access to health services may be influenced by social factors such as income or gender. However, it is often impossible to study all these factors within the same study design. An important task in any kind of research is to identify a research question from the complex web of factors that impact on the issue of interest.

What is a research question?

In your professional role, you may be faced with a variety of practice and policy problems. Carrying out research is not always an appropriate response. The next activity is designed to prompt you to think about when it might be appropriate to consider using or conducting research. This could involve:

- thinking about whether it is possible to carry out research on the question;
- searching for research done by others that is relevant to your experience;

- carrying out your own study;
- commissioning a larger project from an experienced researcher or research team.

 Activity 1.2

Think about a problem that you currently face in your workplace, or one you have faced recently. Did you consider either carrying out or commissioning your own research to help make a decision about what to do? Jot down the main reasons why you answered 'yes' or 'no'.

Feedback

If you answered 'no', some of the reasons might be:

- the solution was already well known but difficult to implement;
- resource constraints;
- a solution was needed quickly and there was no time to wait for research results;
- there were no resources (such as skills, library facilities or personnel) to carry out research;
- it was hard to think of an appropriate study design to answer the question.

If you answered 'yes', some of the reasons might be:

- there was uncertainty about the best solution;
- there were conflicting accounts of what the solution or even 'the problem' was;
- carrying out research provided more time to develop an acceptable solution;
- the research was perceived as relatively easy to perform (e.g., it may have been possible to use data that had already been collected for other purposes).

Research is perhaps most appropriately carried out when there is uncertainty; when we recognize that we need to know more about a problem in order to solve it or when we have identified a gap in our knowledge. Before undertaking any research, it is clearly important to establish whether or not there is a relevant body of existing research literature which might help to solve one's identified problem, and avoid unnecessarily replicating research activity. Guides to undertaking literature searches, and to reviewing research literature, including conducting systematic reviews in the health and social sciences, are widely available.

In practice, however, there may be many motivations for doing research, such as the furtherance of career aims, the furtherance of a political agenda, or for an agency to 'be seen to be doing something' about an intractable problem. Social research is relevant when the 'problem' relates to aspects of human attitudes or behaviour, either of individuals or of groups in society. As the effectiveness, efficiency and acceptability of health care systems are influenced by human behaviour and attitudes at many levels, social research methods are often relevant.

Activity 1.3

In this activity you are asked to consider the problems faced by the manager of an accident and emergency department based at a busy urban hospital. First read the case scenario in the paragraph below.

Scenario

The accident and emergency department treats 70,000 new cases a year, and staff feel that the majority of these patients do not need hospitals to provide their treatment. These patients attend with minor illnesses or injuries that do not require emergency treatment and their needs could be met in local primary care facilities. However, junior doctors tend to investigate and treat patients with minor problems intensively, and the department overspent last year. The department has had some very bad publicity recently as local newspapers have reported that patients often wait up to 24 hours on trolleys before being found a bed, and there have been high-profile cases of patient dissatisfaction with treatment received. Waits for treatment are very long, contributing to an often hostile environment in the waiting room. Nurse turnover is high, and it has been difficult to recruit good staff. The management team meets tomorrow to discuss whether there is any research that could usefully address these problems.

Now think about what the areas of uncertainty are for the manager and how they relate to human behaviour. Which questions would you suggest the team addresses? Consider investigating both the need for hospital care, and patient and staff attitudes. Jot down those that you think could be addressed through research.

Feedback

Compare your notes with the possibilities outlined below.

From the manager's perspective, there are a number of questions which could be researched. Here are some of them.

On the need for hospital care:
(a) Which patients can be safely treated at the primary care level?
(b) How many of our patients are attending 'inappropriately'?
(c) When is primary care unavailable, so that patients have to go to hospital for treatment?
(d) How could the primary care level cope with the influx of new patients?

On patient attitudes and behaviour:
(e) Why do patients choose to attend the hospital for treatment?
(f) What are the sources of patient dissatisfaction with current hospital care and primary care?

On staff attitudes and behaviour:

(g) Why do junior doctors treat patients with minor problems 'intensively', rather than treating more appropriately or referring back to primary care?

(h) Why do nurses feel dissatisfied with working here?

(i) What are the barriers to nurse recruitment?

(j) What would improve staff morale?

You may have identified other questions, perhaps economic ones about how to reduce costs. Others might be about 'public relations', such as how to improve the public's perception of your hospital. Look at your list to check that your questions are about health care need and human behaviour, and that they address areas of uncertainty that could be clarified through research. Other questions raised by this scenario are also of interest to social scientists. These include examining the role of the media in presenting and contributing to the public 'image' of an institution, or investigating why patients and professionals appear to have different ideas about where to go for appropriate treatment for minor health care problems.

Quantitative or qualitative methods?

The questions listed in Activity 1.3 are diverse, and a range of methods would be needed to address them. One way of dividing them up is to separate them into questions that are best addressed by qualitative or quantitative methods.

Quantitative methods are best used for questions that relate to 'quantities': they are about counting or measuring events or phenomena (such as questions that start 'when?', 'which?', 'how many?', 'how frequently?' or 'how much?').

Qualitative methods are best used for questions that relate to the 'quality' of or variations in experience, or the meaning of experience for different people, such as questions starting with 'why?' or 'what?'. Qualitative methods are primarily used to classify events or phenomena, such as the nature of patient dissatisfaction, or barriers to nurse recruitment.

✏ Activity 1.4

Which of the questions listed in the feedback for Activity 1.3 would be best addressed by quantitative methods and which by qualitative methods?

Feedback

Questions (a), (b) and (c) would be best addressed by quantitative methods (they are about measurement) and the rest by qualitative methods (they are about identifying a range of attitudes, developing strategies, or exploring the meaning of events).

Section 2 will introduce some of the qualitative methods used in the social sciences, and Section 3 will introduce some quantitative methods. Qualitative research is more likely to use methods such as observation or in-depth interviewing, which produce words as data, whereas quantitative researchers are more likely to use face-to-face surveys or self-completed questionnaires, which produce numbers as data. However, the contrast between the two kinds of data collection methods should not be exaggerated, and many researchers use both qualitative and quantitative techniques within a single research project. Public health policies and interventions, for example, are becoming increasingly complex, and researchers may need to employ a range of research methods when attempting to comprehensively assess their impacts. The use of multiple methods in a single study may also potentially serve to increase the validity of a study's findings. Section 4 is concerned with multiple-methods research, and research which is multi-disciplinary in nature. Documentary research, also explored in Section 4, uses both qualitative and quantitative methods, depending on the research question. In addition, you should be aware that researchers sometimes perform a quantitative analysis of data produced through qualitative techniques, for instance in counting the different themes that emerge in interviews or focus groups. Furthermore, quantitative research findings (e.g., survey results) may generate research questions which can only be answered using qualitative methods. Regardless of the research methods or data collection techniques they employ, a principle governing all research carried out by social scientists is that it is conducted in accordance with four key ethical principles: autonomy, beneficence, non-maleficence and justice. These principles will be explored in Section 4 of this book.

As you read the scenario in Activity 1.3, you may have drawn on your own experience of management or working in similar departments to think of some explanations and possible solutions for the accident and emergency department manager's problems. What can social research add to this kind of professional experience? Unlike personal experience, 'common sense' or anecdote, research seeks systematically to collect and analyse data, and has a commitment to examining 'counter-explanations', or alternative interpretations. This approach is sometimes characterized as 'scientific'. In the next chapter, you will examine what 'science' means, and why social research methodology is described as 'scientific', even though the research subject of interest is individual people or groups of people. Before addressing this, however, it is important to consider the different stages in the research process.

The research process

Any social research undertaking can be viewed as a process. In general terms, this process often starts with the identification of a problem, and the subsequent refinement of that problem or issue into a researchable question, be it one which is exploratory or descriptive in nature, or framed as a hypothesis to be tested. This is generally followed by the choice of a research design(s) which will allow one to feasibly and appropriately answer one's research question(s), along with the selection of appropriate data collection techniques or tools. Fieldwork or data collection generally constitutes the next stage in the process, followed by the analysis and interpretation of the data collected, and culminating in the writing up and presentation of one's findings. It is important to stress though that not all social research studies fall neatly into these chronological stages, or indeed necessarily involve all of these stages in the form outlined: in qualitative studies, for example, data analysis will generally commence and progress in parallel with data collection; fieldwork, as traditionally conceptualized, may not usually form part of all documentary research studies; and early, preliminary fieldwork may perhaps lead one to reassess the appropriateness of one's research question. Furthermore, individual social science disciplines may differentially emphasize the importance of different parts of, or stages in, the process. However, conceptualizing your research as a 'process' may help you to plan forward and think strategically, for example, about the amount of time required for each stage of your research project, or at which points in time specific tasks need to be undertaken, or decisions need to be made, in order to ensure the smooth running and timely completion of the project.

Summary

There are many social influences on health, health behaviour and the organization of health services. Social science can contribute to investigating these influences through research in disciplines such as sociology, anthropology, psychology and history. Social research addresses both qualitative questions, which explore the meaning of events and phenomena (how they are classified) and quantitative questions that address measurement (when, which, how often, or how much).

Further reading

Bowling, A. (2009) *Research Methods in Health: Investigating Health and Health Services* (3rd edn). Maidenhead: Open University Press.
This is a comprehensive introduction to the range of methods used in health and health services research. It is particularly good on the more quantitative approaches.

Gilbert, N. (2008) Research, theory and method. In N. Gilbert (ed.) *Researching Social Life* (3rd edn). London: Sage.
For those new to research methods, this is an introductory account of the process of social research based on sociological methods and examples.

Petticrew, M. and Roberts, H. (2006) *Systematic Reviews in the Social Sciences: A Practical Guide*. Oxford: Blackwell.
This book provides a comprehensive guide to the rationale for conducting systematic reviews in the social sciences and a practical step-by-step guide to conducting such reviews.

2 | Science and social science

Overview

In this chapter you will learn about some basic concepts in the philosophy of science – what science is, what makes a discipline 'scientific' and how knowledge becomes legitimate. Many students find these ideas difficult if they have had no previous contact with social sciences or other humanities, and have difficulty seeing why they are relevant to the study of research methods. However, some understanding of theories of how knowledge is produced and of the different principles underlying various approaches in the social sciences is essential for understanding the different aims of research, and how to judge the value of research findings appropriately. If you find this chapter difficult at this point, or cannot see how it is relevant, do not worry: read it now and then return to it again when you have finished the rest of the book. Some students find these ideas easier to think about when they can relate them to some substantive knowledge of health research studies.

Readers who already have considerable knowledge and understanding of the philosophy of science may feel that this chapter provides too basic a rendering of major epistemological debates; that our description of the key differences between the positivist and relativist positions, for example, is too stark and inadequately nuanced, or that the classic texts referred to in the chapter appear dated. An in-depth discussion of current debates is, however, beyond the scope of this chapter. The objective is rather to provide a brief account of the emergence and substance of a number of key perspectives on how scientific knowledge is generated and legitimized. Additional reading material is referenced at the end of the chapter for readers who would like to explore the topic further.

Learning objectives

When you have completed this chapter, you will be better able to:

- appreciate the social context of science
- identify different methodological approaches within the social sciences

Key terms

Hypothesis: A provisional explanation for the phenomena under study.

Paradigm: A set of beliefs, values and practices shared by a scientific community at a particular point in time.

> **Positivism:**   A philosophy of science which assumes that reality is stable and can be researched by measuring observable indicators.
>
> **Relativism:**   An alternative to positivism, which assumes that reality can change depending on who is observing it and from what perspective.

What is science?

 Activity 2.1

What does 'science' mean to you? What kinds of research would you describe as 'scientific'?

Feedback

Science means different things to different people, but for many the word has connotations of laboratories, experiments and people in white coats. Scientific research is often associated predominately with the 'natural' sciences such as biology, chemistry or physics, and is seen as an enterprise that generates objective knowledge about the world.

Research in the natural sciences is often perceived to be more 'objective' than that in the social sciences because scientists appear to agree on how to classify natural phenomena and how to study them. In the social sciences, by contrast, there is (as we have seen already) a range of approaches and methods, and findings can seem more 'subjective' in that their interpretation may depend on the approach taken by the researcher. In most contemporary societies, in most fields of endeavour (and certainly in medicine and health care), scientific knowledge has a status and legitimacy not afforded to other sources of knowledge: it is seen as more valid and credible than knowledge derived from non-scientific sources (such as personal experience, religious texts, or the wisdom of elders).

So what characterizes the 'scientific method' that produces this kind of legitimate knowledge about the world? Philosophers of science have disagreed on what makes science 'scientific', but many accounts focus on a number of features that are often seen to apply to the natural sciences. The characteristics of scientific enquiry can be summarized as follows.

Empiricism

For many scientists, a key feature of the scientific method is empiricism: a belief that scientific knowledge can only be derived from observable data. Such things as emotions, motives or inner meanings are thus not a legitimate source of scientific knowledge. We can only research the empirical indicators of such phenomena (such as laughing, or particular actions).

Logical induction

Following on from the empirical approach is logical induction. This is the process by which theories, or laws, about the physical world are inferred from repeated empirical observations. An example of the inductive approach is research into the relationship between high blood pressure and stroke: repeated observation of a higher rate of stroke in people with high blood pressure leads to theories about the causes of stroke.

Realism

A key assumption for many scientists is that reality is stable, and exists outside our attempts to describe it. For example, a realist assumption is that there is a 'real' disease called malaria, caused by a plasmodium parasite, passed on by mosquitoes. It may be that in different historical times the causes of malaria have been differently understood (as the result of bad air, for instance). Some sufferers may believe their malaria has been caused by evil spirits. Others may believe that the phenomenon is not a distinct disease at all and is simply an extreme version of other diseases such as influenza. However, for the realist scientist, malaria is always a distinct disease with invariable causes, however we attempt to explain it.

Value-free nature of scientific inquiry

For many, science should exist outside the influences of society, such as religious, political or emotional views.

Together, the features characterize what is often called a *positivist* view of science. Positivism is a philosophy that holds that there are 'laws' governing the behaviour of the natural world and that the proper object of science is to discover them. To do this, scientists must study observable phenomena, which can be objectively measured. There have been many criticisms of the positivist view of science. We will come to them later in this chapter. However, positivism has had a significant influence on many social science methods, particularly the quantitative ones, so it is useful to start with an understanding of both positivism and the implications it has for scientific logic. Positivist social scientists attempt to study 'observable' facets or consequences of human behaviour, which can be measured, and attempt to derive general laws about behaviour from their observations.

Positivist social science – an example

In the social sciences, the work of the French sociologist Emile Durkheim (1858–1917) is often cited as an example of early positivist research. His study of records of suicide rates across Europe (Durkheim [1897] 1963) demonstrated that different societies had different 'propensities' to suicide; that individuals were more likely to kill themselves if, for instance, they lived in Protestant rather than Catholic societies, if economic conditions were poor, and if they were unmarried. From his analysis of suicide statistics, he developed a theory that linked the rate of suicide to a lack of social integration: when a community had close bonds, and individuals felt part of it, the suicide rate would be lower. Durkheim's findings are of less interest here than his approach, which illustrates the positivist tradition in social science.

Activity 2.2

Why would you characterize Durkheim's approach to the study of suicide as a positivist one?

Feedback

Durkheim used observable facts (recorded rates of suicide) rather than those that would have to be interpreted (such as motivations or moral views) and he attempted to derive general laws from his data (that suicide rates vary with the level of social integration in a society).

Although few present-day researchers would describe themselves as 'positivist', positivism continues as an orientation of much social science, particularly quantitative social science, and it underpins the methodological approaches of many other health science disciplines.

However, there are a number of alternative approaches to scientific enquiry. These alternatives arise from two rather different kinds of criticisms of positivism:

- That the characteristics you read about above do not really describe any kind of scientific research, even in the natural sciences. In this view, these characteristics are seen as either a simplistic, stereotypical description of how science works, or as a naïve view.
- That the characteristics you read about are *inappropriate* for researching questions to do with human behaviour, so positivism is an inadequate starting point for social scientific research.

A number of philosophers have taken the first of these positions: that it is naïve to assume that any kind of scientific research really progresses through the processes of empiricism and induction.

Is science really based on empiricism, induction, realism and value-free enquiry?

First, Karl Popper (1968), writing in the twentieth century, rejected the positivist view of scientific progress, suggesting that knowledge did not grow incrementally, by repeated observations to develop laws about the world, but by a more creative process that might include intuition, hunches, or inspiration. These creative processes generate *hypotheses* – provisional explanations for some aspect of the world. In a sense, it does not matter where initial hypotheses come from – what is important is that they are tested. For Popper, a scientific law or theory can never be proved, but it can be disproved. This model of scientific research is thus called the *hypothetico-deductive model*. The hypothesis is generated, and then tested through research, in order to try to falsify it. For Popper, it is the testability of hypotheses that characterizes scientific knowledge.

Alan Chalmers (1982) further argues that empiricism and naïve logical induction are not convincing as guarantors of the validity of scientific knowledge. Key to his critique is the logical impossibility of observing without presupposing a theory. However mundane our empirical observations, they require a set of expectations about the world and how it is for us to interpret them: we cannot 'see' (or use any other sense) without first having a theory (however low-level) to frame what we are seeing. Thus, we can make repeated observations of the symptoms of malaria, but unless we have a pre-existing 'theory' of malaria, which distinguishes it from other causes of fever for instance, these observations will mean very little.

A third critique of the naïve positivist position comes from Thomas Kuhn (1962), whose ideas undermined a pure realist perspective. For Kuhn, scientific knowledge does not increase incrementally, but by radical changes in world views, which determine the kinds of questions scientists can ask and the theories they work with. He called these revolutionary changes *paradigm shifts*. The dominant paradigm of the day will shape what kinds of research can be carried out, in that anyone working outside the paradigm will find it very difficult to get their research funded or their results published. Paradigms shift as particular disciplines enter a 'crisis' mode, in which there are competing explanations, and existing theories cannot accommodate new knowledge that is generated. New paradigms emerge that can, for the moment, account for new knowledge. The implications of Kuhn's ideas are that science is a social process, in that research happens within a social world that is managed by elite scientists, and that explanations only make sense within a particular paradigm.

It is difficult when inside a paradigm to imagine science outside it: the dominant theories are so widely held that it would seem like nonsense to think outside them. However, it is perhaps a little easier to see the social influences on science. The kinds of research with which you feel driven to become involved, and that are funded and published, are inevitably shaped by influences outside those of science itself, particularly in areas such as public health. Your own values, education, current national and local policies, the political needs of the communities you work with and the business activities of organizations such as drug companies will all shape the topics that it is possible to work on, and the kinds of questions you ask about those topics.

Relativist perspectives and the social sciences

There have, then, been a number of criticisms of positivism as a description of how scientific research happens. These have suggested that science is an activity rooted in society, and that social values will have an influence on what is researched and what kinds of answers we will find. More important, for a discussion of methodology, is that many social scientists believe that positivist approaches are inappropriate for research on human behaviour. Key to many of these criticisms is the rejection of realism. Instead of seeing reality as something that is unchanging and that pre-exists our attempts to research it, relativists believe that reality, and our knowledge of it, are 'socially constructed' in that they are a product of particular social, political and historical circumstances. Various kinds of relativist philosophy have had a major influence on social science methodology, particularly for the more qualitative traditions. When one adopts a particular relativist perspective on, for instance, illness, one accepts that other perspectives on it are equally legitimate. For instance, if we are studying the beliefs people with malaria have about how it is caused, we could treat beliefs such as 'it is a result of witchcraft' not as mistaken or ill educated, but as legitimate beliefs, if we understand the cultural perspective of those with this belief. This is not the same as 'agreeing' that malaria is caused by witchcraft but is a stance that says that this is a legitimate belief and that we can research it as such, rather than as a 'mistake'. This is a perspective known as *cultural relativism*.

A more extreme relativist position is that of *social constructionism*. For social construction-ists, 'observable' facts (such as death rates, or symptoms of disease) are not objective facts, reflecting an underlying reality about the number of deaths from a disease, or the existence of disease in an individual. These labels merely reflect human attempts to cate-gorize nature: there is nothing inevitable or natural about our definitions of such things as 'malaria' or 'a family' or 'virus'. Their meaning changes depending on how the reality is constructed. Symptoms of disease, for instance, are classified in different ways in different countries, and the category 'virus' only has a meaning within a particular biological theory.

 Activity 2.3

How might a relativist criticize Durkheim's analysis of suicide rates?

Feedback

Relativist criticisms of Durkheim's analysis might include the following arguments. First, what we understand by 'suicide' is socially constructed and can change over time and from culture to culture. For example, the decision to not accept life-saving treatment for a fatal disease might be considered suicide by some people and not others. It is poss-ible to imagine a future where death caused by tobacco smoking is considered 'suicide' (a deliberate action that leads to one's own death). Second, various social processes also 'construct' the recorded rate of suicide in a particular country. The actions of such officials as doctors, coroners and police officers are likely to be influenced by the very factors that Durkheim suggested influenced the rate of suicide. Thus, in a Catholic soci-ety, where the social stigma attached to suicide might be higher than in a Protestant country, there may be more incentive to record an accidental death in the same circum-stances. Death rates reflect the ways in which deaths are recorded and classified, not any 'objective' reality about the number of deaths from different diseases.

You may also want to reflect at this point on your own assumptions and beliefs about how we can 'know' the world. Are you a 'positivist' who believes that there is a stable reality, which research should strive to represent, or are you a 'relativist' who believes that reality is constructed differently, depending on who is looking at it and from where? Many people have a shifting perspective, taking a more positivist position on some questions and a more relativist position on others. On suicide, for instance, they might accept that it is impossible to come up with an objective definition that would always represent the same 'reality', whereas they might feel more comfortable with the idea that there 'really is' a disease called malaria, which is always the same, irrespective of how it has been constructed in different times and places.

Interpretive approaches

Even if we accept a realist position, we may be more interested not in researching that reality but in researching people's *interpretations* of reality. For instance, if we are working in an area where people's understanding of malaria is very different from that of the dominant medical paradigm, the key research questions may be around *how* malaria is understood, rather than what malaria is. If we are interested, for instance, in changing people's health behaviour, what is important is an understanding of why they behave as they do and what their beliefs are. This is a principle of interpretive approaches to social research, where the aim is to understand the perspectives of those we are researching. Many qualitative researchers start from an interpretive approach, in that they are addressing questions about the *meaning* of reality (whether it is malaria symptoms, satisfaction with health services, or the aims of a policy), rather than trying to determine what reality is. A key principle of this type of research is the acceptance that there is no one 'right' interpretation of meaning. For example, which definition of 'success' should we accept when judging the outcome of hip replacement: the patient's or the surgeon's? One might argue that patients have a more intimate understanding of their pain and quality of life, or that surgeons are in a better position to compare a single patient with all the other patients whom they have treated. However, we are no closer to proving that the one definition is more correct than another because we have no 'gold standard' of success with which to compare them.

This chapter has provided an introduction to methodology, the general study of research methods and how they can produce valid knowledge about the world from different perspectives. In the next chapter we return to a practical issue concerning methods: how to frame a research question.

Summary

'Positivism' has been described as an approach to scientific research that assumes that reality is stable (is always the same, whoever is looking at it) and that research ought to measure observable features of that reality. In social sciences, there are alternative views. One is relativism, which in its extreme form assumes that reality changes and is constructed differently in different times and places. More common in health research are less strong versions of relativism, which assume that other perspectives on reality are worth studying to aid our understanding of people's health beliefs and behaviour. In practice, these distinctions may not be quite so clear-cut: for example, many social researchers would not wish to classify themselves definitively as either positivists or relativists. Furthermore, studies which employ multiple methods (see Chapter 16), some of which have their basis in the positivist tradition and others in variants of the relativist tradition, in order to address complex public health research questions, bear testimony to the value that can be derived from adopting and integrating, as appropriate, methods drawn from different philosophical perspectives and traditions.

References

Chalmers, A. (1982) *What Is This Thing Called Science?* (2nd edn). Milton Keynes: Open University Press.
Durkheim, E. [1897] (1963) *Suicide: A Study in Sociology*. London: Routledge & Kegan Paul.
Kuhn, T. (1962) *The Structure of Scientific Revolutions*. Chicago: University of Chicago Press.
Popper, K. (1968) *The Logic of Scientific Discovery*. London: Hutchinson.

Further reading

Burr, V, (2003) *Social Constructionism* (2nd edn). London: Routledge

Chalmers, A. (2013) *What Is This Thing Called Science?* (4th edn). Maidenhead: Open University Press.
An accessible book for readers wanting to find out more about the philosophy of science. Chalmers looks at criticisms of science as observation and experiment, and at twentieth-century debates in the philosophy of science. This revised and extended edition offers an account of developments in the field in recent years. The Bayesian approach and the new experimentalism are explored.

Conrad, P. and Barker, K.K. (2010) The social construction of illness: key insights and policy implications. *Journal of Health and Social Behaviour*, 51: 67–69.

Smith, M.J. (1998) *Social Science in Question: Towards a Postdisciplinary Framework*. London: Sage.
This book looks at how the social sciences have researched society, from the early influences of natural sciences models through to more contemporary perspectives.

3 | Framing a research question

Overview

Fundamental to any research study is a good research question. Students or professionals who are new to research sometimes find that while they can readily identify a problem or issue that they want to research, formulating a specific research question which is relevant and appropriate to their identified problem and can be feasibly addressed is far more difficult than they might have initially anticipated. Time invested in developing the specifics of one's research question is never wasted. This chapter examines how broad topic areas of interest can generate more specific research questions. Good research questions are framed in appropriate terms, so that it is clear how the research will answer them.

Learning objectives

After working through this chapter, you will be better able to:

- distinguish concepts, variables and indicators in research
- formulate research questions

Key terms

Concepts: The phenomena that the researcher are interested in (such as 'inequalities in health', 'social status' or 'quality of health care'). These phenomena are not directly observable, but are assumed to exist because they give rise to measurable attributes.

Variables: Aspects of those phenomena being investigated that are subject to change (such as 'disease severity' or 'income').

Indicators: The empirical attributes of variables that can be observed and measured (such as 'blood pressure' or 'monthly wage').

Operationalization: The process of identifying the appropriate variables from concepts or constructs, and then finding adequate and specific indicators of variables.

From 'problems' to research questions

In Activity 1.3 you identified the kinds of problems that might be relevant to a health service manager and suggested that social science research might have a role to play in informing solutions to those problems. But how do you turn the problems faced by the manager in that scenario into questions that can be researched rigorously?

One possibility: developing a hypothesis to test

One way of turning problems into research questions was suggested in the previous chapter – think of provisional explanations for the observed phenomena and then develop 'falsifiable' hypotheses to test.

 Activity 3.1

If you carried out a series of interviews with patients about their dissatisfaction with the service received from the department, one common answer might be 'I don't mind waiting, but I don't like not knowing how long I have to wait'. You want to carry out some research to find out whether telling people how long they will have to wait makes them less dissatisfied. What hypothesis would this study test?

Feedback

The hypothesis you suggested is likely to be along the following lines: 'patients who know how long the wait is will be less dissatisfied than those who do not know'.

We could then plan some research, possibly using an experimental design (see Chapter 4), to test this hypothesis by, for instance, informing one group of patients of the likely wait and then distributing a questionnaire to compare their satisfaction with that of a control group, which was not informed.

Although it is sometimes possible in health research to frame a formal hypothesis of this sort, it is not always appropriate. It might not be appropriate because the question you need to answer is an *exploratory* one – the topic area could be one about which not enough is known to generate even a provisional explanation. One outcome of the research might then be to generate hypotheses as a result of the findings.

 Activity 3.2

Think back to the accident and emergency department scenario in Activity 1.3 and specifically to the issue of junior doctors' treatment of the patients with minor problems.

1 Note down some of the reasons why junior doctors might investigate and treat these patients so intensively.
2 Why might we be interested in doctors' views?

If we wanted to find out more about doctors' beliefs about their patients, and about their
motivations for treating them intensively, we would not necessarily have a hypothesis
to test. Rather, we would want to answer a more open question, such as 'Why do junior
doctors intensively treat patients with minor illnesses?' Much qualitative research
starts with these more open, exploratory questions, rather than formal hypotheses. The
methods and data collection techniques routinely used in research designed to address
exploratory questions are discussed in Section 2.

Concepts, variables and indicators

In social science research, then, not all research questions can be framed as hypotheses.
Sometimes research is focused more on understanding the nature of the concepts under
study and how they relate to each other. This is often achieved by simply asking people
questions or allowing them to tell their own stories, rather than attempting to control and
intervene in the research context. The research question might therefore be about understanding different perspectives, or exploring a topic to generate hypotheses. For example,
young children and older people are known to be particularly vulnerable to hot tap water
scalding – an issue of some public health concern in the UK. As part of a study on scald
prevention, Durand et al. (2012) undertook qualitative interviews (qualitative interviewing
techniques are introduced in Chapter 6) with older people and parents of young children living
in settings where hot tap water temperatures were very high, but not amenable to change in
individual dwellings. Perceptions of tap water temperatures and scald risk were explored, as
well as scald prevention strategies. The researchers found that although participants were
concerned about how hot their water was and the potential for scalding, they also viewed
scald prevention as a personal responsibility. Older people saw hot water management as
evidence of their 'risk hardiness' and ability to live independently, while parents viewed managing hot water risks to their children as evidence of 'good parenting'. The use of an exploratory research question allowed concepts such as 'risk hardiness', which might not normally
be considered by those involved in developing scald prevention strategies, to be identified.

Research questions in quantitative work

However, whatever the area of interest and the aim of the research, researchers must still
frame their question in an appropriate way to answer it satisfactorily. In quantitative work,

in particular, the process of developing a research question from a broad area of interest is sometimes called *operationalizing*. There are three stages that are typically involved.

Think about the concepts

First, think about the *concepts* you are interested in: the phenomena that are crucial to the problem or issue you are concerned with. These are generally abstract constructs that have some theoretical meaning, but are hard to define exactly, such as equity, or social status, or occupational mobility, or health status. Concepts have many *dimensions*: health status, for instance, combines a number of factors, which might include life expectancy, presence or absence of symptoms, feelings of wellbeing, measures of physical strength or endurance, the intensity or severity of symptoms, and the relative importance of symptoms to the individual patient. Dimensions can be thought of as different aspects of the concept.

Identify the variables

The next stage is to separate out the different dimensions or aspects of the concept, and identify which of them are relevant to the research. The relevant dimensions are the *variables* that will be used in the research: they should 'capture' something about the concept. While for some people the term 'variable' may have associations with laboratory research or statistical analysis, in social research terms a 'variable' is simply a factor that changes (varies) in different circumstances, such as from individual to individual, or across time in the same individual. Thus, in Britain, 'social status' is a complex concept, often summed up by the term 'social class', which is hard to define precisely. For most it conjures up an interrelated set of factors, including people's income, their job, their educational level and aspects of their lifestyle. In other societies, the concept of social class may not be important at all, or may involve other dimensions such as religion, ethnicity, or caste. These dimensions of the concept are variables: they are not the same as the concept 'social class' but they do reflect one particular aspect of it. In Britain, the variables often used in research on social class and health are income levels and occupation. These are not identical to social class, but they do reflect important aspects of it.

Decide on the indicators

Even though variables are more specific than concepts, they are still not usually observable or 'measurable'. You cannot go out and 'measure' someone's occupation, or feelings of 'wellbeing'. In quantitative research, variables themselves need operationalizing into empirical *indicators*, which can then be observed or 'measured' in the research. Indicators are operational-level categories. For example:

- In a study of health status, the variable 'feelings of wellbeing' could be operationalized in terms of replies to questionnaire items such as 'How would you rate your own health for someone of your age group, on a scale of 1 to 5?'
- The variable 'occupation' could be operationalized as self-reports of primary occupation on a questionnaire.

Research questions in qualitative work

This process of operationalizing concepts is perhaps easier to think about when the research question is framed as a hypothesis, or for quantitative research designs. However, even for exploratory questions, with the more 'open' research questions typical of qualitative work, it is still necessary to consider carefully how the question is framed. Thinking about the concepts involved is a useful exercise in ensuring that you have identified the most appropriate ones. Considering how you will gather empirical data to answer an exploratory question involves thinking carefully about what the evidence (the indicators) will be for those concepts. For instance, we suggested above the exploratory question: 'Why do junior doctors intensively treat patients with minor illnesses?' In thinking about how this will be answered, and perhaps reframed as a more specific research question, we need to consider the concepts of 'intensive treatment' and 'minor illness', as they may not mean the same things to the accident and emergency manager, the junior doctors and the researchers. We also need to consider how the 'why' question will be answered. Is this a question about doctors' motivations? In which case, what indicators will provide us with evidence about these 'motivations'? Or is it a question about how junior doctors make decisions about appropriate treatment? Thinking in detail about exactly what it is that the research will address will help refine the most feasible and appropriate research question.

An example

Concepts, variables and indicators are not distinct: a particular category (such as health status) could be a concept in one context, but a variable in another. They can be thought of as being increasingly precise formulations. Formulating a research question involves specifying, as precisely as possible, the variables you are interested in and then identifying suitable indicators for them.

 Activity 3.3

Read the following extract, which summarizes the introduction to a paper by Henderson *et al.* (1994), on the utilization of health services in China. As you read, make notes identifying the concepts, variables and indicators mentioned. When you have finished, compare your notes with the feedback below.

> **Equity and the utilization of health services**
>
> This study investigated equity with respect to the provision and use of welfare services in eight Chinese provinces. In China, central government policies attempt to redistribute health resources to those in greatest need, but questions remain about whether services are available to those who need them. In an equitable system, individuals with similar health care problems will have equal access to health care, whatever their income level or other social attributes. In this study, a large sample of working-age adults who identified themselves as ill or injured in the four weeks prior to an interview was used to answer the question: 'What predicts use of health services for those sick or injured?' The

researchers predicted first several predisposing factors (variables that influence the variable being studied) which would increase the use of health care services (including gender, occupation, educational level and age). Second was a range of enabling factors that were predicted to increase use. These included income, insurance levels and geographic location. Finally, they predicted that self-reported severity would be related to utilization.

In the survey, respondents were asked about the severity of their illness or injury; their experiences with the formal health care sector (although a large number also used folk healers); distance from the nearest health care facility, in terms of number of minutes taken by bike; and a range of demographic information such as primary and secondary occupation, household income (including subsidies) and number of years in education.

Feedback

The main concept used here is 'equity', which has been operationalized as 'equal access to health care for similar needs'. The variables the researchers are interested in include gender, occupation, educational level, age, income, insurance levels, geographic location, morbidity and severity, and access to health care. Most variables have been operationalized as answers to a survey question, such as self-reports of use of formal health care, how many minutes it takes to cycle to the nearest health care facility and what the household income is.

This example shows that choice of indicator for a particular variable is a difficult task: no indicator is perfect. These researchers chose self-reports of illness or injury over the last four weeks and its severity as their indicator for 'need for health care'. These reports are relatively easy to collect compared with other indicators as respondents can be asked for the information, but other indicators could have logically (if not practically) been chosen.

 Activity 3.4

1 Can you think of any limitations of using self-reports of incidence and severity as an indicator for measuring 'need for health care'?
2 Which other indicators for 'need for health care' could you use in a population survey, if you wanted to study how equitable your health care system was?

Feedback

1 Self-reports of severity are influenced by people's later health-seeking behaviour: if patients went to a secondary care facility rather than a primary health care clinic they may reconstruct the illness as more serious. Also, reporting behaviour is influenced by the very demographic variables that are being investigated, such as gender and educational level. Those people who are more likely to report the need for health care are not necessarily the same people who have more needs.

2 Other possible indicators include:
- mortality rates for different population groups;
- time taken off work due to illness in a certain period;
- self-reports of severe chronic illness;
- measurements of markers for physical health, such as height, cholesterol levels, body mass index or low peak flow rates.

Sometimes indicators are described as *proxy indicators* because they do not measure some aspect of the variable directly, but are known or assumed to be fair approximations for variables that cannot be measured directly. Thus self-reported weight can be used as a proxy indicator for clinician-measured weight, as there is a high correlation between the two measures. An example of a less exact proxy measure is postal district, which is often used as an indicator for the concept of 'deprivation', even though it is obvious that there will be much variation in deprivation within the same postal district.

Whatever indicator is chosen, it will not be a perfect measure of the concept you want to research. Framing a research question always involves some compromise between what you would ideally like to know and what it is possible to measure. The possible indicators you may have thought of for 'need for health care' in Activity 3.4 may be more valid than those used by the researchers, but perhaps impossible to collect, or not feasible given the resource constraints of the project. The questions suggested in Activity 1.3, such as 'why do people attend the hospital with primary care problems?' are too vague to investigate as they are, but the process of turning them into researchable questions, with measurable indicators, compromises some of the meaning of the original concepts.

Activity 3.5

1 How would you frame 'Why do people attend the hospital for primary care problems?' as a researchable question?
2 Think about the main dimensions or variables you would want to investigate, and list some possible indicators of them, which would be both appropriate and feasible to collect in a research study.

Feedback

1 First the different dimensions of the construct of 'primary care problems' need to be identified, in order to develop indicators that can be used in a research study. The other concept of interest is patient motivation: what factors influence patients' decisions to attend a hospital?
2 Table 3.1 suggests one way of thinking about some possible variables for research; you may have developed others of relevance to the health care system you are familiar with, such as lack of health insurance or lack of appropriate primary care facilities.

Considering the concepts and possible indicators for them helps with the process of deciding exactly what to research, and what kind of data will be most appropriate to collect or generate. One outcome of the process suggested above for the research on those attending accident and emergency with minor problems might be deciding that a survey was needed to answer a research question about patients' motivations, such as: 'To what extent is lack of access to primary care a determinant of patients' decisions to attend the accident and emergency department with minor illness or injury?'

If enough is known already about some of the variables that are listed in Table 3.1 it might be possible to move to a more formal hypothesis, such as: 'Patients attend accident and emergency departments with minor illnesses because they make inappropriate assessments of need for care'.

In Section 3 you will return to the design of quantitative research, including surveys using questionnaires, which can address these sorts of questions. However, you may have noted that it is only possible to develop the kinds of variables in Table 3.1 if you already have some speculative theories about the problem. In the example discussed, such theories may, for instance, include the theory that lack of health insurance impacts on hospital use, or that patients and professionals have conflicting attitudes to the proper role of the accident and emergency department. These theories can come from professional experience, or from reviews of existing literature on the topic of interest. Often, though, these theories are at the level of untested 'common sense', or there may be conflicting accounts of possible explanations. When this is the case, a qualitative research study may be more appropriate. In Section 2, you will examine the various kinds of qualitative methods that are used in health services research. First, though, there is a more general decision to take. Once we have refined a researchable question, and decided what *kind* of data might answer it (such as records from case notes, answers in interviews, blood pressure readings), we need to decide what kind of research design is most appropriate for organizing these data. The next chapter introduces some common designs in social research.

Table 3.1 Why people attend hospital for primary care problems: refining concepts, variables and indicators

Concept	Possible variables	Possible indicators
Primary care problem	Minor illness or injury	Patient left department without treatment
		Specific conditions identified in case notes
	Problem treatable by primary care practitioner	Triage nurse's assessment of problem
		Doctor's assessment of problem
	Duration of symptoms	Onset of problem more than 48 hours ago
Patient motivation to attend hospital	Dissatisfaction with local primary care facility	Answer to questionnaire item on satisfaction with local primary care
	Lack of access to primary care	Answer to questionnaire item on availability of primary care
		Availability of local primary care as recorded in official records
	Inappropriate assessment of need for care	Answers to case vignettes asking where you would go for treatment

Summary

Developing a good research question involves thinking about the concepts of interest, and which variables represent the important dimensions of that concept. A feasible quantitative research question must also define operational level indicators for those variables. For qualitative work, it is also helpful to think through what would provide evidence for the concepts you are interested in. In public health and health services research, choice of indicator is problematic and often involves a compromise between what is possible to collect and what adequately reflects the variables of interest.

References

Durand, M.A., Green, J., Edwards, P., Milton, S. and Lutchmun, S. (2012) Perceptions of tap water temperatures, scald risk and prevention among parents and older people in social housing: A qualitative study. *Burns* 38: 585–590.

Henderson, G., Akin, J., Zhiming, L., Shuigao, J., Haijiang, M. and Keyou, G. (1994) Equity and the utilisation of health services: report of an eight-province study of China. *Social Science and Medicine* 39: 687–700.

Further reading

Mason, J. (2002) Finding a focus and knowing where you stand. In J. Mason (ed.) *Qualitative Researching* (2nd edn). London: Sage.
This chapter describes a very useful approach to developing and refining qualitative research questions, involving thinking through a series of questions about the research project and the nature of the phenomena to be investigated.

Miller, D.C. and Salkind, N.J. (eds) (2002) *Handbook of Research Design and Social Measurement*. London: Sage.

Research design

4

Overview

To answer a research question adequately we need to choose the most appropriate research design: that is, we need to choose a plan or structure for our research study that will allow us to collect or generate the kind of data that are most likely to provide us with the answer to the question. A research design is more than just the data collection methods used (such as interviews) – it refers to the *logic* of how the data will be collected. There are a number of ways of thinking about the range of research designs used in the social sciences. Here we will introduce five common kinds of design used in quantitative and qualitative social science research: experimental (this generally refers to 'trials' such as randomized controlled trials), cross-sectional, observational, documentary and participatory. Readers should note that different taxonomies of research design are used in epidemiology.

It is likely that the use of one of these designs on its own will allow you to answer your research question. However, researchers sometimes need to combine various designs, or elements of them, in the same study, depending on the nature and complexity of their research question(s) (see Chapter 16). In addition, the distinction between 'design' and data collection methods may in some instances appear confusing: researchers from different disciplines may use the same terminology in different ways. The key distinction is that 'design' refers to the overall study plan or strategy which will allow us to answer our research question, while data collection methods refer to the specific techniques or tools we use in conducting the study and generating the data. Furthermore, as we will see, while some data collection techniques or tools are typically more closely associated with particular research designs than others (e.g., quantitative questionnaires are often used in cross-sectional designs), there is not an inevitable relationship between the design of a study and the methods used to collect data for it. Qualitative interviews could, for example, be used in randomized controlled trials.

Learning objectives

When you have completed this chapter, you will be better able to:

- identify the most appropriate research design for a particular research question
- identify the strengths and weaknesses of experimental, cross-sectional, observational, documentary and participatory designs in the social sciences

Key terms

Controlled trial or experiment: Compares outcomes in the 'experimental' group to those in a 'control' group.

Cross-sectional design: Aims to collect the same data from each member of a study sample at one particular point in time.

Observational design: Aims to record, describe and understand the meaning of what is happening in a particular setting.

Introduction

So far in the preceding chapters, you have seen that social research in health involves both quantitative and qualitative approaches, and a range of types of question, from formal hypotheses that can be tested to more exploratory questions. Selecting an appropriate research design is essential for ensuring that your study is capable of answering your research question. Consider, for instance, the questions that might face a public health specialist who wanted to reduce smoking among the teenage population of a particular district. If planning a research programme to support this, they might want to know:

* How many teenagers smoke cigarettes regularly and are there particular subgroups (such as girls, those in urban areas) who are more likely to smoke?
* Why do teenagers start smoking? Why do they stop?
* Would a health promotion campaign in schools be an effective way to stop teenagers taking up smoking?

The first is a *descriptive* question, which needs a design that can provide good data about the prevalence of smoking among particular groups. The second is a more *exploratory* question and would require a design that accessed the meanings smoking has for teenagers. The third is a question about *effectiveness*, and a design capable of addressing causal effects would be needed. Choosing an appropriate research design involves thinking in detail about whether the kind of study you are proposing will generate the right kind of data to answer the research question you posed.

There are a number of ways of thinking about research designs and considering the choices to be made between them. The five common types of design listed above (experimental, cross-sectional, observational, documentary and participatory) are considered in this chapter. This is certainly not an exhaustive list of study designs and (as we will see) it is not a perfect typology as many studies in practice will borrow elements of different designs and many will not fit neatly into any one of these formats. However, thinking about the particular strengths and weaknesses of these particular designs will suggest the issues that need to be considered in any project.

Experimental design

In medical research, and increasingly in health services research, one commonly used experimental design is the *randomized controlled trial* (RCT). The RCT has often been described as the 'gold standard' design for testing the effects of interventions (e.g., new medications and therapies), and for this reason, and because RCTs are not considered in detail elsewhere in this book, we are considering this design in some depth in this section. In an RCT, the key features are that those receiving the intervention (the 'experimental' group) are compared with those who do not (the 'control' group) and that participants are randomly allocated to either the control or experimental group. Random allocation controls for selection biases and for known and unknown confounders which, if not controlled for, might have an impact on the study outcomes. Experiments in general are strong designs for looking at research questions that are about cause and effect. Examples of such questions would be: 'Do bed nets sprayed with insecticide prevent more malaria infections than those without?' and 'Do exercise classes for older citizens reduce the incidence of falls for this age group?' These questions require a research design that enables us to see whether the intervention being tested (insecticide-treated bed nets, exercise classes) has a particular effect (reducing malaria or falls) in a particular population.

✏ Activity 4.1

In a randomized controlled trial to investigate the effect of Insecticide-treated bed nets, you randomly allocate 30 villages in your district to either the control group, given ordinary bed nets for each resident, or the experimental group, given treated bed nets. A nurse, who does not know which group the villages are in, visits each village each month to carry out household Interviews to find out how many cases of malaria there have been. After a year, the incidence is much lower in the villages that have been given treated bed nets.

1 Why does this design enable us to be fairly confident that the intervention (treated bed nets) has caused the reduction in malaria, rather than other factors, such as higher use of prophylactics or a fall in the number of mosquitoes locally?
2 How do we know that the differences between the experimental and control villages are not due to differences in the populations of those villages (such as numbers of children), rather than in the effectiveness of the interventions?
3 How do we know that the lower incidence in the experimental villages is not due to the nurse's bias (for instance, she is likely to expect fewer cases and thus be less likely to record them)?

Feedback

1 Comparing the control and experimental groups enables us to test the specific contribution of the intervention, given that (in theory) the villagers should be subject to the same other factors.
2 Randomly allocating villages to the two groups should, in principle, ensure that differences are due to chance, and not any systematic differences that would influence malaria incidence.
3 The nurse is 'blind' to whether the village has received the intervention or not.

Studies involving single interventions, such as new drugs, are relatively easy to organize, at least in principle. In public health, however, we are usually interested in more complex interventions such as health promotion campaigns or the introduction of new services. Even a relatively straightforward intervention, such as the bed net in Activity 4.1, involves, in practice, a rather complex series of human behaviours. Insecticide must be applied and paid for; the bed nets must be used appropriately; villages may trade the bed nets between them; bed nets may be taken out of the village by those who travel. In testing any complex intervention it is much more difficult to answer a simple question about cause and effect because we are often looking at complicated chains of causes, and at behaviour that is embedded in everyday life. In health services research, the term *pragmatic trial* is used to describe randomized controlled trials in which the aim is to try to test these kinds of interventions in the 'real world'. Testing the effectiveness of an intervention in the type of 'real world' setting in which it is likely to be used increases the generalizability of a study's findings. One example of a pragmatic trial is an experiment that looked at whether additional social support for pregnant women would improve outcomes for them and their babies. The following is a summary of Ann Oakley's (1990) account of this trial. While this trial was conducted over 20 years ago, the issues it raises remain relevant today.

A pragmatic trial of social support in pregnancy

There is a large research literature suggesting that social support is important for women who are pregnant, and that those with little social support (from, for instance, family and friends) experience poorer outcomes. The research team was interested in whether a research intervention providing additional social support could improve outcomes for women and their babies. An experimental design was chosen to answer this question because previous research on this topic had been limited by potential confounding variables; it is impossible to say whether the better outcomes associated with better social support were really the result of social support, or just reflecting the fact that those with better social support are different in some way from those without. An RCT was planned that provided midwives to visit women at home and offer emotional support. The population consisted of pregnant women who had previously given birth to a low-birthweight baby. Those consenting to being entered into the trial were randomly allocated to either receive this extra support or to be in the control group and receive normal maternity care only. Outcomes measured included women's satisfaction and birthweight.

Although an RCT is the strongest design for addressing the question about whether this kind of support does improve maternal and child outcomes, Oakley's account illustrates the difficulties of organizing this kind of pragmatic trial in real health service settings. Some of the problems she encountered were:

* Professionals are often uncomfortable about random allocation to services. If the midwives felt that women were in desperate need for social support, it was difficult for them knowing there was only a 50:50 chance of being allocated it. For professionals used to allocating services on the basis of perceived need, random allocation is difficult.
* Contamination. If participants are informed about a trial, many will want the potential benefits of the intervention. If they are not allocated to the experimental group they may try to get the same benefits in other ways, or may well talk to women they know in the other group.

- The conflicts between informed consent and rigorous testing. The research team were concerned to inform participants fully about the trial aims so they could make a decision about whether to take part. However, the more trial participants know about the study aims (e.g., that social support may improve satisfaction) the more likely it is that the outcomes will be biased.

A key issue for trials like this is *uncertainty*. It is only when we are genuinely uncertain of the benefits of an intervention that it is ethical to test it (otherwise, it would be unethical to withhold the intervention from the control group). However, 'uncertainty' (sometimes called 'equipoise') may be difficult to agree on. Most medical interventions may never have been rigorously tested, yet it would not be ethical now to test them experimentally (see Chapter 14 for a discussion of ethical principles in research). In the case described here, many professionals believed that there was already enough evidence to suggest the benefits of social support and that an expensive RCT, which withheld the service for many in apparent need, was not needed. Oakley comments that genuine scepticism is very rare. However, experiments provide the most rigorous evidence we can have of whether something 'works' or not, and are likely to be much more convincing for policy-makers.

Experiments are, then, a strong design for answering *causal questions*, when we need to be fairly confident that a particular intervention does have a particular effect in a given population. However, there are many reasons why this design may not be appropriate:

- First, not all questions are about causes. We may be more interested in describing a phenomenon, or exploring its meaning, than in determining what effects it has. A legitimate aim of much social science research is not predicting the effect of a variable or intervention (such as gender, or social support, or diagnosis) but understanding the meaning given to it by different participants. People, unlike the objects studied by natural scientists, reflect on their own behaviour (and on researchers' accounts of it) and change as a result. Research has to explore understanding as well as describing behaviour.
- Secondly, in much social research it may be impossible to separate out one particular intervention to study. In much health research you might be interested in examining the range of different factors that impact on behaviour, and how they interact, rather than just testing those that you predict will have an influence. Thus, if carrying out the study described in Activity 4.1, we might want to study such activities as bed-net trading, and how nets are used within households. Rather than being factors that 'interfere' with our research, these are the interesting aspects of behaviour that we need to understand in order to understand how bed nets are used in everyday life.
- Third, even if an experiment were the design of choice, it might not be possible for ethical or practical reasons. Imagine, for instance, that we were to hand out bed nets to only half of the villagers in a district. This might well cause resentment among the control villagers, and the villagers themselves might attempt to redistribute nets more fairly.
- Finally, experiments, in the form of RCTs, can be very expensive and resource intensive, particularly if we are interested in long-term outcomes.

 Activity 4.2

How many of the key ethical issues described above might be faced in carrying out the study described in Activity 4.1?

Feedback

A key ethical issue here is uncertainty. Given that there might already be good evidence that insecticide-treated bed nets are effective, some might consider it unnecessary to carry out a trial to test this. Gaining informed consent from all participants without jeopardizing the aims of the trial might also be difficult. If all villagers are informed of the aim (testing insecticide), they may ensure that all nets are treated, perhaps by buying insecticide to treat their nets from other outlets. This is called contamination.

In public health, the debate has shifted from the early focus on the methodological and practical difficulties involved in designing and conducting trials, such as the Oakley and bed nets examples described above, which were interested in the impact of one specific and relatively straightforward intervention (although, as we have already noted, this may be more complex than it initially seems), to the problems associated with attempts to measure the equity, public health, or general health and wellbeing impact(s) of more complex, multi-faceted interventions (e.g., large-scale programmes or policies). While noting that the boundaries between what constitute simple and more complex interventions are not clear-cut, Craig et al. (2008) suggest that the latter typically consist of a number of interacting components. The other characteristics which make interventions complex, and which they recommend that evaluators should take into account, include the 'number and difficulty of behaviours required by those delivering or receiving the intervention; number of groups or organisational levels targeted by the intervention; number and variability of outcomes; degree of flexibility or tailoring of the intervention permitted' (Craig et al. 2008: 979). For a brief guide to developing and evaluating complex interventions see Craig et al. (2008).

Two key questions that researchers evaluating complex interventions will often seek to address are whether and how they work in 'everyday practice' (Craig et al. 2008). Although RCTs may be the design of choice for researchers seeking to answer questions concerning the effectiveness and impact of complex interventions, they may not be feasible or appropriate as the researcher may not, for example, have any control over how and when an intervention is designed and implemented. Where the evaluation of the health impacts and/or effectiveness of population-level policies or large environmental or social interventions is required, such interventions may not be amenable to experimental manipulation, may be implemented in ways that make conducting planned experiments challenging, or may not be suitable for experimental evaluation for ethical or political reasons (Craig et al. 2012). The implementation of such interventions may, however, provide opportunities for conducting 'natural experiments', with potential health impacts investigated through the use of quasi-experimental and/or other research designs. Designed to evaluate the impact, over a 10-year period, of a housing-led regeneration project on the health and wellbeing of residents of disadvantaged neighbourhoods in Glasgow, the GoWell study (Egan et al. 2010) is an example of how the potential impacts of a complex multi-component intervention can be evaluated using a combination of research designs and data collection methods, where a large-scale trial is neither feasible nor appropriate. For readers interested in this topic, Craig et al. (2012) have produced a guide to using 'natural experiments' to evaluate population-level health interventions, including discussion of the associated challenges, drawbacks, and merits involved.

Cross-sectional design

Some research questions, such as the one posed earlier in this chapter concerning the number of teenagers in a particular district who smoke regularly, require us to collect data in a way that provides us with a 'snapshot' of a selected population regarding, for example, their attitudes, views or behaviours, or their exposure to specific risk factors. For this we use a cross-sectional design. The hallmark of the cross-sectional design is that data are collected from the population of interest at one point in time only. Cross-sectional designs or studies often, but not exclusively, employ surveys to collect data. Using a standardized questionnaire, for example, as our survey instrument, we can collect the same data from, and about, each member of our study sample at a particular time point. Examples include household surveys to collect data about family circumstances, or surveys of patients to evaluate their satisfaction with services. The issues to consider in designing and conducting a survey are discussed in Chapter 12, but these are some illustrations of the kinds of questions that cross-sectional designs can address:

- Descriptive questions about population health and health behaviour. National surveys such as the Health Survey for England collect data on health and health-related issues each year. These are invaluable data for such descriptive questions as: How many people smoke? How many men or women have limiting long-standing illnesses?
- Descriptive questions about public attitudes. Cross-sectional studies using surveys are a useful way of taking a 'snapshot' of public attitudes or knowledge. One example is the British National Surveys of Sexual Attitudes and Lifestyles, or Natsal. These are among the largest and most detailed studies of sexual behaviour in the world. Three Natsal surveys have taken place: Natsal-1 in 1990–1991, Natsal-2 in 1999–2001 and Natsal-3 in 2010–2012. The third survey covers an extended age range (up to 74, compared to 59 and 44 in previous surveys) allowing exploration of the interplay between ageing and sexual behaviour. By combining data from all three surveys it has been possible to conduct both period and cohort analyses, as the surveys include people born from the 1930s to the 1990s (http://www.natsal.ac.uk).

   Another example is the Eurobarometer, which, since 1974, has questioned people within each member state of the European Union to monitor social and political attitudes. This includes information useful for public health policy, such as public concerns about food safety, or trust in public information. Here we could use the data to answer comparative questions, such as where in Europe consumers are most concerned about the risks of food infection. However, comparing data across countries needs care and we need to be sure the instrument used has validity for the population. Surveys of attitudes are also used within health care organizations to look at users' perspectives.
- Studies of association. As well as descriptive analysis, we can use survey data to look at associations between different variables. Young people's consumption of alcohol, tobacco and illegal drugs is a public health concern in the UK. Using data from a nationally representative cross-sectional survey of school children in England, Farmer and Hanratty (2012) explored relationships between subjective wellbeing, low household income (eligibility for free school meals being used as a proxy indicator), and self-reported regular substance use among 3903 school children, aged 10–15 years, and living in two local authority areas in the North-West of England. Multivariate analysis revealed older age to be the most important factor associated with regular substance use. The study findings also indicated that living in a low-income household was associated with substance use, adjusting for subjective wellbeing and age. Children

who reported being able to communicate with their families, or being happy, were less likely to be regular substance users.

In general, well-designed cross-sectional studies are good for answering descriptive research questions. If we can be sure that our cross-sectional survey included a representative sample of the population (see Chapter 12), and used a reliable and valid survey instrument, we can be fairly confident that the results will be applicable to the whole population of interest.

However, cross-sectional studies cannot address questions about causation. To take the example above on the relationships between subjective wellbeing, low household income and substance use, we cannot conclude that living in a low-income household causes children to use substances; the survey findings simply indicate that there is an association between the two. This is one of the drawbacks of the cross-sectional design. If we need to look at causal relationships, ideally an experimental design is needed. In the case above, this would be impossible: we could not randomly assign children and their families to live on different income levels for the sake of research.

An alternative to experimental designs for addressing causal relationships, where randomization is not possible or appropriate, is the longitudinal design. This type of research design is mentioned here because, like the cross-sectional design, it is often used in public health and social research. Longitudinal designs involve repeating data collection at several time points with the same people. An example of a longitudinal design is a prospective *cohort study*, which follows the same sample of people who share a common characteristic, such as their year of birth, over time. Large cohort studies can look at how, for instance, health behaviour or social circumstances affect future health. However, it should be noted that longitudinal studies are not without their challenges (e.g., they tend to be expensive; attrition from samples may occur over time; and there can be significant problems with attributing direction of causality). Note also that RCTs are themselves 'longitudinal' in nature as participants are generally followed up at several time points.

Observational designs

In the social sciences, an observational design is one that enables the researcher to observe behaviour in as 'natural' a setting as possible (note that it has a rather different meaning in epidemiology, where it would include cross-sectional and cohort designs). In experiments, the researcher deliberately introduces an intervention. In cross-sectional surveys, the researcher asks for responses to a predetermined set of questions. Observational designs are orientated towards describing and analysing everyday lives and behaviours.

Ethnography has become popular across the social sciences as one example of observational studies. In traditional ethnographies in anthropology the researcher lives amongst those being studied for extended periods of time, from several months to many years, in order to understand the world from their perspective. It is a research approach characterized by flexibility, depth and iteration (repetition over time, for instance, by going back to ask interviewees further questions as the research evolves). The primary method of generating data in ethnographic research is through participant observation. Data collected during periods of observation help researchers focus in on topics, which need further exploration in interviews. This symbiotic relationship between observation and interviews allows researchers to explore and compare what people say with what they do.

Anthropologists strive to understand local and *emic* ('insider') perspectives and ways of doing things. To do this they use the most open-ended and unstructured methods possible. For many ethnographers, who have undergone training in anthropology, this has meant a mandatory rite of passage of fieldwork at one or many points in their lives; that is, total immersion, participant observation and the holistic study of a community. The product of long-term fieldwork, called an ethnography, does not necessarily have a researcher-driven focal topic, but instead comprises a comprehensive study of the interrelationships between environment, economic and social organization, politics, science, religion, medicine, and so forth, in a community. Applied medical anthropologists usually work within multidisciplinary teams on studies with time-bound public health agendas. In this instance long-term fieldwork is not always feasible or necessary to provide contextual information relevant to study outcomes. In applied social research observational designs are often combined with other designs. For instance, we might use observational work at the beginning of a study to look at how a health care setting 'worked' before moving on to design an intervention study, or combine observations of meetings with interviews.

The key advantage of observational designs is that they allow researchers to answer questions about people's behaviour in everyday contexts: how people talk and act in their working and home lives. Ethnographic observational studies, if done well, can generate rich, deep information about one particular context. The disadvantage is that this is time-consuming, and research projects can usually only include one or a couple of sites within the study. They might then be limited in terms of generalizability.

Other kinds of observational design use 'naturally occurring' behaviour and inter-actions, such as consultations in health care settings, as the data. Here, audio or video recordings of consultations are transcribed in detail and analysed to answer questions about how health care providers and patients communicate. More quantitative approaches to observational data (such as counting the number of times nurses wash their hands on a hospital ward) resemble surveys.

Documentary approaches

The three designs discussed so far generally involve collecting, or generating, new data. Documentary approaches are those that use existing documentary resources as data. Modern organizations produce large numbers of documents: a hospital, for instance, pro-duces medical and nursing notes on individual patients, summary reports of patient sta-tistics such as numbers treated, management reports including statements of current strategies and annual reports, internal memoranda and emails between staff, and possi-bly patient information leaflets or health promotion materials. Individuals also produce documents such as diaries and letters. Mass media also include documents such as newspapers, magazines and television programmes. There is, then, an enormous wealth of potential 'data' for health research that already exists. Documentary research approaches are particularly useful when sensitive or adversarial research needs to be undertaken (e.g., until recently the tobacco industry was under no obligation to provide researchers with its research data, so publicly available documentary sources constituted an important source of information for interested researchers), for historical research, or for conducting research on health-related communication (e.g., an analysis of the differ-ent media used to communicate health-related messages).

As will be described in Chapter 15, three broad approaches are used by documentary researchers, depending on the nature of the research question to be addressed: a qualitative interpretive analysis involves the critical analysis of a set of qualitative documents; quantitative reconstruction involves the analysis of historical statistics; and content analysis consists of the construction and analysis of a quantitative data set based on qualitative sources (e.g., counting the frequency of media reports on a given health issue, and categorizing them into a number of emerging themes).

Documentary designs have practical strengths. The use of existing documents can save time and money, although it is important to remember that documents cannot be used in any simplistic way as data about reality. In discussing how documents can be used in studies of organizations, Paul Atkinson and Amanda Coffey (1997: 47) note that:

> one must be quite clear what they can and cannot be used for. They are 'social facts', in that they are produced, shared and used in socially organized ways. They are not, however, transparent representations of organizational routines, decision-making process or medical diagnoses. They construct particular kinds of representations within their own conventions. We should not use documentary sources as surrogates for other kinds of data.

Documents in the public domain, such as newspaper articles or reports of national statistics, are easily accessed. However, accessing documents such as medical records will require ethical approval and may be time-consuming. Chapter 15 looks in detail at some of the methodological issues raised by using documentary sources.

Participatory research designs

The final type of design to be introduced in this chapter is that of participatory research. For some researchers, the aim of research is not just to document or analyse the social world but to change it: this kind of research is often called *action research*. As Elizabeth Hart and Meg Bond (1995) note, action research 'may be particularly appropriate where problem-solving and improvement are on the agenda'. Participatory action research covers a number of perspectives, ranging from radical attempts at changing the social order through to more limited projects working on professional practice. Studies in these traditions include ambitious projects aiming at empowerment of rural villagers in developed country settings as well as smaller studies based on single hospital wards that are designed to improve nursing practice. What these perspectives share is a belief in research processes that include elements of working with (rather than researching on) participants in order for them to control the research agenda and outcomes and to identify desired changes. There is also usually an explicit commitment to viewing the knowledge of participants as essential to the process. Many studies in health include elements of participatory design. This can be at a minimal level of including representatives of user groups in steering committees (such as those from patients' associations) through to full participatory designs that attempt to redress radically the traditional power relationships within research. A short example of a participatory approach is described by Paine *et al.* (2002):

> The Stepping Stones project aims to empower communities to take control of their own sexual and emotional health. In evaluating the impact of Stepping Stones in the Gambia, the research team used a participatory approach that included the use of workshops with separate age and gender groups from the intervention villages. In

these, villagers were invited to set priorities for action. Villagers changed the focus from 'family planning' to 'infertility prevention', in line with their own priorities about sexual health. Thus, rather than designing research using the agenda and priorities of the researchers, participatory approaches focus on changes identified by participants.

Participatory designs are not without their challenges. These include the demarcation of boundaries between those evaluating projects and those implementing change, and the difficultly in objectively documenting the processes of change and attributing significance to specific actions or factors.

Other designs

The approaches we have suggested here are clearly not exhaustive, nor are they mutually exclusive. First, many projects include a number of designs used in sequence or in tandem (see Chapter 16). Also, individual studies may not 'fit' any of these designs. One example is that of the qualitative interview study, which is a little like a survey in that it collects data from a sample of individuals, but not the same data, and the data collected are not amenable to statistical analysis. Instead, the qualitative interview study utilizes some of the logic of observational designs, in that the idea is to encourage respondents to talk 'as if' they were in naturalistic settings.

Research design and data collection methods

There is no inevitable relationship between the design of a study and the methods used to collect or generate data. Although experiments may be more associated with quantitative data collection methods, sometimes in-depth interviews or focus groups are used. In the trial of social support in pregnancy, the researchers used interviews to collect data post-intervention on women's views of the services they received as well as collecting data on the meaning of certain events. Similarly, an observational study could quantify observations. An example might be research on adverse events in a hospital ward. Although the design is observational, the researchers might want to classify particular events (drug errors, falls and so on) and count them. It is, then, important to distinguish between the design of the study and the data collection methods used.

Summary

In this chapter, you have learnt about the importance of selecting an appropriate study design for the research question. Experiments are the strongest design for answering questions about causal relationships. However, they are not as commonly used in social as in medical research. First, there are often limitations on how far we can 'intervene' in human behaviour. Second, most of the questions social researchers are interested in are not primarily about cause and effect but are about describing or understanding health and health-related behaviour. For these sorts of questions, cross-sectional designs offer advantages for many descriptive questions, whereas observational designs may be strongest for questions reliant on in-depth understanding of human behaviour.

References

Atkinson, P, and Coffey, A. (1997) Analysing documentary realities. In D. Silverman (ed.) *Qualitative Research: Theory, Method and Practice*. London: Sage.

Craig, P., Cooper, C., Gunnell, D. *et al.* (2012) Using natural experiments to evaluate population health interventions: New Medical Research Council guidance. *Journal of Epidemiology and Community Health* 66: 1182–1186.

Craig, P., Dieppe, P., Macintyre, S., Michie, S., Nazareth, I. and Petticrew, M. (2008) Developing and evaluating complex interventions: The new Medical Research Council guidance. *British Medical Journal* 337: a1655.

Egan, M., Kearns, A., Mason, P. *et al.* (2010) Protocol for a mixed methods study investigating the impact of investment in housing, regeneration and neighbourhood renewal on the health and wellbeing of residents: The GoWell programme. *BMC Medical Research Methodology* 10: 41. http://www.biomedcentral.com/1471-2288/10/41

Famer, S. and Hanratty, B. (2012) The relationship between subjective wellbeing, low income and substance use among schoolchildren in the northwest of England: A cross-sectional study. *Journal of Public Health* 34: 512–522.

Hart, E. and Bond, M. (1995) *Action Research for Health and Social Care: A Guide to Practice*. Buckingham: Open University Press.

Oakley, A. (1990) Who's afraid of the randomized controlled trial? In H. Roberts (ed.) *Women's Health Counts*. London: Routledge.

Paine, K., Hart, G., Jawo, M., Ceesay, S., Jallow, M., Morison, L., Walraven, G., McAdam, K. and Shaw, M. (2002) 'Before we were sleeping, now we are awake': Preliminary evaluation of the Stepping Stones sexual health programme in The Gambia. *African Journal of AIDS Research* 1: 41–52.

Further reading

Creswell, J.W. (2009) *Research Design: Qualitative, Quantitative and Mixed Method Approaches* (3rd edn). London: Sage.

This is aimed mainly at postgraduate students planning a dissertation or thesis, but is a useful and readable guide to the steps in designing a proposal, from reviewing the literature through to writing it up in an appropriate way.

Geissler, P.W. and Prince, R.J. (2010) *The Land is Dying: Contingency, Creativity and Conflict in Western Kenya* (Epistemologies of Healing, Vol. 5). New York and Oxford: Berghahn Books.

Reynolds Whyte, S., Whyte, M.A., Meinert, L. and Twebaze. J. (2013) Therapeutic clientship: Belonging in Uganda's projectified landscape of AIDS care. In J. Biehl and A. Petryna (eds) *When People Come First: Critical Studies in Global Health*. Princeton, NJ: Princeton University Press.

For students interested in the topic, the above two references are good examples of how ethnographic research is written up and published.

SECTION 2

Qualitative methods of data collection and analysis

Second edition revised and updated by Tracey Chantler

Introduction to qualitative research methods

5

Overview

Over the past two decades the contribution of qualitative research to the field of public health has grown significantly, and is evident in the increasing publication of qualitative studies in high-impact academic health journals. There is keen interest in the way that qualitative methods can complement quantitative methods in multi-methods research approaches (see Chapter 16), but the value of stand-alone qualitative research (the main focus of this section) is also widely recognized as a way of addressing questions which are not amenable to experimental or survey methods. Qualitative methods used in public health have their roots in the disciplines of sociology and anthropology. Chapters 5–7 introduce some of the methods used by sociologists and anthropologists in observational and participatory research designs (see Chapter 4). The present chapter starts by providing an overview of the orientations, aims and potential uses of qualitative methods, and then Chapters 6 and 7 look more closely at the use of interviews and focus groups. These data collection methods may seem diverse, but they do have in common some basic orientations towards research, apart from their tendency to produce language, rather than numerical data. The activities included in these chapters and the references to classic as well as more recent literature will enable you to explore how qualitative research methods can be used to address problems and questions in public health. Chapter 8 provides an introduction to qualitative data analysis, and Chapter 9 is a practical exercise designed to give you some experience in using qualitative data collection and analysis methods.

Studying Chapters 5–9 will enable you to appreciate the value of qualitative health research, identify the advantages and disadvantages of qualitative interviews, focus groups and participant observation as qualitative data collection methods, and help you to understand different approaches and techniques used to analyse qualitative data.

Learning objectives

After working through this chapter, you will be better able to:

- identify the main methods used in qualitative research
- identify the main aims of qualitative research
- comprehend core orientations which characterize qualitative research

Key terms

Interpretive approaches: Approaches that focus on understanding human behaviour from the perspective of those being studied.

Naturalism: Studying social behaviour in the context in which it 'naturally' occurs.

Qualitative research methods and the aims of qualitative research

Qualitative research methods are characterized as those that aim to explore meaning and that produce non-numerical data. Qualitative data can be produced by a range of data collection techniques. These include:

- *participant observation* in which the researcher participates, to some extent, with the group he or she is studying – this is a hallmark of ethnographic research;
- *in-depth or semi-structured interviewing* to explore the attitudes and experiences of individuals;
- *focus groups* or group interviews;
- *audio-recording or filming naturally occurring talk*, such as consultations between health professionals and patients;
- *analysing textual or pictorial data*, such as diaries or photographs, to explore what they can tell us about the individuals or societies that produced them.

However, these data collection techniques can also produce quantitative data. Certain forms of observation can, for example, be designed to quantify aspects of human behaviour, such as counting the number of times nurses speak to patients, or the number of questions patients ask in a consultation. Similarly, textual data (diaries, magazine articles, newspaper reports) could be quantitatively analysed by counting the number of times a concept is mentioned, or the number of column inches devoted to a topic.

What makes a research study qualitative is not the data collection strategy used, but the aim of the study, the questions posed (the what, how and why), and how the data produced are analysed. Health research that employs qualitative approaches has a range of different aims, but common ones include those of *understanding* the experiences and attitudes of patients, the community, or health care workers. In public health research, this is often done with the goal of informing policy-makers or practitioners.

In an article arguing for the greater use of qualitative methods for assessing health care, for instance, Ray Fitzpatrick and Mary Boulton (1994) summarize their view of the aims of qualitative research:

> Qualitative research depends upon not numerical but conceptual analysis and presentation. It is used where it is important to understand the meaning and interpretation of human social arrangements such as hospitals, clinics, forms of management, or decision making. Qualitative methods are intended to convey to policy makers the experiences of individuals, groups, and organisations, who may be affected by policies.

Building on this understanding of the purpose of qualitative research, and in view of the increasing acceptance of qualitative evidence, Nicky Britten (2011) argues that qualitative researchers need to develop expertise in synthesizing findings from primary qualitative research studies:

> Although qualitative research is often characterised as providing descriptions of patients' experiences, the challenge for qualitative researchers is to become more ambitious than this. By moving beyond description and emphasising the development of new concepts and theories, qualitative researchers can help to unpack the processes surrounding healthcare communication and explain 'how, why and what' is going on. The synthesis of qualitative research offers the opportunity of building up a

cumulative evidence base comparable to the growing evidence base of quantitative research, which is based on much larger and more diverse populations than those of single studies. In this way, the early criticism of qualitative research – that it is based on small and unrepresentative samples – is less and less relevant. Qualitative synthesis also offers the opportunity of developing more comprehensive theoretical and explanatory models.

Qualitative systematic reviews which include this kind of synthesis are becoming more commonplace (for an example, see Campbell *et al.* 2011), and prior to undertaking qualitative research it is important to undertake a literature search to identify any relevant reviews in your topic area. The methods used to undertake qualitative meta-synthesis fall outside the scope of this book, but it is important to be aware of this development in the field of qualitative research.

Orientations of qualitative research

Many qualitative researchers share a set of assumptions about the research process, including the aims of research and how research ought to proceed. Three of these orientations are outlined here. They are an interpretive approach, a commitment to naturalism, and the adoption of flexible research strategies. Of course, not all qualitative studies or research will feature these orientations at all times.

Interpretive approach

Much qualitative research has a relativist starting point. As the aim is to explore how people understand events and phenomena, qualitative researchers start by assuming that there are different possible and legitimate understandings. In other words, qualitative researchers are interested in multiple social realities and they try to avoid assuming that their view of the world is the only valid and rational one. Thus what appears common sense to one social actor may not be to another. A good example of this is research on lay health beliefs – which to the professional may appear irrational and unscientific but which have a consistency and rationality for the patient and may lead to very different ways of conceptualizing health and disease. This is sometimes called an *interpretive approach* in that it aims to interpret how people conceptualize the world. The orientation towards interpretation and understanding is illustrated by the work of the American sociologist Erving Goffman in his study of large psychiatric institutions (Goffman 1961). He used participant observation to understand the lives of patients who lived in them and staff who worked there and wrote of the importance of seeing the world through the eyes of those being studied:

> any group of persons develops a life of their own that becomes meaningful, reasonable and normal once you get close to it and a good way to learn about any of these worlds is to submit oneself in the company of the members to the daily round of petty contingencies to which they are subject.

In contrast to positivist social science, which assumes there is only one 'reality', interpretive social science takes seriously the possibility that there may be different realities depending on people's circumstances.

Naturalism

A second orientation of many qualitative studies is a commitment to *naturalism* – the importance of trying to study behaviour in its natural context rather than, for instance, in the laboratory or in terms of answers to questionnaires. What people say and do is related to where they are – behaviour is contextual. People take medications in their home, when out, to fit in with the rest of their lives, not in the controlled conditions of a drug trial. Health workers relate to their clients in hospitals, clinics and in clients' homes, not in their offices where they fill in your survey questionnaires. One of the advantages of qualitative research is that it can inform practitioners and policy-makers about how policies are put into practice (or not) in 'real life'. A summary of a study of asthma patients in the UK by Adams *et al.* (1997), illustrates this.

Using qualitative research: an example

Stephanie Adams, Roisin Pill and Alan Jones were interested in the general problem of 'why patients do or do not take their medication as prescribed' (Adams *et al.* 1997) and how qualitative research can contribute to our understanding of how decisions that might seem irrational (such as not taking prescribed medication) can be understood better by taking a patient-centred perspective. Asthma is a common condition, and, from the perspective of health professionals, poor compliance with prophylactic medication (the 'preventer' inhaler) and overuse of the 'reliever' inhaler (intended only for relieving symptoms) contribute to high rates of morbidity and mortality. Adams *et al.* used in-depth interviews with 30 patients to understand medication behaviour from the patients' perspective.

When they analysed the interviews, the researchers identified three broad patterns of response to asthma diagnosis and symptoms. For about half the sample, 'denial' or 'distancing' characterized their accounts. Most denied that they had asthma, preferring to describe themselves as having chest trouble or short-term conditions. Although denying they had asthma, detailed stories from their interviews suggested that their symptoms did interfere with everyday life, entailing avoidance of exercise or of going outdoors on occasion. This group also hid their medication use to a large extent, reporting using inhalers only out of sight of others, and had negative views of asthmatics – an identity they did not accept for themselves. Most did not use preventative medications at all – partly because of worry that they would become dependent on drugs that have to be taken daily, but also because taking medication regularly, whether there are symptoms or not, relies on accepting an asthmatic identity, which these 'deniers' did not. Given that they did not see themselves as having asthma, they did not attend special clinics for asthma.

A smaller group within the sample accepted both the diagnosis and their doctors' advice completely, using medications as prescribed and taking pride in doing so. For this group, the route to 'normal life' was gaining adequate control over symptoms through medication. Their definitions of asthma coincided with those of medical professionals. For them, 'asthmatic' was not a stigmatized identity, and they used inhalers in public.

The final response was identified among a few respondents, described as 'pragmatists'. This group did use preventative medication, but usually not as prescribed and only when their asthma was particularly bad. They also had a pragmatic approach to disclosing asthma diagnosis, for instance, in telling family, but not employers in case it prejudiced their employment prospects. This group accepted they had asthma, but usually perceived it as mild, or as an acute rather than a chronic illness.

Looking at medication use from the point of view of patients enabled the researchers to see how health behaviour was tied tightly to people's beliefs about asthma and what kind of chest problems they had, as well as social circumstances and the threat of an asthmatic identity to other social identities. For patients, health, defined in medical terms, may not be the top priority all the time, and the meaning of symptoms for professionals may be rather different from the meaning of symptoms for patients.

✎ Activity 5.1

How might these findings be useful to primary care practitioners who are planning a special asthma clinic in their practice? How might they help them address factors which mean asthma sufferers do not benefit fully from prescribed medicine?

Feedback

For service providers and health promoters this kind of information is very useful. First, it suggests that providing designated asthma clinics may not appeal to the majority of sufferers, either because they do not identify themselves as having asthma or because they see themselves as in control of their condition. Second, professionals can see that what appears to be irrational use of medication and the result of ignorance Is actually deeply embedded in complex social identities that have to be managed.

Flexible research strategy

A third orientation of qualitative research is the adoption of a flexible or 'open' research strategy. Quantitative studies tend to follow standardized research stages, which are reproduced when writing up for publication. Studies start perhaps with the definition of a hypothesis to test, then proceed to designing a data collection instrument, collecting the data, and then analysing data to produce results. This is, of course, a proper way to proceed if there is a firm hypothesis to test. However, in qualitative studles the research question may be informed by the priorities and experiences of participants such as interviewees, and become refined as a result of early data collection and analysis. Analysis starts as soon as data are collected, rather than at the end of the study. This initial analysis can also inform later sampling. This is known as *theoretical sampling*, when cases or sites are included in the study on the basis of an emerging theory about relationships between variables rather than as a result of an initial, one-off sampling decision (for more about theoretical sampling and grounded theory, see Chapter 8).

When is it appropriate to use qualitative methods?

Before we can count events or phenomena in a quantitative study, we have to know what *should* be counted: what the relevant variables are and how they should be defined to inform the researchers about the concepts they are interested in. Qualitative research is an important part of this, especially if the research topic is a relatively new one. In this situation, qualitative research can help generate hypotheses, which can later be tested using quantitative methods. Qualitative research is useful for generating theory and developing new concepts. At a more practical level, qualitative work is essential in questionnaire design to ensure that the phrases and language used are meaningful to those who will be completing the questionnaire.

However, qualitative methods are not just a precursor to quantitative studies, nor are they just complementary to quantitative research or a component of multi-methods research (see Chapter 16). Qualitative methods can be used independently in observational or participatory research designs to answer questions which are not amenable to experimental design or survey methods. The following is a summary of an ethnographic study by Madeleine Gantley *et al.* (1993) which shows how qualitative research can help explain statistical variations: in this case the finding that ethnicity is related to rates of sudden infant death syndrome.

Using ethnographic methods: an example

Sudden infant death syndrome is the most important cause of death for infants aged between 1 and 12 months in the UK. The rate varies across the different ethnic groups that make up the UK population, with babies born to mothers from Bangladesh having significantly lower rates that those born to mothers born in the UK, Northern Ireland or the Caribbean. Epidemiological evidence and current knowledge about risk factors do not help explain this difference, and the researchers were interested in whether infant care practices might contribute to this low rate. To investigate infant care practices, they undertook a qualitative study in which they asked parents to describe a day in the life of their infant. They interviewed mothers born either in south Wales or Bangladesh who had children under 1 year old.

From these interviews, they identified some themes that suggested some differences in the ways in which infant care happened in Bangladeshi or Welsh households. For example, in Bangladeshi families, infants were more likely to be in households where child care was shared between a number of adults, such as brothers and their wives living together in extended families, whereas the mothers born in Wales were more likely to be in nuclear households with just parents and their children. Extended Bangladeshi families of cousins and grandparents meant that people other than parents were more likely to be involved with child care than in the Welsh households. Bangladeshi families were more likely to have larger numbers of children, meaning there was more general familiarity with infant care. For the Welsh mothers, the arrival of a child was more likely to lead to dramatic changes in lifestyle. Welsh mothers were more likely to focus on regularity and routine in household management and infant care, in contrast to Bangladeshi mothers who stressed fluidity and flexibility. Bangladeshi infants sleep close to other people, but Welsh mothers felt it important to get babies used to sleeping alone, in their own cots at first, and in their own rooms where this was possible.

It is not possible from this kind of study to identify which practices might protect against sudden infant death, but the findings do suggest some useful pointers to explore potential physiological mechanisms, such as the sensory stimulation from others that might help regulate breathing for human infants.

Activity 5.2

Why do you think the researchers used qualitative methods for this study?

Feedback

They were interested in the broad area of 'infant care practices', and wanted to explore differences between two ethnic groups in the UK. Not enough was known about how these might affect child health either to develop a structured survey, or to start testing cause and effect. Qualitative methods are particularly useful for these kinds of exploratory questions.

Summary

Qualitative methods aim to focus on how people interpret their social worlds and to explore the meaning of phenomena and events for participants. They contribute to health and health services research by investigating issues not amenable to quantitative analysis, by informing the development of quantitative tools and by exploring the processes described by statistical research.

References

Adams, S., Pill, R. and Jones, A. (1997) Medication, chronic illness and identity: The perspective of people with asthma. *Social Science & Medicine*, 45: 189–201.

Britten, N. (2011) Qualitative research on health communication: What can it contribute? *Patient Education and Counseling*, 82: 384–388.

Campbell, R., Pound, P., Morgan, M., Daker-White, G., Britten, N., Pill, R., Yardley, L., Pope, C. and Donovan, J. (2011) Evaluating meta-ethnography: Systematic analysis and synthesis of qualitative research. *Health Technology Assessment*, 15(43): 1–164.

Fitzpatrick, R. and Boulton, M. (1994) Qualitative methods for assessing health care. *Quality in Health Care*, 3: 107–113.

Gantley, M., Davies, D.P. and Murcott, A. (1993) Sudden infant death syndrome: Links with infant care practices. *British Medical Journal*, 306: 16–20.

Goffman, E. (1961) *Asylums*. Harmondsworth: Penguin.

Further reading

Green, J. and Thorogood, N. (2013) *Qualitative Methods for Health Research* (3rd rev. edn). London: Sage.
This introduction to qualitative methods is aimed at health professionals who need to use qualitative findings or conduct their own studies, and introduces key issues in research design, data collection and analysis. It uses examples from a range of health care systems.

6 Qualitative interviewing

Overview

Qualitative interviewing involves using a semi-structured or more open topic guide to explore how respondents experience, conceptualize or construct their social worlds. This method has been widely used in health research to explore the beliefs and views of users and providers of health care.

Learning objectives

After studying this chapter, you will be able to:

- identify the uses of qualitative interviewing
- develop your skills in designing topic guides
- develop your skills in asking questions and listening to answers

Key terms

In-depth interviews: The interviewer uses a broad topic guide, but respondents' priorities influence the final range of questions covered.

Rapport: Relaxed, natural communication between interviewer and respondent.

Semi-structured interviews: The interviewer uses a more defined topic guide in which set questions are covered, but can prompt for more information.

Structured interviews: The interviewer uses a schedule in which questions are asked in a predetermined standard order.

Research interview methods

Interviewing is one of the most commonly used methods in social research in health, and qualitative interviews are only one form of research interview. Table 6.1 illustrates one typology of interviews, where they are classified by how *structured* they are, or the extent to which the questions asked by the researcher are predetermined.

Table 6.1 Types of interview

	Format of questions	Example of uses
Structured	Standardized, predetermined, asked in the same order	Survey research
Semi-structured	List of questions or interviewer prompts	Surveys or qualitative studies
In-depth (sometimes called narrative)	Broad topic guide	Qualitative study

Many surveys, especially those aiming to generate data that are generalizable to the whole population, favour the use of standardized structured interview formats, where the same questions are asked in the same order of each respondent, and the interviewer's job is to be as neutral as possible, so they do not influence, or bias, the respondents' answers. This is more likely to produce standardized data amenable to statistical analysis. In these kinds of surveys, if interviewers are used, they are, in effect, a tool for collecting responses, and interaction between interviewer and respondent is seen as a problem to be managed – it potentially interferes with reliability. From the more positivist perspective, the aim is to minimize the influence that interviewers have on the data they collect – to remove, as far as possible, interviewer bias. We will return to standardized, or structured, interviews in Chapters 10–13, when survey research is introduced.

In qualitative approaches, researchers are more likely to start with other assumptions about the nature of an interview, the status of data collected and the role of the interviewer. The role of the interviewer shifts depending on the perspective employed in the research. The qualitative interview provides a method of gaining in-depth information about people's knowledge, beliefs and interpretations of the world.

In qualitative work, interviews are therefore more commonly *semi-structured* (with a set of questions to cover, but which can be rephrased to suit the understanding and vocabulary of the respondent, and supplemented to probe for more information), or *unstructured*. You will see a number of different terms to describe unstructured interviews, such as in-depth interviews and narrative interviews. These terms generally refer to interviews in which the interviewer has a list of prompts or topics to focus the interview but the conversation is guided by the priorities of the respondent. The advantage of using semi-structured approaches is that similar data can be gathered from all respondents; the advantage of using unstructured interviews is that they are more likely to elicit the views and priorities of the respondents rather than merely gathering their responses to the researcher's concerns. The best approach to use depends on the aims of the research. When it is important to explore in detail the respondents' own perceptions and accounts, a less structured approach will be most useful. This might be the case if researching a topic on which little is known, or when it is important to gain an in-depth understanding of a topic.

What makes a good qualitative interview?

In both the qualitative and structured interview setting interviewers need to demonstrate interpersonal skills, which engender trust, and allow interviewees to feel comfortable talking about their experiences and attitudes. In qualitative interviews these skills are especially important and it is essential for the interviewer to establish good rapport with the interviewee. The aim is to create a flow of 'natural' conversation, which requires skills in active listening and the ability to ask questions which demonstrate an appreciation for interviewees' personal and social context.

Developing rapport and considering context

The sociologist Richard Sennett (2003), in reflecting on his early experiences as a field researcher, describes how he came to develop interview skills:

> In-depth interviewing is a distinctive, often frustrating craft. Unlike a pollster asking questions, the in-depth interviewer wants to probe the responses people give. To probe, the interviewer cannot be stonily impersonal: he or she has to give something of himself or herself in order to merit an open response. Yet the conversation lists in one direction; the point is not to talk the way friends do . . . The craft consists in calibrating social distances without making the subject feel like an insect under the microscope.

This reflection suggests that interviewing is a craft – the skills needed are developed through practice – and that it requires insights into how to develop appropriate relationships with interviewees. The development of a good relationship is referred to as 'rapport': the establishment of a relaxed interchange in which interviewees feel able to talk without feeling judged and have the space to tell their story. This is a skill that builds on the techniques we use in everyday life to listen to the stories and opinions of others, although, as Sennett notes, it is not quite like the kind of interchange you might have with your friends. First, the conversation is more directed in that you are trying to elicit talk on a more or less defined topic. Second, the aim is usually not for you to expound your opinions and beliefs as well, but solely to elicit those of your interviewee.

The interviewer must be aware of cultural and social differences, not because these should be eliminated but because they need to be taken into account in qualitative work. Often we are interviewing people from very different backgrounds: from different professions, genders, ethnicities, ages or social status. These differences have an effect on all aspects of the interview: how likely it is that someone will agree to be interviewed, how much they feel they can disclose, and how they frame their answers to your questions. On some very sensitive topics it may be sensible to 'match' interviewers with interviewees in terms of characteristics such as ethnicity or gender. However, it is also important to ensure a level of social distance in order to facilitate open interactions between interviewers and interviewees. It can be easier to talk about a sensitive issue with someone who is not part of your social circle, and an outsider asks questions an insider may take for granted or never have associated with the topic of study. In short, in order to understand how research participants think (and gain some insight into how they behave from their accounts) it can be helpful if interviewers and interviewees do not share the same assumptions and world view.

Although we cannot change our social characteristics, we can adopt the kinds of behaviours that are more likely to engender rapport. The specific behaviours will differ from setting to setting, and depend on what the normal 'rules' for interpersonal interactions are in the setting in which you are working. In general, though, the key is to practise active listening skills, be interested, non-judgmental and encouraging. So if you want, for instance, to probe your respondent on an unusual opinion, or extreme view, do not look surprised or disapproving, but perhaps probe with some more neutral questions: 'Do you think that is a view shared by most people?' or 'Other people might think X: what would you say to them?'

To maintain rapport in an interview, the interviewer needs to listen carefully to answers so that the next question follows on and so that respondents do not have to repeat themselves. Some of the ways in which this is achieved will include:

- Eye contact. In many cultures, it is important to maintain eye contact, but without staring at the interviewee.
- Making the appropriate non-verbal noises or prompts (such as 'um-hm', 'yes', 'um' in English) and nods of encouragement that make people feel they are being listened to and can carry on speaking.
- Following up points where appropriate, or making appropriate neutral and non-leading comments in response ('that sounds difficult', 'was anything else important?').
- Not interrupting. This is often difficult to start with, as interviewers can be anxious not to leave a long space in the conversation, or to continue through the topic guide.
- Not giving our own opinions or disagreeing.

Nicky Britten (1995) notes that those experienced in clinical interviewing already have some of the skills needed to be a good qualitative interviewer, but these skills do need adapting to generate good data from in-depth interviews, rather than clinical history-taking interviews:

> To achieve the transition from consultation to research interview, clinical researchers need to monitor their own interviewing technique, critically appraising tape recordings of their interviews and asking others for their comments. The novice interviewer needs to notice how directive he or she is being, whether leading questions are being asked, whether cues are picked up or ignored, and whether interviewees are being given enough time to explain what they mean.
>
> (1995: 252)

The general context of the interview will also have an effect on the kind of data you obtain. People talk differently in 'private' space (such as their home) than they do in public spaces (such as their workplace) and as you get to know people they are more likely to disclose less socially acceptable views and experiences. Jocelyn Cornwell (1984), in her study of people's accounts of health and illness in east London, interviewed her participants at different points, and she noted that in early interviews they gave different explanations and stories than in later ones, when they trusted her more as a friend rather than an 'outsider'. She called these accounts 'public' and 'private' accounts. It is not that the 'private' accounts are more accurate, or that her interviewees were lying in the more 'public', earlier ones, but just that people frame their responses differently in different contexts.

Practical and ethical considerations

Interviews in qualitative research are usually recorded and then fully transcribed, both to allow a good rapport to develop between interviewer and respondent, and to allow full analysis of the interview based on the respondent's real words. This can be time-consuming: one hour of recorded conversation can take five hours to transcribe fully. Recording reduces the need to take written notes of respondents' answers during the interview, which allows the interviewer to engage fully with the interviewee. This said, it can be very useful to have a notebook at hand to jot down interesting points you want to return to in the course of the interview. It is also good practice to write a short summary of the interview shortly after you have completed it. In this summary you can make a note of the flow of the conversation, non-verbal communication and any particular or surprising topics which came up and might need to be explored in subsequent interviews with the current and other interviewees. When planning qualitative interviews you need to pace yourself as this type of interaction requires significant energy. Therefore be realistic about the number of interviews you can manage well in a day, and allow yourself sufficient time to complete summary notes between interviews.

Qualitative interviews, particularly those covering sensitive topic areas, can provoke emotional responses from interviewees. Interviewers need to be prepared to pause the recording of interviews should this occur, and ensure that the interviewee is willing to continue the interview. Researchers have a number of responsibilities to research participants, including ensuring confidentiality, avoidance of harm, reciprocity and feedback of results. Participants need to be assured that they will not be able to be identified in research publications.

Qualitative interview topic guides

A key element of a good interview is developing the right questions to ask. Even if using less structured approaches, it is worth spending some time on thinking about the best ways to elicit the most useful data for your research question. Your respondents (whether they are patients or professionals) are unlikely to share your perspectives on the world, your classifications, or your vocabulary, so you need to develop questions that allow them to frame appropriate answers.

✎ Activity 6.1

A hospital psychiatric department is concerned at the high drop-out rate from its treatment programmes. You want to interview people who have been diagnosed with schizophrenia, but who have not returned to the clinic, to see what their perceptions are of their health problem and what kind of help they think the hospital can provide for them. The first two questions on your proposed topic guide are:

- How has schizophrenia affected your life?
- Why have you dropped out of the hospital treatment programme?

Why might these not work very well at establishing rapport or eliciting useful information?

Feedback

First, patients may not share the interviewer's classification of their diagnosis. It might be better to elicit first how patients think about their (mental) health problems, rather than using a medical diagnosis. Look back at the example in Chapter 5 on exploring patients' understanding of asthma: here the researchers found that many people who had been diagnosed with asthma did not share this view of their 'chest troubles'. The second question again uses the researcher's frame of reference: that 'dropping out' is a problem and that the interviewee can account for it as a 'problem'. It would be more useful to ask about views of hospital treatment in a more neutral way by, for instance, asking about what interviewees' expectations were of treatment, and whether they had been met.

One temptation is always to simply ask interviewees our research question, but this is rarely a useful question to ask directly in an interview. For instance, the following are reasonable questions for researchers to consider, but neither would generate useful information if asked directly of an interviewee:

- 'Is poor knowledge about malaria transmission a barrier to using bed nets in this village?'
- 'Is inappropriate antibiotic prescribing the result of doctors being unaware of current guidelines?'

It is not just that these questions use vocabulary that might be unfamiliar. More importantly, they would merely generate respondents' views about your research question, which is not the intention. In an interview you want to generate data that, when analysed, will answer your research question – not generate a list of rather superficial thoughts on the answer to that question.

So how can we ask questions that are likely to generate useful data? There are no hard-and-fast rules on how to do this. We need to think first very carefully about what kind of data will be useful. If we are interested in why villagers do not use bed nets, we might want to start by generating lists of all the possible causes of malaria, from their perspectives, or talk more generally about what they think about bed nets and how they are used. If we want to understand why doctors prescribe antibiotics 'inappropriately' it may be more useful to ask questions that generate data on why and in what circumstances they prescribe. We need then to think about what kinds of questions generally elicit these kinds of data from the people we want to interview. Direct simple questions sometimes work, but often we need to think more imaginatively.

Rules of thumb for interview questions

- Start with *general* questions. To begin, use a general question both to orientate your interviewees to the topic, and to elicit the kind of language they prefer to use. For instance, 'Tell me about how you came to be a patient in this hospital' or 'Can you start by telling me a bit about your working day here as a nurse?'
- Ask *open* questions. These are questions that require more than a 'yes' or 'no' in answer.
- Ask *neutral* questions. Instead of 'Why haven't you had your children immunized?' ask 'How did you make the decision about whether to immunize your children or not?'
- Use *appropriate everyday vocabulary*, not medical terminology. Ask about 'your heart trouble' not 'your ischaemic heart disease', for instance.
- Use *concrete* rather than *abstract* questions. Talking about specific incidents rather than abstract ones is often easier. So instead of asking 'What do you like and dislike

about maternity services?' ask 'Think about last time you were pregnant. What did you like about the services you received then?'

Sometimes we need to think more imaginatively about how to elicit particular kinds of information. Knowledge is sometimes difficult to access and tied to particular contexts. Here are some suggestions of types of question that can be used as alternatives to simple questions:

- *Diary questions*. Asking people to describe 'a day in their life' or 'a typical shift at work' can be a useful way to both introduce a topic, and to elicit what is important to them to talk about.
- *Critical incidents*. Asking about the best or worst experience people have had may be a useful way to elicit what is important to them about a topic. For instance, asking about 'the best dentist you ever had' and why might be more productive in generating data about what people think are important criteria for 'good dentists' than asking directly 'What do you think makes a good dentist?'
- *Free listing*. This can be useful in more structured interviews, and involves asking people to list all the examples they can think of in a certain category, such as all the possible causes of malaria, or all the possible treatments they use for fever in children.
- *Ranking*. Interviewees can be asked to rank items generated by free listing in order of importance or efficacy.

✎ Activity 6.2

A team of primary care physicians want to find out what their patients think of the family planning services they offer from their practice, and what their understanding is of various contraceptives available. They plan to interview patients in the waiting room as they are waiting to see the clinic nurse. What comments would you have on the kind of data they are likely to generate?

Feedback

Patients may be very reluctant to disclose their negative views of services to those who are clearly clinic staff. The practice staff will need to consider who would be best placed to interview patients: they might want to contract the services of independent researchers, or ask new team members or colleagues from other practices to perform the interviews. Patients also may be inhibited by talking in a medical setting, particularly if there is no private space. If the interviewers are hoping to access more 'personal' accounts of understanding, they may need to interview patients in their homes, and perhaps match by gender. If more private accounts are needed, which might be a better guide to patients' behaviour, they may need to do repeat interviews.

How can qualitative interviews contribute to understanding health care?

As stated, the qualitative interview provides a method of gaining rich information about people's beliefs and interpretations of the world. Interviews are used widely in health care research across the different social science disciplines. In the following paragraphs we will look at how interviews are used in historical, anthropological and sociological research.

Interviews in historical research (oral history)

Much experience of interest to historians is neither quantified nor written down. Oral accounts can therefore be very valuable and relevant. These are usually gathered from individuals through interviewing. This limits current research to those who have been born within the last 90 years. However, there are also oral history archives in some countries where earlier interviews have been deposited and are available to researchers. Here we outline three different kinds of interviews which are used in 'oral history', which we define as 'interview-based recollection of events in the past': life history interviews, key inform-ant interviews and witness seminars.

Life history interviews are used to reconstruct the experience of people who do not always appear in historical documentary sources (see Chapter 15 for more information about historical documentary sources). To paraphrase Nigel Fielding (2006), they are a form of individual interview which is directed to documenting the respondent's life, or an aspect of it that has developed over the life course. These types of interviews contribute to the social history of medicine, which is also referred to as 'history from below'. For an example of historical research which used life history interviews in this way, you could read Stuart Anderson and Virginia Berridge's (2000) work on the role of community pharmacists in health and welfare in Britain.

Key informant interviews are interviews with people who have played a role in events, such as a scientific discovery, the establishment of a speciality, or key health policy decision-making. The idea is not to explore the interviewees' whole life history but rather their involvement in a particular set of events.

Witness seminars are a relatively recent development within oral history. Participants are those who have been involved in a particular set of events; they discuss these events in a group discussion, which is then recorded and transcribed. The interaction between participants sometimes achieves more than might emerge from individual face-to-face interviews. Until recently witness seminars on health topics mainly dealt with events in countries in the West – for example, the 1979 Black Report on inequalities in health and the subsequent impact of the report on health research (Berridge and Blume 2003).

There is an increasing interest in historical research in the field of international public health, and a recent paper by Nadja van Ginneken *et al.* (2010) on 'The emergence of community health worker programmes in the late apartheid era in South Africa' illustrates well the use of witness seminar and oral history interviews.

There are of course limitations associated with oral history. Depending on the time frame of interest, you may be more or less limited in terms of who is available for inter-view and where they are based. You also need to think carefully about the accounts which can be collected in such interviews. This comes back to broader epistemological ques-tions about the status of interview data in social research, what it can tell us, how reliable it is, and how we can account for recall bias. In essence, we need to learn to decipher how people tell stories and consider how interviews convey factual data from different perspectives. For example, in health policy related interviews, participants may use the interview to settle old scores, or to present a view of events that they hope the researcher will use uncritically. Other interviewees may have become celebrities who have been interviewed too often. Such people often develop a standard official story, which they offer to interviewers. As indicated, this is relevant for all types of qualitative interviews, hence interviewers need to take care in how they prepare for and conduct interviews and how they analyse the accounts gathered.

Interviews in medical anthropology

In medical anthropology interviewing is usually conducted 'in the context of a relationship with interviewees with whom the researcher has, through an ongoing presence, estab-lished relations of rapport and respect sufficient for a genuine "meeting of minds" and that enable a mutual exploration of the meanings the interviewee applies to their social world' (Heyl 2011). Hence it can be difficult to make a clear differentiation between interviewing and observational activities. This type of interviewing, also used by other social researchers, is generally referred to as 'ethnographic interviewing'. Ethnographic interviews are normally conducted in unstructured and in-depth formats, which can be likened to natural conversations, and what distinguishes them from other forms of interviews is relatively long-term and frequent contact. Medical anthropologists, who tend to apply ethnographic methods, usually spend extended periods in the field and the interdependent relationship between participant observation and interviews allows them to explore and compare the relationship between what people say and what they do. Ethnography as outlined in Chapter 4 is a research design, and whilst interviews and participant observation are core features of ethnography, other data collection techniques can be used. To learn more about ethnography we recommend the book by David Fetterman (1998).

In ethnographic research observations are often characterized according to the pres-ence of the researcher (open or hidden), the extent of his/her participation in the event being observed, and whether a phenomenon, such as smoking behaviour, is directly observed (people smoking in a bar) versus indirectly observed (the number of cigarette stubs in ashtrays). Different types of observation may be used in the same study, as will become apparent in Activity 6.3.

✎ Activity 6.3

Quantitative data collected from nutritional centres in the northern region of a Central American country suggest that malnutrition is more prevalent in female children under the age of 4 than their male counterparts. You have been asked to undertake some research to explore possible reasons for this at household and community level. You are particularly interested in observing and documenting whether there is any gender bias in child feeding practices. How would you go about this, what methods would you use and in what sequence?

Feedback

You could spend an initial phase of research observing child care, including feeding practices in households. You may or may not participate directly in household activities. After some time, by means of your presence in households, you may have gained enough understanding of some basic criteria to be able to draw up a structured checklist to focus observations around measurable aspects of child feeding practices (such as amount of food, types of food, when meals are taken, and who eats together), and to design a semi-structured interview topic guide which you can use to interview parents, grandparents and others who assume responsibility for child care in the communities in question.

Note that the data generated during the initial phase of research not only serve an instrumental purpose of informing the development of quantitative and qualitative data collection tools, but provide rich, contextual information that can bring to life quantitative data collected via checklists, and textual data collected in interviews.

Activity 6.3 illustrates how observations can inform the development of interview topic guides and other data collection instruments. Participant observations can also ensure that your interviews and your research adequately reflect the local context in both content and conduct.

Another way interviews are used in medical anthropology is to elicit information about people's illness experiences in order to develop an *explanatory model* for an illness (Kleinman 1981). An explanatory model is a systematic set of knowledge, beliefs and attitudes with regard to a particular illness which offers explanations of illness and treatment to guide choices among available therapies and to cast personal and social meaning on the experience of illness. The method you use to elicit information about the illness experience produces an *illness narrative*. This generally covers perceived symptomatology, patterns of resort (those ways in which people navigate their way through the popular, folk and professional sectors of the medical system in search of treatment and relief), perceived course of illness, perceived aetiology and perceived outcome. If you had collected a hundred illness narratives for the 'common cold' and organized the information in a systematic way, you would be able to develop an *explanatory model* of the common cold. The idea of an explanatory model is linked to a central distinction that medical anthropologists make between *disease* and *illness*. While a bio-medical definition of disease is largely based on demonstrable physical changes in the body's structure or function that can be quantified by reference to 'normal' physiological measurements, illness is the subjective evaluation or response of a patient to his or her feeling unwell. It includes experience but also the meanings given to that experience. Social research interviews are a good conduit for documenting these types of experiences and other phenomena which can influence people's health behaviours.

Interviews in sociological research

In sociological studies it is common to rely on interviews as the primary method of collecting data. While this has the potential to produce useful and rich data on perceptions and world views, there are limits to how far we can use interview data as a good guide to behaviour without considering the difference in what people say and what people do. This is why some sociological studies include observational data or are preceded by a period of informal observations – see the case study below and Simon Carmel's (2006) work on health care practices. However despite the limitations of interview data, it can provide rich insights into how people experience phenomena and the places in which these events occur.

For example, interviews can be used as a method for providing insight into how organizations are perceived by those who work within them, and how their 'talk' helps to construct organization. The structures that deliver health care – hospitals, the division of health care labour, the family (within which decisions about seeking health care are made, for instance) – are in part made real by the ways in which they are talked about; what it is possible to say, and in what contexts it is said. The following is an example of one research study that took this approach, in looking at how managers' talk contributed to the effectiveness of hospital organization (Green and Armstrong 1993, 1995).

Bed management: a qualitative study

Many London hospitals experience problems in finding enough in-patient beds for admitting emergency patients. One solution examined in this study was the introduction of 'bed managers' in nine London hospitals. These were designated managers who monitored and controlled access to beds across the hospital, in all specialties and wards, in order to make maximum use of the resources available and to balance the needs of emergency patients and those booked for elective surgery. In some hospitals these managers appeared to have successfully achieved authority over areas that were traditionally seen as areas of clinical decision-making, such as the decision to admit or discharge a patient, or to place a patient on a particular ward. The researchers used semi-structured interviews with senior nurses, clinicians and managers, in which a topic list included questions on respondents' perceptions of the problem of emergency admissions and their experience of responses to it. They also used observation of the work of the bed managers. The researchers found a high level of consensus about the success of bed management. How had these managers achieved this, given the traditional conflict between clinical and managerial authority within hospital organizations? Analysis of the interview data suggested that there were three 'rhetorics' used by bed managers, which contributed to their successful presentation of management as the solution to the problem (rather than more resources, for instance).

The first of these rhetorics was that of a 'constant crisis', as illustrated by this comment from an interview with a bed manager: 'I mean, it's crisis management all the time and bed management won't be anything else unless there is no casualty, no emergency services, no referrals from GPs – it's always going to be crisis management.' Staff from all professions agreed with this perception of the problem as one of constant crisis – which required constant management.

The second rhetoric utilized by managers was that of neutrality, which was used to present themselves as separate from vested interests and conflicts between the clinical specialties that were a normal feature of hospital organization. The bed managers presented themselves as 'honest brokers' who could act as unbiased arbiters of bed allocation, as this comment from a general manager suggests: 'Somebody has to play heavy honest broker really and say you've got too many beds, you've not got enough, you need to give them to him and so on.'

The third rhetoric was that of rationality, in which the new system was presented as a rational, well-informed alternative to the previous *ad hoc* system, which had clearly not worked. As this quote from a consultant illustrates, the informed, rational basis of the new system was accepted by clinical staff: '[Bed managers] literally know every acute patient – and they've got their finger on the pulse so they know exactly what's going on – they're thinking ahead for the whole week.'

Activity 6.4

1 Would a study like this one be able to evaluate how successful bed management had been in these hospitals?
2 Why do you think the researchers used observation as well as interviews in this study?
3 What sources of bias might affect the findings of this study? How can such sources of bias be reduced?

Feedback

1 In-depth interview data cannot address quantitative questions such as 'How many more patients were admitted in the new system?' They can, however, address questions about process, such as how acceptable the new system was to professionals affected.
2 Observation would provide information about what bed managers did, as well as what they said. It would also provide data about how they interacted with other professionals, as well as their accounts of this interaction.
3 Respondents might want to present their own practice in a positive light, for instance in emphasizing the problems they face (the 'crisis') and their ability to deal with them (the success of bed management). They may tailor their account to what they believe the interviewer wants to hear, so may be influenced by the interviewer's account of the aims of the study. Using other methods (such as observation, examination of hospital records) can help reduce this bias, as can interviewing other professionals. The findings could also be biased as respondents were from only nine hospitals in one city (London) and there is no information about how representative they were. Finally, there is no information here about how the researchers analysed the data, so we cannot know if their selection of illustrative quotes might be biased.

Qualitative interviews, then, unlike participant observation, provide information about what people say rather than what they do. Although this can be a poor guide to what happens in practice, it is useful information in its own right. Language is the main way in which we construct our social world, and examining what, for instance, clinicians and managers say and how they say it provides an account of not only how they perceive the health care system within which they work, but also how they construct it.

As the case study in Activity 6.4 illustrated, researchers might be interested in how people interact in practice, as well as their accounts of interaction with, for example, other health care professionals. In the next chapter you will examine focus group interviews, a method that can be used to observe and record interaction amongst homogeneous groups.

Summary

Interviews are a very important means of collecting data in across different disciplines in health research and they can be more or less structured. Good rapport, sensitive use of observation, careful sampling of participants and thoughtful development of interview topic guides are essential for good data collection. In qualitative work, the interview is mainly used to look at how respondents perceive their world and how what they say ('their talk') helps construct that world.

References

Anderson, S.C. and Berridge, V.S. (2000) The role of the community pharmacist in health and welfare 1911 to 1986. In J. Bornat, R.B. Perks, P. Thompson and J. Walmsley (eds) *Oral history, Health and Welfare*, pp. 48–74. London: Routledge.

Berridge, V. and Blume, S. (eds) (2003) *Poor Health. Social Inequality before and after the Black Report*. London: Frank Cass.

Britten, N. (1995) Qualitative interviewing in medical research. *British Medical Journal* 311: 251–3.

Carmel, S. (2006) Health care practices, professions and perspectives: A case study in intensive care. *Social Science & Medicine* 62: 2079–2090.

Cornwell, J. (1984) *Hard Earned Lives: Accounts of Health and Illness in East London*. London: Tavistock.

Fetterman, D.M. (1998) *Ethnography: Step by Step*. Thousand Oaks, CA: Sage.

Fielding, N. (2006) Life history interviewing. In V. Jupp (ed.) *The Sage Dictionary of Social Research Methods*. London: Sage. Accessed online at http://srmo.sagepub.com/view/the-sage-dictionary-of-social-research-methods/n107.xml on 17 December 2013.

Green, J. and Armstrong, D. (1993) Controlling the bed state: Negotiating hospital organisation. *Sociology of Health and Illness* 15: 337–352.

Green, J. and Armstrong, D. (1995) Achieving rational management: Bed managers and the crisis in emergency admissions. *Sociological Review* 43: 744–764.

Heyl, B. (2001) Ethnographic interviewing. In P. Atkinson, A. Coffey, S. Delamont and J. Lofland (eds) *Handbook of Ethnography*. London: Sage.

Kleinman, A. (1981) *Patients and Healers in the Context of Culture*. Berkeley: University of California Press.

Sennett, R. (2003) *Respect: The Formation of Character in an Age of Inequality*. London: Penguin.

van Ginneken, N., Lewin, S. and Berridge, V. (2010) The emergence of community health worker programmes in the late apartheid era in South Africa: An historical analysis. *Social Science & Medicine* 71(6): 1110–1118.

Further reading

Wengraf, T (2001) *Qualitative Research Interviewing*. London: Sage.

Most social science research methods textbooks have a chapter on interviewing. Two that might be particularly useful as further reading for those doing health research or more applied evaluative research are:

Green, J. and Thorogood, N. (2013) In-depth interviews. In J. Green and N. Thorogood (eds) *Qualitative Methods for Health Research* (3rd edn). London: Sage.

Patton, M.Q. (1990) Qualitative interviewing. In M.Q. Patton (ed.) *Qualitative Evaluation and Research Methods* (2nd edn). Newbury Park, CA: Sage.

Focus groups and other group methods

7

Overview

Various kinds of group interview have become popular both as methods for collecting data in qualitative studies, and as methods for involving participants in the research process itself. This chapter introduces you to focus groups and also briefly to some other uses for group processes in health research.

Learning objectives

After working through this chapter, you will be better able to:

- identify the benefits and disadvantages of different kinds of group interview as data collection methods
- describe the practical issues to consider when planning to use focus groups in a study
- identify how consensus groups can be used in participatory and deliberative projects

Key terms

Deliberative methods: Those that enable the participants to develop their own views as part of the process.

Focus groups: Groups of people brought together to discuss a topic, with one or more facilitators who introduce and guide the discussion and record it in some way.

Interaction: Communication between people.

Natural groups: Groups which occur 'naturally', such as workmates or household members.

Group methods

The previous chapter considered the one-to-one interview, which has been widely used in health research. One disadvantage of this kind of interview is that it does not provide any access to how people talk to each other in more 'natural' settings. To offset this disadvantage, various kinds of group methods are becoming increasingly popular in health and health services research. These are used both to collect data from groups of people at the same time, and as a way of involving participants more in the research process. The

Table 7.1 Coreil's typology of group interviews

Interview type	Features	Typical uses
Consensus group	Often composed of key informants or experts Aim to develop group consensus More narrow, closed-ended stimulus material	Agreeing clinical protocols, resource prioritization
Focus group	Participants selected to meet sampling criteria Seeks broad range of ideas on open-ended topics Formal, controlled, pre-arranged time and place Usually audio-taped and transcribed for analysis	Piloting and testing health promotion materials or questionnaires; exploring service users' views and involving them in developing and evaluating interventions; generating hypotheses; observing social interaction
Natural group	Group exists independently of the research study Can be formal or informal (e.g., an opportunistic interview in the field) Interview guide loosely followed Recorded by written notes (informal) or audio-taped (formal)	Ethnographic data collection (informal), social research (formal), understanding the social and cultural and how this relates to health care decision-making
Community interview	Open to all or large segments of a community Usually recorded by written notes	Project planning, programme evaluation

Source: adapted from Coreil (1995).

defining feature of group interviews is that the interaction between participants produces important insights into how opinions are voiced, formed and discussed in peer groups.

Jeannine Coreil (1995) makes a useful distinction between four types of groups that are used in qualitative health research (see Table 7.1). In practice, many groups have elements of more than one of these types, but in general, these four headings each encapsulate some common aims and processes you might encounter in health research.

Before describing the main uses of focus groups and natural groups, we will briefly discuss the role of consensus groups. We do not expand on the role of community inter-views in this text as they are used less frequently in health research. They play an impor-tant role in health development work where community members can be asked to participate in needs appraisals. In health research community interviews can be used as a forum for informing community members about research and disseminating and dis-cussing research findings.

Consensus groups

Consensus groups bring together participants with the explicit aim of coming to a decision about something – perhaps community representatives to identify priorities for health service funding, or clinicians to develop protocols for use in clinical practice. In rural settings, particularly in low-income countries, various kinds of consensus groups have a long history as a way of involving local people in research projects. They are also becoming more widely used in high-income countries, with a growing recognition of the usefulness of involving users in policy-making and decisions about how to implement services.

There are a number of ways of organizing consensus groups, depending on how much deliberation the group needs and how far the members have to be representative of some wider constituency. Maggie Murphy *et al.* (1998) reviewed consensus methods in the particular context of their uses for developing clinical guidelines. They identify three main types of consensus group. These are:

- *Delphi methods*. In these, the group does not actually meet, but the members all complete a questionnaire on their views on a particular topic. Examples might be priorities for research in a certain area, or the most important elements to include on a new training curriculum. Participants then receive a collated summary of all responses, and are asked to revise their judgements in the light of these responses from others in the group. This cycle might be repeated until a group consensus or summary of differing views can be reported.
- *Nominal group techniques*. These are ways of formalizing group decision-making such that all members contribute, and have an opportunity to deliberate on their views. This is a useful method for coming up with priorities for action. The basic process involves each participant first individually noting their own ideas. These are then all listed in a group setting, discussed by the group, then voted on. Votes are statistically analysed to identify strength of agreement and disagreement.
- *Consensus development conference*. This usually involves an open meeting, at which the participants discuss the topic, but also hear evidence from experts in order to deliberate on areas of agreement, rather like a jury in a legal trial. Murphy *et al.* (1998) identified a number of topics in the health field in which consensus conferences had been used, including treatment of stroke, the management of hypertension and the diagnosis of depression in later life.

Delphi groups, nominal group techniques and consensus development conferences are typically used with professionals as formal methods for collecting expert opinion when there is insufficient other evidence on which to base policy. The UK-based James Lind Alliance (http://www.lindalliance.org/) also applies consensus methods in its work of determining patients' and clinicians' views on setting the research agenda. It has established a research approach which incorporates quantitative and qualitative methods to achieve inclusive stakeholder participation. An article by Artitaya Lophatananon *et al.* (2011) describes how this research approach was used to set up a priority setting partnership to identify research priorities for prostate cancer. Patients and community members are increasingly being regarded as experts on their own health and the services that their communities need. Citizens' juries have become popular as a way of involving lay people and communities in decisions about, for instance, the management of environmental hazards, or the development of guidelines for managing health problems. Similar to consensus development conferences, these are facilitated meetings that involve deliberations in which the participants hear evidence from various experts during the decision-making process.

Group techniques that aim to allow participants to come to some informed decisions are often called *deliberative group processes*: such techniques are especially useful when the researcher wants access to how decisions are made. Although the aim of group techniques is usually policy development (for instance, to include users' views in the shaping of policy implementation) they are also used to produce research data. This was the case in a study which used two modified one-day citizen juries to explore barriers and facilitators to e-health implementation and the priorities for future e-health research from the perspective of health service users and lay representatives based in rural and urban communities in Scotland (King *et al.* 2011). The citizen juries proved to be a practical means of public engagement and conveyed support for e-health interventions as enhancements rather than substitutes for existing health services.

Focus groups and natural groups

Focus groups consist of a number of people (typically from eight to 12, although this depends on the aim of the study) brought together to discuss a topic, with one or more facilitators who introduce and guide the discussion and record it in some way. Sometimes the group is also asked to carry out exercises together, such as sorting cards with statements on them, or ranking a list of priorities. Focus groups provide an opportunity to research not only people's experiences and attitudes, but also how these are communicated in a relatively 'naturalistic' setting. In community development projects they are also a research technique that can help to involve a community with the research process. For instance, carrying out a focus group study before introducing a vaccination programme for villages in a rural area not only informs the researchers about the villagers' attitudes to vaccination but also potentially informs the villagers about the research programme. If the results from focus groups do inform the research, then a community may be more committed to the results of that research.

 Activity 7.1

What advantages might focus groups have over participant observation?

Feedback

They can be a more efficient method of collecting data on a topic, as the facilitators can set the agenda and prompt for particular areas to be discussed in more depth. They allow facilitators to observe how opinions are voiced and deliberated on in a particular social and cultural context and can be potentially less intrusive than participant observation.

Choice of participants is important. The sample does not usually represent the larger population in any statistical way but may be chosen to reflect the range of people in whom the researcher is interested. Traditionally, focus groups were used in market research where participants did not know each other before the group met. In health research, researchers often sample *peer groups*, or participants who already know each other or at least have something in common. Natural groups are a particular kind of focus group in which the participants already know each other, perhaps as work colleagues, as friends or as members of the same social club. This could be groups of nurses who work on the same ward, patients who run a self-help group, or people who live together in the same household. There is a wide range of possible uses for focus group methods, including using them to test research instruments (such as questionnaires) to observe how the language used in the questions is understood by different groups in the population. In developing health care interventions, such as health education campaigns, focus groups can be used to see how messages are received, understood and communicated to others.

M. Khan and Lenore Manderson (1992) suggest that, in practice, many interviews in developing country settings will be informal 'natural' group interviews. As researchers start asking questions, more people will join in, and a group interview happens spontaneously. The everyday demands of people coming and going or work being done often interrupt attempts at more structured interview formats. As they note, this can be a real bonus as:

> Such natural clusterings of people represent, in a loose fashion, the resources upon which any member of the group might draw . . . This is a group that may weave or mend nets together . . . It is precisely this natural social network which provides the scripting for the management of an illness event – what to do with a child with bloody diarrhoea, for example . . . Decisions about such matters are rarely carried out by one care-giver alone: people draw on those around them. As a result, discussions with such groups provide fairly accurate data regarding the diagnosis and treatment of ill-ness, choices of health services, and so on.

Thus natural groups are an invaluable resource for accessing not only what kind of health knowledge a community has but also how that knowledge is transmitted to others, discussed in everyday contexts and acted upon.

In more formal settings than those described by Khan and Manderson (1992), natural groups can be brought together in a research setting with the aim of recreating (to some extent) the kinds of everyday discussions that might occur around health topics. Jenny Kitzinger (1994) used such groups in a study of how media messages about HIV/AIDS were understood by various audiences in a UK context. She notes that in the study:

> We chose to work with pre-existing groups – clusters of people who already knew each other through living, working or socialising together. We did this is order to explore how people might talk about AIDS within the various and overlapping groupings within which they actually operate. Flatmates, colleagues and friends – these are precisely the people with whom one might 'naturally' discuss such topics . . . The fact that research participants already knew each other had the additional advantage that [they] could relate each other's comments to actual incidents in their daily shared lives. They often challenged each other on contradictions between what they were professing to believe and how they actually behaved.

Thus Kitzinger (1994) is also suggesting that group discussion can provide some access to what people do, as well as what they say they do. Again, this is a potential advantage compared with one-to-one interviews. However, it should be remembered that a focus group – even if the participants know each other already – is still not a 'natural' setting. Few groups of friends will gather to discuss one topic for an hour or two, and what they say to a moderator may well not reflect what they might say if no researchers were present. This relates back to a similar point made in Chapter 6 about public and private accounts.

Activity 7.2

What do focus groups provide that one-to-one interviews cannot?

Feedback

Focus groups provide access to *how* participants interact with each other. This can be useful because the researcher can see how opinions are received by others – whether they are challenged or agreed with, for instance. The relatively informal group setting can also encourage talk about topics that might be sensitive, such as sexual behaviour. However, groups may be inhibiting for some participants, who may feel unable to give their opinions, particularly if they are likely to be marginal to those of the rest of the group.

In many health care systems, focus groups can be a good way to access patient attitudes to health care services, or staff attitudes to quality standards. They can also be used to inform resource allocation by, for instance, asking groups from the population about priorities for health care spending.

Adapting methods for the setting

Bilkis Vissandjée *et al.* (2002) discuss the need to adapt the methods used to the particular setting you are working in. Drawing on their experiences of running focus groups in rural India for a project on the influence of rural women's autonomy on their health, they make some suggestions for designing what they call 'culturally competent' focus groups:

- Detailed and careful planning and implementation, so that participants know what to expect from the research (and, as importantly, what not to expect) and to build relationships. This must be done in collaboration with those who know the setting well.
- Consider the daily lives of participants – what timing and location will fit best for the men and women you would like to talk to? In rural India, it was important to find locations in which women could talk without being overheard.
- How will you deal with onlookers? In many settings, it would be typical for all villagers to be asked to a social occasion, so inviting only some may well mean that others gather to watch.
- Consider local hierarchies, and how they will affect both how willing all participants are to speak and what can be said. In rural India, the researchers had to consider age, gender, caste, religion and family position (such as daughter-in-law relative to mother-in-law). Although they could hold separate focus groups for men and women, it was not possible to separate groups by caste. This meant that those women who were of lower caste or education often did not speak in the groups. Similarly, daughters-in-law had less autonomy to speak in meetings than their mothers-in-law.
- Ethics. Written assurances of confidentiality and written consent forms were negatively viewed in this context, as they were associated with government affairs. The researchers

thus had to use verbal explanations and assurances. Another ethical issue to consider when discussing sensitive topics in rural settings (and arguably in other settings) is that of 'over-disclosure'. Participants should not be encouraged to disclose information that could be difficult to manage in future everyday contexts.

- Follow-up. In this research, women might feel that the focus group discussion raised difficult issues for them, or led them to question taken-for-granted ways of life. It was important to follow up with oral interviews to give women a chance to reflect on the group discussion.

In conclusion, Vissandjée *et al.* (2002) suggest that developing appropriate methods for the setting requires detailed ethnographic work as a prerequisite, and a good understanding of local social, cultural and political contexts. The former may not always be feasible depending on project logistics: nevertheless, researchers should familiarize themselves carefully with the environment, review relevant literature and work very closely with local collaborators and gatekeepers. Authors of a paper documenting experiences and dilemmas of conducting focus group discussions on HIV and tuberculosis in resource-poor settings stress the importance of 'being aware of and embedded within a culture and working to build culturally competent practice' (Theobald *et al.* 2011). In particular, they stress the importance of choosing the right facilitator to moderate focus groups. Facilitators need to have excellent interpersonal skills, the ability to inspire confidence in others, be a good judge and interpreter of group dynamics, be empathetic but not judgemental, and keep the discussion focused without driving it. Facilitators also need to have a good understanding of the cultural context and the issues at stake. In most cases this requires facilitators to originate from the host country or area where the research is taking place.

 Activity 7.3

1 Can you think of some research topics that might be particularly suitable for focus group interviews?
2 Are there any kinds of research for which you would avoid using focus groups?

Feedback

1 Your ideas will be informed by your knowledge of topics likely to generate group discussion. In most cultures, there are some topics on which respondents have a 'story' to tell: for example, about experience of childbirth, or of visiting a general practitioner. These stories are often told more readily (and differently) in group settings than in one-to-one interviews.
2 Again, the answer to this will depend on social context. Every culture has areas of behaviour that are seen as 'private' and may be unsuitable for group discussions. Political constraints might also limit the use of focus groups. In a hierarchical work setting (such as most hospital departments), including workers from all grades might inhibit some in giving their opinions.

Running focus groups

The key to successful focus groups is careful preparation. We have already suggested that this involves thinking about appropriate methods for the cultural setting, thinking about what kind of data you need, and who will provide it: whether natural groups, if you want to maximize interaction between participants, or perhaps a more heterogeneous group if you want a broad range of opinions within each group. Sampling appropriately usually means some kind of purposive sampling, in which you think about which participants and groups of participants will best generate data to answer your research question. Some possibilities for recruitment include:

- Advertising for volunteers, for instance on community notice boards, through email lists or in hospital waiting rooms. This is fine for some pilot studies, or for accessing participants who might be hard to reach, although often response rates are very low.
- Working with established community groups to recruit volunteers, such as schools, voluntary organizations or patients' associations.
- Using existing sampling frames (lists of medical professionals, addresses from electoral rolls) to invite people to participate. Care must be taken that it is legal and ethical to use lists in this way.

Some of the issues you need to consider in planning a focus group study are: the topic guide, facilitation, location and resources.

The topic guide

A focus group topic guide is similar to a topic guide for semi-structured interviews (see Chapter 6) in that it should list the topics you want to cover, and some prompts that will stimulate discussion. Here are some suggested tips for developing focus group topic guides.

The introduction is a brief summary of the aims of the group, how long it will take, what will happen to the data and assurances of confidentiality.

Start with 'ice-breaker' exercises to ensure everyone speaks and gets to know each other a little. These should include the participants' identifying themselves by the name they like to use.

You might want to follow up with a *focusing exercise* designed to get participants thinking about the topic. This might, for instance, ask participants to rank words or pictures in order of importance.

Start with *general questions* about the topic. Move on to more *specific questions*, but do not include more than about five key questions. These might include:

- Questions on experiences. (What happened? What did you do?)
- Questions on attitudes to experiences. (How did you feel about that?)
- Questions on what participants like/dislike about services.
- Questions about what could be improved now/in an ideal world.

Avoid asking questions starting 'Why?' These are ambiguous, and can often sound interrogative. Make sure questions are *simple*, easy to understand, and open-ended. Pilot them first with colleagues.

Think about some *prompts and probes* to get the group to expand on these and to broaden discussion if one person is dominating. These might include:

- Has anyone else had this experience?
- What else do you like/dislike?
- OK, thanks for that contribution. Do other people feel as strongly?

Finish by *summarizing* the key points raised in the discussion. Ask if anything has been missed or if participants want to add anything. Thank participants for attending, and compensate them for their time and travel expenses.

The topic guide should be piloted to ensure that the questions and instructions for tasks are understood by participants and work well to generate discussion.

Facilitation

Focus groups are usually facilitated by one person (often called the moderator), assisted by one or more others to record discussion and/or make sure that the recording equipment is running, help with meeting and greeting, and organizing refreshments. Moderators need skills in running discussions and making participants feel respected and listened to. For some groups you will need particular skills or attributes, such as competence in local languages, or perhaps social attributes (e.g., gender, age, profession, kinship relations, religious affiliation) or experiences that match those of the participants.

Location

Choosing an appropriate venue and time is essential, and should be done with the comfort of participants in mind. Often a room in a community centre or local school is more familiar than a hospital location or university seminar room. Make sure there is a quiet room in which to hold the discussion, and that the location is one all participants can get to and into easily. Consider whether you will also need to provide child care facilities or transport. Set out furniture so that there are no physical barriers to interaction: a circle of chairs usually works best. In cultures where it is the norm for people to bring others, consider how you will accommodate them: do you need a separate room for these 'extras' or will you be able to fit them into the group discussion?

Resources

It is usual to offer refreshments, depending on local norms. You may also want to consider how you will compensate participants for their time and any travel expenses. In high-income countries, market research companies usually pay participants, and many focus group volunteers may now expect to be compensated for their time. However, in other settings this could be insensitive or divisive and may be seen as unethical. Other means of compensation may be preferable, such as store vouchers, gifts or household goods.

Resources for running the group will include recording equipment, perhaps flip charts for writing up key points and summaries, any materials you need for the ice-breaker and other exercises and travel expenses for the participants.

Activity 7.4

You have been asked to organize some focus groups to explore how mothers prevent accidents to their children. The women have been recruited from primary care centres and do not know each other.

1 Think of one appropriate ice-breaking and one appropriate focusing exercise for your groups.
2 Think of three or four questions for a topic guide that would generate discussion on this issue.

Feedback

1 One possibility is to ask each participant to introduce themselves by saying their name, and one kind of food they like, and one they do not like. You could then ask each participant to turn to the person or sitting on their right to find out if what she/he does to relax, any hobbies (sports, art, singing, reading)? This information could be fed back to the group by the person who asked the question, depending on your time constraints. You want to foster a positive ambience, and key to this is to think of questions that people will not be embarrassed to answer, and will not generate discomfort: this is clearly dependent on the participants and the cultural setting. A focusing exercise might get the group to look at pictures of playgrounds, kitchens and outdoor environments to rank them in order of how likely children are to have accidents there, or to identify the main risks of injury to children.
2 Some suggestions might be:

- Has anyone's child had an accident recently? Anyone else?
- What happened? How did it happen?
- What did you do?
- What do you do in the house/while out to prevent accidents?

If possible, try out your exercises and questions with mothers of young children. Do they work?

Focus groups for needs assessment

In many health care systems there are policy initiatives that encourage those who provide or commission health care services to seek the views of users on their perceived needs for health care and their attitudes to services currently offered. Focus groups have been increasingly used to assist in this kind of needs assessment. In the next activity, there are some extracts from a British report to the National Health Service Executive, which is an example of this kind of use of focus group methods. Read the following extract by Judith Allsop et al. (1995).

South Asians with diabetes: experiences of primary care and the relevance of current satisfaction methods

The incidence of diabetes is significantly higher in the British south Asian communities than in the British population as a whole. It has also been shown that there is a high proportion of undiagnosed cases in these communities. [One aim of] this research was to obtain indicative views from south Asians with diabetes about their experiences of care and their satisfaction and dissatisfaction with the provision they had received . . . We collected and analysed three types of data: data from short questionnaires, focus groups, and notes from meetings with community coordinators and interpreters. Focus group participants were recruited by community workers.

[Focus group] discussion was based on a *questioning route* which is a logical sequence of open-ended questions which encourage universal participation within the group . . . The themes we included in the questioning route began with each individual's personal history of diabetes following their own illness pathway. The themes were when, and how, people were diagnosed and their reactions to their diagnosis. This was followed by a section asking about their contact with health care professionals . . . Two focus groups met in each of three inner-city sites. Overall, the focus groups included members of the main ethnic groups which make up the south Asian population in Britain.

Groups were single sex on two sites, where local custom required segregation of the sexes. The dominant attitude in all groups was one of acceptance of the diagnosis of diabetes and indeed good humour. There was also a degree of fatalism. The overwhelming impression was that while a minority were well controlled [in managing their diabetes] and understood their condition, many were not. [Problems were reported] in relation to the ease of communication with health care professionals and access to information and advice in their own language and within the context of their own customs and practices. This resulted in most participants lacking adequate information, advice and support . . .

Because of their reluctance to voice dissatisfaction, many of the participants' concerns were implicit. Directly expressed dissatisfaction included concerns about the numbers of different doctors seen in hospital settings, long waiting times in clinics, conflicting advice given by various people involved in their care, receptionists who acted inappropriately as interpreters. Implicitly expressed dissatisfaction included concerns about health problems not being addressed, absence of information on diet in a form people could understand, and lack of low-cost facilities for taking exercise.

 Activity 7.5

1 Suggest some reasons why focus groups may have been chosen for this study.
2 How did the researchers try to ensure that all members of the groups could contribute?
3 What are the possible limitations of this kind of data?

Feedback

1 There is a suggestion that access to health care may be limited (as diabetes may be underdiagnosed), so discussions may raise some reasons for this. South Asians

in Britain, although from a range of different backgrounds, may share common problems in dealing with a health service which is not responsive to their needs, and focus groups allow participants to draw on shared experience. Given that patients are often reluctant to criticize health services, the informal approach of the focus group may be a more effective way of uncovering dissatisfaction.

2 They used a 'questioning route' to canvass experiences from all members in the groups. They also held single-sex groups when this was appropriate.

3 The three sites are unlikely to be representative of the whole south Asian population, even if the participants were similar in terms of ethnicity. As the members were recruited by community coordinators, the groups themselves might not be representative. It would be difficult to gauge the views of undiagnosed diabetics. Data from focus groups, like those from qualitative interviews and participant observation, can be difficult to organize and analyse for novice researchers. If the discussion is audio- or video-taped and transcribed, an enormous amount of data can be collected. The task of analysing these data is the subject of the next chapter.

Summary

Group interviews are a useful method for generating data about how social knowledge is constructed and can be particularly suitable for participatory research. Given the current emphasis on public involvement in research and health care decision-making, there is also renewed interest in the use of consensus groups. Group interviews need to be conducted in a culturally sensitive manner with the support of researchers who know the research context well. They have an advantage over one-to-one interviews in that they provide access to social interaction. This is particularly important when time restrictions are not conducive to more detailed participant observation of social interaction. The disadvantages are that they can take considerable time and effort to set up. Groups need skilled moderators, recruitment can be slow and data can be difficult and time-consuming to analyse.

References

Allsop, J., Tritter, J., Turner, G. and Elliot, B. (1995) South Asians with diabetes: Their experiences of primary care and the relevance of current satisfaction methods. Social Science Research Centre, South Bank University, London.

Coreil, J. (1995) Group interview methods in community health research. Medical Anthropology, 16: 193–210.

Khan, M. and Manderson, L. (1992) Focus groups in tropical diseases research. Health Policy and Planning, 7: 56–66.

King, G., Heaney, D.J., Boddy, D., O'Donnell, C.A., Clark, J.S. and Mair, F.S. (2011) Exploring public perspectives on e-health: Findings from two citizen juries. Health Expectations, 14: 351–360.

Kitzinger, J. (1994) The methodology of focus groups: The importance of interaction between research participants. Sociology of Health & Illness, 16: 103–121.

Lophatananon, A., Tyndale-Biscoe, S., Malcolm, E., Ripon, H.J., Holmes, K., Firkins, L.A., Fenton, M., Crowe, S., Stewart Brown, S., Gnanapragasam, V.J. and Muir, K.R. (2011) The James Lind Alliance approach to priority setting for prostate cancer research: An integrative methodology based on patient and clinician participation. BJU International, 108: 1040–1043.

Murphy, M.K., Black, N.A., Lamping, D.L., McKee, C.M., Sanderson, C.F.B., Askham, J. and Marteau, T. (1998) Consensus development methods, and their use in clinical guideline development. *Health Technology Assessment*, 2(3): 1–88.

Theobald, S., Nyirenda, L., Tulloch, O., Makwiza, I., Soonthorndhada, A., Tolhurst, R., Bongololo, G., Sanou, A., Katjire, M., Kilonzo, N., Yan, F., Al-Aghbari, N., Al-Sonboli, N., Cuevas, R.A.D. and Fergusson, P. (2011) Sharing experiences and dilemmas of conducting focus group discussions on HIV and tuberculosis in resource-poor settings. *International Health*, 3: 7–14.

Vissandjée, B., Abdool, S. N. and Dupéré, S. 2002. Focus groups in Rural Gujarat, India: A modified approach. *Qualitative Health Research*, 12: 826–843.

Further reading

Barbour, R. and Kitzinger, J. (eds) (1999) *Developing Focus Group Research: Politics, Theory and Practice*. London: Sage.

A collection of chapters drawing on the authors' empirical experiences of focus group research that cover methodological issues including the impact of context, using focus groups in feminist and participatory research, and using focus groups for sensitive topics and approaches to analysis. This collection gives a good flavour of the range of uses, advantages and limitations of various kinds of group interviews.

Krueger, R. and Casey, M.A. (2009) *Focus Groups: A Practical Guide for Applied Research* (4th edn). Thousand Oaks, CA: Sage.

A useful guidebook full of practical advice on the whole process of focus group research, from planning, recruiting, and running groups through to analysing and reporting the data generated. The authors draw from their own experiences of running different kinds of focus groups, largely in North America.

8

Analysing qualitative data

Overview

This chapter describes the basics of thematic analysis of qualitative data, introduces some approaches for more sophisticated analysis and suggests some ways of improving the quality of qualitative analysis.

Learning objectives

After working through this chapter, you will be better able to:

- identify the main objectives of qualitative analysis
- undertake a basic thematic analysis of qualitative data
- understand how reliability and validity can be maximized in qualitative research

Key terms

Coding: The process by which data extracts are labelled as indicators of a concept.

Typology: A means of describing individual or group patterns of behaviours, attitudes or views of the world, or the systematic classification of types that have characteristics or traits in common.

Transferability: The degree to which the results of qualitative research can be applied to other contexts or settings

Introduction

To illustrate some of the principles of qualitative analysis, this chapter draws on some examples of data from a small qualitative study carried out in the UK of bilingual young people's accounts of interpreting in health care settings (Free *et al.* 2003). Here is a summary of the study.

The bilingual young people's study

In London, many GPs report that they are often asked to consult with patients who do not speak English and who bring their children to the consultation to help interpret. This raises a number of problems. First, children may not have sufficient language skills to interpret accurately. Second, GPs feel that for many health care problems children are inappropriate interpreters, either because they will have to translate personal information for their parents or they will lack general knowledge about health and illness. Third, having to help their families may mean that children miss school or college. There was already a large literature on these problems and how they could be addressed by improving the professional interpreting services on offer. However, there was no literature on what young people thought about their contribution. This study was carried out to find out what the young interpreters themselves felt about their experiences: why they helped their families, what they liked and did not like about this work and what suggestions could be made to improve their families' access to health care. Interviews were held with 77 young people aged between 9 and 18 who spoke English and at least one other language and who had some experience of interpreting for others. The findings from this study suggested why young interpreters are sometimes used by preference, and also had some implications for GPs.

Approaches to analysing qualitative data

One of the most difficult stages of research for the novice qualitative researcher is that of analysis: what to do with the data (field notes or transcripts of interviews) that are produced. This section introduces some of the principles of coding and analysing data from interviews, focus groups, or field notes from participant observation studies. There are a number of different ways of approaching analysis, depending on your theoretical orientation, disciplinary background and the aims of the study, but there are several objectives that many of these approaches share. These are as follows.

Describing the form and nature of phenomena and developing conceptual definitions

In Chapters 1 and 5 you learnt about the idea that qualitative research aims to explore the meaning of phenomena. Analysis is often, then, directed at developing in-depth descriptions of phenomena that reflect the complexity of social life and the development of conceptual definitions that contribute to further research.

Generating typologies and classifications

As well as representing the complexity of your data, analysis also has to represent the major findings or key themes for the reader. Typologies are one way of doing this. If you look back at Chapter 5, you will see how the researchers generated a typology of responses to asthma diagnosis: 'deniers', 'acceptors' and 'pragmatists'. These typologies are drawn up by looking for patterns in how people give accounts of their health and illness, or health-seeking behaviour. Note that they are derived from the data, not from looking for comparisons between pre-existing variables such as gender or age. As well as looking at the content of what is said, it is sometimes helpful to examine how people talk about things. For example, one typology developed in the bilingual young people's study was that of 'straightforward' and 'problematic' consultations. There was a key difference between how these were described in the interviews, with 'straightforward' consultations being described in very brief accounts of the encounter (such as 'I just explained to my mum what the doctor said, and that was that') whereas 'problematic' encounters were often told as longer and more elaborated stories.

Identifying associations between attitudes, behaviours and experiences

Qualitative research does not aim to find statistical associations, but nevertheless explores connections within the data by comparing patterns in accounts of attitudes, behaviours and experiences. In the study of asthma patients you looked at in Chapter 5, these included associations between patients' attitudes to their diagnosis (denial, acceptance or pragmatism) and their behaviour – in this case their use of medication (using reliever medication only, using medications exactly as prescribed by the doctor or adapting the doctor's advice).

New ideas and theories

Although health research is often orientated towards practical outcomes and may be addressing a tight research question, ideally new ideas and theories will also emerge from the data. Some of these will be useful for sensitizing practitioners or policy-makers to issues they may not have thought about, or different ways of looking at some aspect of health. Some may not have immediate relevance to the provision of better health care but may feed into a broader understanding of the context in which health care happens, or may help us think differently about some taken-for-granted aspect of practice. For instance, in the bilingual young people's study, one outcome of the analysis was a reconceptualization of young people's contribution as 'work' rather than as 'poor interpreting'. Thinking about their contribution as 'work' enables us to think differently about it: rather than assuming that it is just a 'problem', and asking how we can remove the need for it, we can ask in what circumstances it is easier or harder to do. Is it ever financially remunerated, and what difference does this make to how they experience it?

First steps in analysis

Whatever the aims of analysis, whether they are primarily orientated towards practical outcomes (e.g., how can we increase healthy services uptake?) or more explorative (e.g., why do teenagers not attend youth-friendly health clinics?) there are some common first steps in organizing and preparing data.

Begin analysis at the beginning of the project

This is essential for qualitative analysis. In quantitative studies, analysis is usually a separate stage after data collection. In qualitative research, analysis should begin as soon as you start collecting data. This is in part to maximize the flexibility of qualitative designs. As you begin analysing, new theories emerge to test, suggesting new data to collect or refinements of the interview topic guide. A good way to ensure that you do this is to write regular field notes, documenting your observations and reflections, and record these in a paper or electronic format. Your first entry can be a summary of your and other team members' assumptions and prior knowledge about the subject you are studying. This is a good way to practice reflexivity and account for the influence researchers' prior experience, professional expertise and background can bring to the research process. It can also help you minimize bias and ensure that your research tools are appropriate – for example, that topic guide questions are not leading. After each interview you can write a summary of the interview commenting on rapport, the main topics that were discussed, new topics that came up, and any non-verbal communication that should be considered in the textual analysis. It is also important for other team members to listen to the interview recordings, read and check the transcripts and make a note of emerging ideas and how these should be reflected in revisions to the topic guide, for example by inserting new questions and prompts or adapting existing ones. It may also become evident that you need to change your sampling frame in order to obtain another perspective on your question (see Chapter 5, in particular the reference to theoretical sampling).

Preparing your data

Interview transcripts should be laid out with enough space to write notes and codes on the manuscript. It is helpful to number both pages and lines for ease of reference. In Figure 8.1 we have reproduced an extract from a transcript from the bilingual young people's study to illustrate what a transcript looks like after initial coding, although you may find it easier to double-space the lines. Field notes and interview notes should be typed up as soon as possible after collection. If you have assured participants of confidentiality, make sure transcripts or field notes do not contain names, only identifiers that are linked with names on a separate record, which should be kept securely.

Organizing the data

Your data must be organized so that you can find extracts easily, refer back to the original source when necessary and keep a record of what has been done. In a large project, it soon becomes difficult to keep track of notes, tapes and transcripts unless you have a good system for labelling and filing them. A number of software packages now exist that are designed to help organize and manage qualitative data. These are briefly discussed below. If you are using one of these, you may need to check the requirements before preparing the data for analysis.

Familiarizing yourself with the data

You need to be familiar with your own data. Read and reread notes and transcripts, listen to recordings and familiarize yourself with the content and format of the data. Write summaries of each interview, or period in the field, if this helps. (If you have kept field notes you will already have written some of this after each interview.)

30   **A** My Dad he has no problems understanding or speaking
31   English, he is alright about that, but, umm basically when   } OBLIGATION/DUTY
32   we go to doctor and things like that, one of us has to go   TO HELP
33   with my Mum

34   **Int** yeah

35   **A** You know, she can't explain certain things and you
36   know, especially with the family doctor now that we change] STRATEGIES to manage
37   to a Bengali doctor, that's fine with her but before she   (FIRST LANGUAGE GP)
38   used to have a lot of problems, you know, like explain and   } PROBLEMS (EMERGENCIES)
39   things that, even making a phone call, emergency phone call   (PHONE ACCESS)
40   or things like that she couldn't, because when you are at }
41   school or at college or things like that and when she has } DISADVANTAGES OF CHILDREN
42   some problems she couldn't speak to anyone so that's why we] STRATEGIES to manage
43   had to change to a Bengali doctor for her   (FIRST LANGUAGE GP)
...
52   ..... but when we go to hospital, they do ask you   } STRATEGIES to manage
54   like, do you need interpreters and things like that -   }   (USE OF FORMAL SERVICES)

55   **Int** - yes -

56   **A** - on the form, you know to send it back so they will   SHARED RESPONSIBILITY/
57   arrange someone for you but we don't do that basically,
58   cause we go with her cause its easier for her, for her to   } REASONS FOR USING CHILDREN
59   explain to us than to the other person, 'cause they don't   (PERSONAL KNOWLEDGE)
60   know what they, how they are going to translate and things }
61   like that, and we know about her, how she is feeling and
62   things like that so we could translate easier for her   ——— UNPROBLEMATIC TRANSLATION
...
81   **Int** You said that before when your Mum used to be with a
82   doctor that wasn't Bangladeshi ....
83   can you sort of tell me about the kinds of problems she had?

89   **A** I mean, she couldn't explain what her problem is, you] } DISRUPTED COMMUNICATION
90   know and although we were more young that time   ]   (INTERPRETER'S SKILLS)
91   and if she explained something to us, we couldn't   (PATIENT'S SKILLS)
92   translate it the way she wanted ...

118   ... but before I was about   ] DISRUPTED COMMUNICATION
120   12, 13 when I used to go with my Mum so that was really }   (LACK of SOPHISTICATION)
121   hard for me basically
123   I used to find it really difficult to explain it for her] DISRUPTED COMMUNICATION
124   ... I don't know, 'cause there is certain problems she has]   (LACK of EXPERIENCE)
127   that I have, I don't have any experience about
129   you know, sort of personal problems and things like] DISRUPTED COMMUNICATION
130   that, I don't know what was she talking about so I just }   (LACK of EXPERIENCE)
                                                                   + inappropriate for
                                                                           age ?

Figure 8.1 Extract from coded interview transcript. This is an interview with a young woman, bilingual and English, discussing her experiences of interpreting for her family. The interviewer's talk is marked (Int) and the interviewee is A.

Thematic analysis

Many approaches to qualitative analysis rely on identifying key themes, or recurring issues, in the data. In many health studies, this is the main aim of analysis: to identify those issues that commonly emerge in interviews or focus groups, or that emerge as general headings under which we can describe most of the data. To identify key themes, we need to look closely at the data to see patterns. This first involves beginning to code the data, a process that has three overlapping stages.

Initial coding

Each transcript, or set of notes, is read in detail, with the analyst making notes in the margin on what is going on: what is the participant referring to, or talking about. As you can see in Figure 8.1, initial coding of this section of transcript has identified a number of issues in this young woman's accounts of her experience, including *strategies to manage* health care interactions when parents do not speak English, causes of *disrupted communication* and accounts of *unproblematic translation* experiences. At this stage and during subsequent stages of analysis it can be helpful to keep a log or audit trail of your analytical thoughts and decisions. This is particularly useful when more than one person is responsible for undertaking the analysis.

Developing a coding scheme

These margin notes are collated and discussed by the project team. They are then sorted into categories and subcategories: this is the coding scheme. For instance, if you look at the codes written on the margin of the transcript in Figure 8.1, some of them refer to 'Disrupted communication'. This was a major category (and one of the three core themes reported on in this study), which was broken down into a number of subcategories to cover the various causes to which participants attributed disruptions in communication in medical settings:

(1) Causes of disrupted communication:

    (a) Communication skills of patient (vocabulary/other)
    (b) Communication skills of interpreter (vocabulary/other)
    (c) Communication skills of professionals (vocabulary/other)
    (d) Experience of interpreter
    (e) etc.

Each of these codes should be named and it is useful to include a definition and description of the code so that it is evident when to assign other text to this code. It is also helpful to keep notes about any emerging ideas about the data as you go through this process. At this stage, it is important to discuss your coding scheme, and get other people to help code if possible. This will minimize the chance of you missing important issues, or being funnelled into narrow interpretations.

Activity 8.1

The transcript in Figure 8.1 has been annotated by one researcher, in the context of a project with specific aims (to document the experiences of young interpreters). However, there are many other potential themes here. Look at the data as if you were interested in the topic of different family members' need for help in terms of accessing health care. Are there any lines that you might code for this topic, and what might you call your code?

Feedback

Lines 30–33 discuss the difference between the interviewee's mother and father in terms of need for interpreting. You might want to provisionally code these 'Parents' needs for interpreting'. In lines 118–120, she discusses her role when younger: this might be 'Young children's roles'. Lines 61–62 refer to the interviewee's accounts of why family members might help (their 'knowing how she is feeling'): this might be something like 'Emotional work'. You may well have come up with different examples or codes. There are no 'right' or 'wrong' codes, only coding schemes that will work more or less well at helping you see what is in the data and what associations there are within them. You might start underlining sections of text, but you will need to label and define this with reference to your research question. You also need to refine your coding, labels and definitions as you compare text from different interviews, and finalize your coding scheme.

Coding the data

New data are then coded as they are added to the data set. New cases will challenge emerging coding schemes, which need to be flexible enough to be adapted as you rethink the labels and definitions you have given to your categories and subcategories and consider how categories relate to each other, whether there are overlaps and which are the main categories that will become your core themes.

Activity 8.2

Here is a short extract from another transcript from the bilingual children's study:

Interviewer: So tell me more about that visit [to the doctor] for your mum's medicine? Why was that one difficult?

Young man: Well, she was telling my mum why she had to have this new medicine, and I was telling my mum, and she understood, but like she didn't want to take the pills, she was happy with the ones she had already, so I'm like telling the doctor 'my mum doesn't want to change to these pills' but like the doctor thinks I haven't explained properly, so she keeps like saying 'tell her again' and it was like, but I can't convince my mum – that's her decision whether she wants the new pills or not.

How might you code this extract?

Feedback

You may have put this under a new subcategory of causes of disrupted communication, such as 'Conflicts between doctor and patient', or you might have decided that this was a new category, such as 'Conflicts between the roles of interpreter and advocate'. If the category 'Causes of disruption' becomes too large, it might be sensible to split it up and think about the subcategories in more detail.

Cut and paste

Once some of the data are coded we can continue exploring the data using 'cut-and-paste' techniques in which the coded extracts from a number of cases are collected under the same headings. This can be done manually, by literally cutting up copies of transcripts and then pasting them onto large sheets of paper, or sorting them into piles, each with a code heading. With small data sets, this can be very effective, and you (and the rest of the team) can see how the data are sorted, and move extracts around. Use different coloured paper, or different fonts, on each transcript so you can refer back to see where each extract came from. An alternative is to use a word processor to electronically 'cut and paste' extracts to a set of files, one for each category (or subcategory) in the coding scheme.

As you start collecting extracts under each heading, they can be compared with each other, and more themes start emerging. You will probably want to revisit your coding scheme to split some categories, or combine others, or rethink completely what some are about.

Such cut-and-paste techniques are 'low technology', but they work. They allow the researcher, or team of researchers, to compare, contrast, start to build up categories and typologies and discuss the meaning of their data. With larger data sets you may have to type in a case identifier for the original transcript after each quote. At this point, the advantages of using computer software to help with the analysis start emerging (see below).

The key headings from your coding scheme can be the basis for sections of your report. For instance, one report from the bilingual young people's project used the following headings, which were derived from three main themes derived from the coding scheme: experiences of interpreting, accounts of 'straightforward' interpreting, and disrupted communication (Free *et al.* 2003).

Developing more intensive qualitative analysis

Often a thematic analysis is appropriate to the study aims. Sometimes, though, if the data are rich enough, we might want to carry out a more thorough analysis and develop a more sophisticated understanding of the data. Two particular approaches to qualitative analysis have become popular in the field of health research: framework analysis and grounded theory. This section does not aim to show you how to do analysis using these methods, but to introduce the main principles so you can judge research reports that claim to have used them.

Framework analysis

This is an approach developed specifically for more applied qualitative research, so it has an appeal to many of those working in public health and related fields. It was developed by researchers at what is now the UK National Centre for Social Research (http://www. natcen.ac.uk) and described by Jane Ritchie and Liz Spencer (1994) as:

> an analytical process which involves a number of distinct, though highly inter-connected, stages . . . although systematic and disciplined, it relies on the creative and conceptual ability of the analyst to determine meaning, salience and connections . . . The strength of an approach like 'Framework' is that by following a well-defined procedure, it is possible to reconsider and rework ideas precisely because the analytical process has been documented and is therefore accessible.

Framework analysis is particularly appropriate when the study is tightly orientated towards policy outcomes and has clear aims and research questions at the outset. Ritchie and Spencer describe five stages in framework analysis:

- *Familiarization*. To get a feel for the whole data set, its range and diversity, and perhaps (if only using a sample of the data for the report) selecting a representative sample for full analysis.
- *Identifying a thematic framework*. This is like the process of developing a coding scheme in the thematic approach. For framework analysis, though, these key themes are likely to reflect the aims of the original proposal as well as those emerging from the data. The headings might, then, reflect the original questions in the topic guide, although it is important to be inductive as well. This is then developed into an index, which lists all the categories to be used in the analysis. It is helpful to number these.
- *Indexing*. The thematic framework is then applied to the whole data set. The number relating to the subcategory in the index is written in the margin of the transcript.
- *Charting*. Charting has the same function as cut and paste, in that data are then rear-ranged according to appropriate thematic references in charts, so that themes can be compared across cases. Table 8.1 is an example of what such charts may look like, using data from the bilingual young people's study. Note that summaries of data can be used as well as direct quotes, but there is still a reference to the original source.
- *Mapping and interpretation*. These charts, and any notes made while developing the thematic framework, are then reviewed to look at patterns across the data and asso-ciations within it. This process involves defining concepts, mapping the range and nature of phenomena, creating typologies and making provisional explanations of associations within the data. For example, in the bilingual young people's study, some key patterns and associations were around the settings in which interpreted communi-cation was most likely to be successful or unsuccessful. We therefore looked for asso-ciations between contexts and reported problems, and the kinds of health care issues being described and whether communication was successful or not.

To learn more about how framework analysis can be applied in health research you may want to read an article by Tolhurst *et al.* (2008) which explores the gendered dynamics of intra-household bargaining around treatment seeking for children with fever revealed through two qualitative research studies in the Volta region of Ghana. The article discusses the influence of different gender and health discourses and the likely policy implications drawn from such findings.

Finally, as this kind of data analysis is aimed at making changes to policies or inter-ventions, an important element is identifying strategies for improving health care. These can be either those identified directly by participants, or those that can be inferred from the kinds of problems they describe facing. Thus, in the bilingual young people's study,

Table 8.1 Sections of possible charts from the bilingual young people's study

1. Disrupters of good communication – Bengali speakers

Number	Age, gender	Summary of experiences	Problematic encounters	Sources of disruption 1 – own language skills	Sources of disruption 2 – parents' behaviour
B1	13, F	Accompanies mum to doctors etc., interprets for officials, translates letters to house	Council officer (p. 6), dentist (p. 10)	'Don't know words' (p. 5)	'Mum interrupts when I'm on phone' (p. 6)
B2	15, F	Helps for past year, now older sister has left home – phoning GP, accompanies mum to parents' evenings	None – all 'no problems' (p. 3)	N/A	N/A
B9	14, M	Interprets for mum and grandmother (hospital, GP, dentist)	One visit abandoned ('woman's problem') (p. 7), dentist (p. 11)	Didn't know Bengali words (p. 12)	Sometimes parents/ grandmother argue with you while you're trying to translate (p. 13)

2. Disrupters of communication – Albanian speakers

Number	Age, gender	Summary of experiences	Problematic encounters	Sources of disruption 1 – own language skills	Sources of disruption 2 – parents' behaviour
A1	16, M	Helps friends (solicitor), helped stranger register with GP	Registering with GP (p. 7)	'English not good when I came' (p. 4)	N/A
A2	15, F	Helps 'others in community'	Social services (p. 9)	Sometimes don't know English words (p. 6).	N/A
A10	14, M				

Source: Free *et al.* (2003).

several young people talked about the difficulty of interpreting when professionals did not look at them, only at the client. Here is one example of a comment about this, from a 14-year-old:

> When I'm with my Mum at the doctor's, what's really difficult is that the doctors sometime just look at my Mum, not me, even if it's me that's doing the talking. I find that really hard, 'cause I don't know if the doctor is hearing me, or what. I expect that if you're talking to a person, they look you in the face, so you can communicate properly. I hate it when they just ignore me.

Activity 8.3

Look at the extract above. How might you use this in making some policy suggestions in a report on this data?

Feedback

Looking at the client, not the interpreter, is of course 'good practice' if working with a professional interpreter, but young people often find it very disruptive. One possible policy suggestion might be to amend advice given to health professionals when working with young informal interpreters, to look at them as well as the client.

Grounded theory

This approach, also called the 'constant comparative method', is a more inductive approach than framework analysis, in that it aims to stay grounded in the empirical data rather than in the original aims of the study. This means that the research question, sampling strategy, sample, and key outputs of the study can be very different from those originally identified. For this reason, it is perhaps less suited to more applied health research, where tight timescales and the need for defined outputs for commissioners mean there can be less flexibility in research design. However, the techniques of grounded theory have been widely used in many social research projects, and many researchers utilize a 'grounded theory' approach to some extent in their analysis.

Grounded theory is associated with two North American sociologists, Barney Glaser and Anselm Strauss (see Strauss 1987), who believed that the process of qualitative analysis could be 'demystified' by developing some rules of thumb for what they called 'the discovery of theory from data'. As this term suggests, the main aim is not necessarily to develop policy-relevant recommendations but to contribute to theory, although of course such contributions are essential for an evidence-based understanding of how policy is likely to be implemented and what its consequences are. Although perhaps more inductive than framework analysis, grounded theory in practice involves a cyclical process of data collection, analysis, developing tentative theory, going back to do more data collection and analysis to test this out, and so on until the emerging theory is, to use Glaser and Strauss's term, 'saturated'. This means that the point is reached at which the analysts are confident that they have a dense theory that is fully grounded in data and accounts for the complexity of the topic. It does not mean merely that 'no new themes emerged from the data'. When the emerging theory is saturated it is also important to consider how it relates to other theory and relevant literature.

The first step in grounded theory is open coding, and intense, line-by-line analysis of the early data to answer the basic question 'what's going on?' There are a number of techniques for helping to do this, including:

- Looking for *in vivo* codes. These are the classifications that participants themselves use to 'divide up the world'. In Figure 8.1, at line 129, the interviewee uses the phrase 'personal problems'. This is an *in vivo* code that suggests that there is a classification of the kinds of problems you might take to the doctor, and one category is 'personal problems'.

- Label all codes provisionally. As you begin to identify codes, these should be labelled. The process of thinking about what to call a category helps us identify what concept it refers to and moves away from a merely descriptive level.
- Asking a battery of questions about each line. For instance, if we just take lines 32–33 in the transcript in Figure 8.1, we could ask: in what other situations might children have to help parents? Does 'has to go' mean that there is an expectation or an obligation? Does 'one of us' refer to the family, the children, or a broader community? What are the consequences of going/not going? The aim is not necessarily to answer these questions but to generate a number of ideas for codes and evolving theories that will later be checked out in the data.

This intense coding is obviously not used for the whole data set but is a useful way of generating potential codes and ideas about the data. It is also a very useful process if you become 'stuck' with data analysis, as a way of generating some new directions to think about. As coding in grounded theory becomes more selective, it concentrates on the key codes and categories that have been identified as core to the emerging theory.

A note on using computer software

A number of software packages have been developed by social researchers to help manage qualitative data (e.g. Ethograph, NVivo (developed by QSR), ATLAS.ti). These packages do not *do* the analysis: the researcher still has to do the hard work of thinking about coding frameworks, attaching codes to data extracts and thinking about the relationships between those codes. In the following extract Pope *et al.* (2000) caution against the notion that software packages in and of themselves increase the quality and validity of qualitative research:

> The prospect of computer assisted analysis may persuade researchers (or those who fund them) that they can manage much larger amounts of data and increase the apparent 'power' of their study. However, qualitative studies are not designed to be representative in terms of statistical generalisability, and they may gain little from an expanded sample size except a more cumbersome dataset. The sample size should be directed by the research question and analytical requirements, such as data saturation, rather than by the available software. In some circumstances, a single case study design may be the most successful way of generating theory. Furthermore, using a computer package may not make the analysis less time consuming, although it may show that the process is systematic.

However, on large projects, computer software can aid the tasks of organizing extensive data sets and can help retrieve relevant sections of the data for comparison and further analysis. Many packages have specific requirements for transcripts in terms of preferred layouts and conventions, so it is important to test a pilot section of your data before, for instance, having it all transcribed. One website with useful information and test versions of software is the CAQDAS (computer-aided qualitative data analysis software) Networking Project, at http://www.surrey.ac.uk/sociology/research/researchcentres/caqdas/index.htm.

Improving the quality of qualitative analysis

Whatever style of analysis you choose, it has to be done in such a way as to convince a reader that your interpretation is credible. This is perhaps particularly important if working in the field of health research, as many readers may be more familiar with more quantitative traditions and may have questions such as:

* How do I know these findings are not just the subjective interpretations of the researcher?
* How do I know the researchers have not just picked out the examples that support their hypothesis?
* The sample is very small – how do I know these participants are representative of a larger population?

Analysis and writing have to be done with this kind of critic in mind: how can you convince them that your analysis was good enough to be credible? There are some criteria that describe good-quality analysis, and paying attention to these will help the credibility of your research. These are: comprehensiveness, thoroughness, transparency and reliability.

Comprehensiveness

Analysis should be systematic and comprehensive. If you are not coding all the data in detail, select the sample with clear criteria. When selecting quotes to illustrate points, make sure you note whether they are typical or unusual. Simple counts can help – instead of saying 'many people said x was the most important factor', say '10 of the 15 interviewed mentioned x as the most important factor'. Do not trawl the data to find examples that back up your theory, but look at all the extracts under each thematic heading and make sure your interpretations account for all of them.

Thoroughness

As well as covering the whole data set, analysis should be thorough, fully accounting for variation within the data set and for the complexity of people's accounts. There are two key strategies for doing this: comparison and being critical.

Comparison

Analysis is driven by comparisons: between cases and within cases (do people say different things when talking about hypothetical cases and real experiences, and do they make different explanations of events in their past history and their current practice?) and (if possible) between data sets (how do your findings differ from others on similar topics/ similar populations?). Asking why things are the same or different is key to answering the basic question of 'what is going on here?'

One example from the bilingual young people's study was the comparison of stories in which young people said that interpreting was 'easy' and stories in which they talked about difficulties and problems. Examination of the two kinds of stories suggested some common features of 'easy' interpreting: it was more likely when children were younger (perhaps they were less aware of the problems) or when the consultation was for themselves rather than their parents, or when the consultation was for a routine problem when the outcome was agreed by all parties.

Being critical

Analysis should be approached in the spirit of testing emerging hypotheses, and constantly looking for disconfirming evidence. Credibility is enhanced if you have accounted for *deviant cases*: those examples that differ in significant ways from the rest of the data set. This could be, for instance, the one person who does not report a problem that all other participants mention, or for whom the consequences of an experience were different than for other participants. When reporting qualitative research you need to present evidence both for and against the theory or argument you are making. It is important to explain and discuss any paradoxes, contradictions or inconsistencies which are present in a data set.

Transparency

If a reader can see exactly how you did your analysis, and what steps you took between data collection and interpretation, they can assess how far your conclusions are credible. Practical details and examples of coding decisions and how you came to agree on the main themes are more useful than general comments like 'we used grounded theory' or 'a framework analysis approach was used'. Essentially it is important to keep an audit trail of your decision-making and reports of discussions with team members. It is also useful to organize your data in a way that would enable independent researchers to review your analysis.

Reliability

A basic prerequisite of credible and trustworthy research findings is that they were collected through rigorous (thorough and systematic) research practice: accurate notes or interview transcripts were used, the topic guide was appropriate, and the interviewer was skilled in qualitative interviews. Triangulation (see Chapter 16) can also be used to increase the reliability of qualitative data analysis. Data can be collected by using different tools (e.g., interviews, focus groups, observation). It is also useful to access data from more than one source, and ideally data analysis should involve a team of researchers. Two or three researchers may be primarily responsible for coding, but the coding scheme should be presented to and discussed with all involved in the research. It is also important to test different propositions, hypotheses or theories which emerge from the data. The research report needs to be plausible, balanced and fair in terms of accounting for multiple perspectives and it should have explanatory power which can be judged by others. For guidance on how to critically appraise qualitative research we would recommend you read Kuper *et al.* (2008) and take a look at a checklist developed by the UK-based Critical Appraisal Skills Programme (CASP) – http://www.casp-uk.net/wp-content/uploads/2011/11/CASP-Qualitative-Research-Checklist-31.05.13.pdf.

 Activity 8.4

Can you think of any ways of improving reliability in analysis?

Feedback

In some approaches, using more than one coder is a key way to improve reliability, especially early in the data analysis when codes are being defined. Some basic quantitative methods might also be useful, such as counting the frequency of certain behaviours, or themes in interviews. The development of computer software packages designed to aid qualitative data analysis has made this easier. Deliberately seeking negative cases, instead of being satisfied with the first 'good story' that emerges from the data, can aid the case that analysis methods used are reliable.

Generalizability and transferability

A common criticism of qualitative studies with small sample sizes is that they may not be generalizable. Methods such as participant observation require an intensive period of fieldwork, and it is often not possible to include more than a small number of sites in the sample. Traditionally, ethnographies were based on a single site, studied in depth. Although this produces rich, detailed data about one setting, the findings may not be generalizable to others. Even in-depth interviews often cover a small number of respondents as the interviewing, transcribing and analysis are time-consuming. Many studies reported in journals are based on 30 or fewer interviews and they may not be sampled as a representative group of the whole population.

 Activity 8.5

In what ways do you think the results from participant observation or small qualitative interviews are generalizable? Think about the summary you read in Chapter 5 on the study of asthma patients. Could these findings be generalized more widely? Can you think of any ways of improving the generalizability of findings from qualitative studies?

Feedback

The aims of qualitative research are not to produce findings that are generalizable in a statistical sense but to produce *concepts* that are transferable. In the example of the study of asthma patients, for instance, we do not know how far the proportions of patients in each group would represent a larger population, but we can find the broad typology transferable. One test of theory in qualitative studies is how transferable the concepts are: could you use them to help understand another setting? This typology might be useful in thinking about patients with other chronic problems.

The key to both the development of theory, generalizability or transferability is *comparison*, both within a set of data and between those data and other published work. It may be possible to find other settings reported in the literature similar to those you have studied to provide comparative data.

The value of qualitative data is, then, not that it 'represents' in any statistical way the views of the whole population, or their behaviour, but that it can generate new concepts and theoretical insights. It can also *sensitize* practitioners or policy-makers to potential issues of concern.

Summary

Qualitative analysis involves careful and theoretically informed coding to identify, in the data, indicators of underlying concepts that interest the researcher. Thorough and systematic data collection and using more than one coder can improve reliability. Attention to theory (to how the concepts emerging from the data are connected, how they are examples of more general social situations, and how they relate to other concepts reported in the existing literature) extends the transferability of qualitative research.

References

Free, C., Green, J., Bhavani, V. and Newman, A. (2003) Bilingual young people's experiences of interpreting in primary care: a qualitative study. *British Journal of General Practice*, 53: 530–535.

Kuper, A., Lingard, L. and Levinson, W. (2008) Critically appraising qualitative research. *British Medical Journal*, 337: a1035.

Pope, C., Ziebland, S. and Mays, N. (2000) Qualitative research in health care. Analysing qualitative data. *British Medical Journal*, 320: 114–116.

Ritchie, J. and Spencer, L. (1994) Qualitative data analysis for applied policy research. In A. Bryman and R.G. Burgess (eds) *Analyzing Qualitative Data*. London: Routledge.

Strauss, A. (1987) *Qualitative Analysis for Social Scientists*. Cambridge Cambridge University Press.

Tolhurst, R., Amekudzi, Y.P., Nyonator, F.K., Bertel Squire, S. and Theobald, S. (2008) 'He will ask why the child gets sick so often': The gendered dynamics of intra-household bargaining over healthcare for children with fever in the Volta region of Ghana. *Social Science & Medicine*, 66: 1106–1117.

Further reading

Miles, M.B. and Huberman, A.M. (1994) *Qualitative Data Analysis: An Expanded Sourcebook* (2nd edn). Thousand Oaks, CA: Sage.

This is a very practical guide to the principles of analysis, and different ways of organizing, analysing and presenting qualitative data, which will appeal to those who like graphic aids to analysis such as grids and data matrices.

Seale, C. (1999) *The Quality of Qualitative Work*. London: Sage.

Clive Seale discusses various methodological positions on issues such as validity, reliability and generalizability and provides some practical approaches to maximizing the quality and credibility of qualitative analysis.

Strauss, A. and Corbin, J. (2008) *Basics of Qualitative Research: Grounded Theory Procedures and Techniques* (3rd edn). London: Sage.

This is an introduction to the processes of grounded theory for those relatively new to qualitative analysis, and many find it more readable than many texts on this approach.

9 Practical: using qualitative methods

Overview

This chapter provides an opportunity to review the methods introduced in this section, and to gain some practical experience in one of them. For this chapter you are required to work through this text and to carry out some fieldwork. To complete the chapter, you will need the help of friends, family or work colleagues who may be your focus group research participants, or, if you decide to conduct an in-depth interview, the cooperation of four people who are not close friends, family or work colleagues.

The time taken to complete this practical will depend on how long the fieldwork takes. You may be able to combine fieldwork with your everyday working role. Thinking about the research question and writing up your notes should take about two hours.

Learning objectives

After working through this chapter, you will be better able to:

- identify an appropriate strategy for collecting qualitative data
- use a strategy that you have selected to carry out qualitative research

Choosing the research method

So far, you have studied a number of interview methods that can be used to generate qualitative data, including in-depth interviewing and focus groups. In this chapter, you will have an opportunity to carry out either interviews or focus groups. You will first choose a qualitative research question from some suggested topics and then decide which of these data collection strategies might appropriately generate useful data.

First, choose a topic for your study. Here are some suggestions, but you may already have a topic from your workplace which you would like to study:

- Patient satisfaction with one health provision with which you are familiar.
- Communication between different professional groups within a hospital or health centre: for instance, managers and doctors, or nurses and doctors.
- Infection control in a hospital or community setting.

Think of an aspect of the topic that is relevant to your own experience. From this, frame a qualitative research question and decide which data collection strategy will be most appropriate. Use the notes below as a guide to carrying out your data collection. Keep any notes you make, as you will need them again to inform your work in Chapter 13 when you design a survey instrument.

Guidance notes

In-depth interviews

Preparation

When you have decided on your research question, write a topic list to cover in the interview. Think of some 'open questions' that will generate more than a 'yes/no' answer, and some prompts (such as nods of the head or encouraging noises) you can use to get your respondents to expand on their answers. Also consider what kind of probes you might use to explore their answers.

Interviewing

Interview four people – if possible people who are not close friends, family or colleagues. Try to audio-record and transcribe a part of at least one interview, and make full notes on the others. When interviewing, remember to question in a non-judgemental and non-directive way. This can be very difficult if your professional background has trained you to ask directive questions, such as those used in a clinical interview. Remember that the aim is not to 'test' the respondents but to try to understand their way of seeing the world.

Reflection

Try coding part of the interviews. Are there common themes? Compare your own notes to the interview transcribed. What did you miss in your own notes? Can anything be added by considering the respondents' own words? Did the findings generate other research questions, or refine your own? How did you do at exploring and gaining insights into interviewees' perspectives, and the factors that influence their views?

Focus group

Preparation

Choose the participants you will invite. If you have willing work colleagues or friends, you might persuade them to give up an hour of their time in return for hospitality! A common experience is that of non-attendance, so invite more people than you need for the discussion. Make sure you have a room available where you will not be interrupted. You might want to plan some games or exercises to make participants feel comfortable with each other as well as generating data. Some to consider are:

* writing attitude statements on cards and asking the group to put them in order of strength of agreement;
* asking participants to rank, for example, health services offered, in order of importance to them;
* inviting them to share with a partner a 'critical incident', such as the best and worst aspect of their hospital stay, or working with other professions.

Consider whether you want all participants to contribute to the discussion, and how you could encourage this, or whether you want a more 'natural' discussion, and how this could be achieved. If you want to simulate a more natural discussion you will need to think about how you observe and record peer interactions and group dynamics. This is also relevant for groups who may not know each other, but is particularly important if you are interested, for example, in exploring how status or gender influences communication in health teams. Make sure you think through the topics that you want the group to discuss, and compose some questions that will generate discussion.

Running the group

Introduce yourself and say why you are running the group. Explain how much time it will take and what the process will be. During the discussion, take notes of what is said and the reaction of other participants. Are there some topics that generate broad agreement? Are some opinions marginalized by the group? Are some topics sensitive?

Reflection

Did your group provide any data on how people interact? How would you run another group, if you were to repeat this exercise? What themes emerged as important for your participants? How useful were the data from any group exercises you ran?

Summary

Completing this practical will give you some really valuable experience and insights into the process of collecting qualitative data. You can use your findings from this practical in the next practical in Chapter 13. This will help demonstrate how different approaches to research can be used in tandem or complementarily to refine data collection instruments and ensure that comprehensive data are collected to address research questions.

SECTION 3

Measurement and quantitative methods

Second edition revised and updated by Sarah Smith

Measurement in the social sciences 10

Overview

This chapter introduces issues in quantitative research through a discussion of some of the principles of measurement. Good measurement of variables is essential for good quantitative research: however well designed a quantitative study is, it will not answer the research question if we have not designed appropriate, precise and reliable ways to measure the variables we are interested in. Often, measurement of variables in quantitative social science is achieved using questionnaires. In the next chapter we will discuss two different types of questionnaires (surveys and psychometric instruments). The development of psychometric instruments is an area of methodology most associated with the discipline of psychology, in which much of the good work on measurement in the social sciences has been generated. For now, though, it is enough to know that a psychometric instrument is a particular type of questionnaire. Sometimes these are also called 'measures'.

Learning objectives

After working through this chapter you will be better able to:

- distinguish between nominal, ordinal, interval and ratio levels of measurement
- appreciate the role of theory in measurement
- identify different kinds of validity and reliability in quantitative research

Key terms

Measurement level: The type of measurement achieved (nominal, ordinal, ratio, interval).

Psychometrics: The statistical techniques used in the science of measurement to ensure that psychometric instruments derived from questionnaires are reliable and valid.

Psychometric instrument: Allows one to derive a score by adding together several individual questions that are administered in a questionnaire.

Reliability: The extent to which an instrument is free from error.

Validity: The extent to which an indicator measures what it purports to measure.

Introduction

Qualitative methods are particularly well suited to research that seeks to understand people's behaviour or the meanings they attribute to the social world. However, public health professionals can also gain understanding of their research topic from quantitative research (research that involves numerical measurement). Often qualitative and quantitative research will be used in a complementary fashion to increase understanding (see Chapter 16).

In the examples examined in the chapters in the previous section on qualitative research, it might be important to follow up qualitative research with studies that *measure* some of the variables identified as important. For instance, in the example of focus groups used to investigate the views of south Asians with diabetes (Chapter 7) you might need to know how many south Asians need information written in languages other than English and which languages are needed. You might need to know how many south Asians have been diagnosed as diabetic in different areas of Britain, in order to plan services, or what level of underdiagnosis is likely, so that you can assess unmet need.

A range of quantitative methods are used in social sciences. Often these apply statistics to data from specially commissioned surveys of samples of the population or from investigations using controlled conditions. This section concentrates on these kinds of methods, although of course there are many other quantitative approaches used in the social sciences, including content analysis of texts and documents, in which the number of times particular themes or issues occurring in the text is counted (see Chapter 15), and quantitative approaches to observational work, involving counting the occurrence of particular behaviours.

Policy-makers, managers and front-line health professionals increasingly rely on quantitative data about the population they serve, their health problems and how the health care system itself functions. This chapter will help you understand the theory of measurement and the importance of developing reliable and valid quantitative indicators.

Statistics

In the early nineteenth century in northern Europe, governments began to collect increasing numbers of 'facts' about their populations. Since then, across most of the world, state governments and their departments have gathered ever more sophisticated measurements of their citizens. As individuals, we are now the objects of considerable surveillance, with details about our homes, health, use of health services, consumer preferences, and views collected not only by government agencies and public bodies, but also by commercial organizations. The health service manager, like managers in any other public or private organization, relies on an increasing range of quantified data to monitor and plan their work. This includes the 'routine statistics' collated by other people, as well as the information that they themselves produce.

 Activity 10.1

What sources of quantified data does your workplace use or collect?

Quantitative research methods

In almost every area of life we contribute to quantitative data collection or use data collected by others. The quantitative social sciences have their roots in this growth of 'official statistics' and have developed a number of techniques for quantifying, or 'measuring', aspects of social life. Quantitative techniques involve the use of standardized and scheduled questionnaires, rather than the more open methods discussed in Chapters 5–9. Methods of analysis rely on manipulation of numerical data, rather than textual analysis. Survey-based studies concentrate on generalities and on 'normality' (in a statistical sense) and departures from it, rather than the in-depth investigation of a particular case or setting that sometimes characterizes qualitative research. However, the contrast between quantitative and qualitative methods should not be exaggerated (these are tendencies, rather than absolute descriptions), and they are often best used in combination.

Chapter 11 describes what is perhaps the most widely used data collection tool in the social sciences, the questionnaire. Chapter 12 introduces survey methods. Before studying how to design questionnaires and use them in surveys, it is important to understand something about what is meant by 'measurement' and how you can ensure that scores derived from questionnaires are as reliable and valid as possible.

Much of the work on the theory of measurement and validity in the social sciences has come from the discipline of psychology. Psychologists have developed statistical techniques for measuring variables that cannot be directly observed, such as 'quality of life', and for testing instruments to demonstrate that they are reliable and valid. This is called *psychometrics*. Although you may never have to develop a psychometric instrument, the principles of this discipline are useful for framing a more general discussion of measurement in quantitative research.

Measurement

In previous chapters, it was suggested that qualitative methods could be used to explore how people *classify* the world: how, for instance, they understand concepts such as health. An in-depth understanding of what is meant by such abstract terms as 'quality of life' or 'social class' is essential, as you have seen, to clarify what indicators are needed to investigate them. In quantitative research, the aim is to 'measure' these indicators in order to answer questions such as:

- 'How much x is there in the population?'
- 'Is there more x than y?'
- 'To what extent is x larger than y?'

These questions imply different levels of measurement. Measurement scales are conventionally divided into four kinds, depending on what kind of category is used to classify the variable being measured and what assumptions can be made about the relationships between categories. These assumptions have implications for the kinds of statistical analysis that can be done on the resulting data. The four levels of measurement are:

- *Nominal*. This is the most basic level of measurement, which involves merely classifying and labelling (naming) two or more categories (such as eye colour, occupation or diagnosis), without making any assumptions about their relative value. A hospital survey that counted how many inpatients were resident in the surgical, medical, and maternity wards would be 'measuring' patients on the nominal scale of 'specialty'. If data are at the nominal level, they can be used to compare distributions across the categories (e.g., to compare the number of surgical and medical patients in any one week), and statistical tests can be applied to see if the distribution is 'normal', or one that would be expected.
- *Ordinal*. An ordinal scale not only labels the categories of interest, but also ranks them in an *order*. To help work out staffing arrangements, a nurse managing a ward might categorize his or her patients into three groups of dependency: 'fully independent', 'needs some help in self care' and 'needs help for all self-care tasks'. Although this scale of 'dependency' does not measure how much more dependent a patient in one group is than another, it does rank them in order.
- *Interval*. An interval scale has more information in that it not only ranks the categories of interest but does so in such a way that there is a known difference between them, although the starting point of the scale (e.g., the 0 on a numerical scale) is arbitrary. Temperature measured in degrees Celsius is a well-known example of an interval scale. Although the difference between 5°C and 10°C may be the same as that between 25°C and 30°C, because the *interval* between the two measures is the same (5°), the beginning of the scale is arbitrary (and different from that used if we were measuring in Fahrenheit). The absence of a 'real' starting point means that we can only answer questions such as 'how many degrees hotter is x than y?' It would be a nonsense to say 'patient x was twice as hot as patient y'.
- *Ratio*. The strongest measurement scale has an absolute starting point (zero), so the distances between points on the scale can not only be compared but can be compared proportionally, or by means of *ratios*. Thus, 'cost' is usually measured on a ratio scale, by attributing a price. Prices can then be compared not only in absolute terms but also in terms of proportion. If, for instance, the average cost of a day surgery procedure is £500, whereas that for inpatient care is £2000, it is possible to say that inpatient care costs four times as much as day care. In a ratio scale, the unit of measurement (whether it is pounds, dollars or any other currency) does not affect the ratio between two measurements. In this example, inpatient care would still cost four times more if it were measured in US dollars. If the characteristic of interest can be measured on a ratio scale, we can use

more powerful statistics to investigate the distribution of variables within the population and relationships between them. However, in the social sciences the concepts we are interested in are often only measurable at a lower level (nominal, ordinal or interval).

✎ Activity 10.2

Four items from a questionnaire used to survey hospital inpatients are listed. Alongside each one, note what level of measurement is being used to rate the responses.

(1) Are you male or female? (circle one)
(2) How many days did you stay in the hospital? _____ days
(3) On a scale of 1 (no pain at all) to 10 (extreme pain), how would you rate your pain level on the day you were discharged? (circle one number)

   1   2   3   4   5   6   7   8   9   10

(4) How satisfied were you with cleanliness of your ward? (circle one answer)

Very satisfied   Satisfied   Neutral   Dissatisfied   Very dissatisfied

Feedback

(1) Gender is measured on a *nominal* scale. By convention, there are usually just two categories called 'male' and 'female'.
(2) Length of stay is measured on a *ratio* scale, by number of days. If patients had instead been given the following choices:

- less than 2 days
- between 2 and 5 days
- more than 5 days

the scale would have been *ordinal*.

(3) This scale is really an *ordinal* scale, as there is no way of knowing whether the points are equidistant. However, response scales like this are sometimes treated as *interval* data for statistical analysis (the distance between the points is assumed to be the same). The extent to which this assumption is tolerated depends among other things on the number of points on the scale: a 10-point scale is often treated as though it were interval, but it would be very rare to treat a three-point scale in this fashion.
(4) This is an *ordinal* scale, where the response categories are merely ranked in order.

Role of theory in social science measurements

In biomedical sciences measurement poses fewer problems than perhaps it does for social scientists. There are a number of reasons for this:

- There is greater clarity over the concepts to be measured (e.g., height, weight, cholesterol levels).

- There are agreed indicators for measuring many of these concepts (e.g., 'amount of mercury pushed up a tube' for blood pressure).
- There are reliable and valid measurement instruments (e.g., the thermometer for temperature).
- There are also agreed units of measurement, which are usually at least at the interval level.

This does not imply that there are no problems in the biomedical sciences, however. For many of the concepts of interest (such as 'fitness for surgery', 'extent of comorbidity') there are problems with the indicators that have been developed in some or all of the areas mentioned above.

In the social sciences, because the concepts used are more abstract, it may be much more difficult to develop appropriate indicators, and they are more likely to be at the nominal or ordinal level. Compare, for instance, the debate about how to measure 'intelligence' with the agreement about how to measure temperature. The problem is not just that there is no equivalent to the thermometer to use but that there is considerable disagreement about what intelligence *is*, and what might be appropriate indicators of it:

- scores on an IQ test which measures non-verbal reasoning;
- skills in 'real-life' problem-solving; or
- educational qualifications gained.

For this reason, indicators for many concepts used in health research reflect an underlying theory of what the concept is and how it is related to other concepts. Theory has an important bearing on how indicators are chosen, whether the researcher is designing a psychometric instrument or a questionnaire for a more general survey. There is currently considerable debate about how 'health' should be defined in order to operationalize it for measurement.

 Activity 10.3

Read the following extract from a report of a conference that considered the definition of health (Huber *et al.* 2011) and consider the following questions:

(1) What are the main limitations of the WHO's 1948 definition of health?
(2) What alternative definition is suggested by Huber *et al.*?
(3) Why is it important to consult a wide group of stakeholders in future discussions about definitions of health?

> The current WHO definition of health, formulated in 1948, describes health as 'a state of complete physical, mental and social well-being and not merely the absence of disease or infirmity.'[1] At that time this formulation was groundbreaking because of its breadth and ambition. It overcame the negative definition of health as absence of disease and included the physical, mental, and social domains. Although the definition has been criticised over the past 60 years, it has never been adapted. Criticism is now intensifying,[2-5] and as populations age and the pattern of illnesses changes the definition may even be counterproductive.

Limitations of WHO definition

Most criticism of the WHO definition concerns the absoluteness of the word 'complete' in relation to wellbeing. The first problem is that it unintentionally contributes to the medicalisation of society. The requirement for complete health 'would leave most of us unhealthy most of the time.'[4] . . . The second problem is that since 1948 the demography of populations and the nature of disease have changed considerably. . . . Disease patterns have changed, with public health measures such as improved nutrition, hygiene, and sanitation and more powerful healthcare interventions. . . . Ageing with chronic illnesses has become the norm, and chronic diseases account for most of the expenditures of the healthcare system, putting pressure on its sustainability. In this context the WHO definition becomes counterproductive as it declares people with chronic diseases and disabilities definitively ill. It minimises the role of the human capacity to cope autonomously with life's ever changing physical, emotional, and social challenges and to function with fulfilment and a feeling of wellbeing with a chronic disease or disability. The third problem is the operationalisation of the definition. WHO has developed several systems to classify diseases and describe aspects of health, disability, functioning, and quality of life. Yet because of the reference to a complete state, the definition remains 'impracticable, because "complete" is neither operational nor measurable.'[3, 4]

Need for reformulation

Various proposals have been made for adapting the definition of health. The best known is the Ottawa Charter,[8] which emphasises social and personal resources as well as physical capacity. However, WHO has taken up none of these proposals. Nevertheless, the limitations of the current definition are increasingly affecting health policy. For example, in prevention programmes and healthcare the definition of health determines the outcome measures: health gain in survival years may be less relevant than societal participation, and an increase in coping capacity may be more relevant and realistic than complete recovery. Redefining health is an ambitious and complex goal; many aspects need to be considered, many stakeholders consulted, and many cultures reflected, and it must also take into account future scientific and technological advances. The discussion of experts at the Dutch conference, however, led to broad support for moving from the present static formulation towards a more dynamic one based on the resilience or capacity to cope and maintain and restore one's integrity, equilibrium, and sense of wellbeing.[6] The preferred view on health was 'the ability to adapt and to self manage.'
. . .

Conclusion

. . . This could be a starting point for a similarly fresh, 21st century way of conceptualising human health with a set of dynamic features and dimensions that can be measured. Discussion about this should continue and involve other stakeholders, including patients and lay members of the public.

References (as per original report)

1. WHO. Constitution of the World Health Organization. 2006. www.who.int/ governance/eb/who_constitution_en.pdf.
2. What is health? The ability to adapt [editorial]. *Lancet* 2009;373:781.
3. Jadad AR, O'Grady L. How should health be defined. *BMJ* 2008;337;a2900.
4. Smith R. The end of disease and the beginning of health. BMJ GroupBlogs 2008. http://blogs.bmj.com/bmj/2008/07/08/richard-smith-the-end-of-disease-and-the-beginning-ofhealth/.
5. Larson JS. The conceptualization of health. *Med Care Res Rev* 1999;56; 123–36.
8. Ottawa Charter for Health Promotion. www.who.int/hpr/NPH/docs/ottawa_ charter_hp.pdf.
6. Health Council of the Netherlands. Publication A10/04. www.gezond-heidsraad.nl/sites/default/files/bijlage%20A1004_1.pdf.

Feedback

1 The traditional WHO definition of health emphasizes a complete state of wellbeing. This places emphasis on the medical model of health and suggests that there is no possibility of considering oneself to be healthy even with only minor ailments. Chronic disease is now much more prevalent than it was in 1948 when WHO developed its definition, and many people live into old age with symptoms of chronic disease, yet may not consider themselves to be unhealthy.

2 There have been several suggested alternative definitions of health. The definition suggested in the Huber *et al.* report places emphasis on the ability of a person to adapt and to cope with their health symptoms (i.e., 'the ability to adapt and to self manage').

3 It is it important to consult a wide group of stakeholders in future discussions about definitions of health because different stakeholders may have different perceptions and understanding of what it means to be healthy. Each of these views should be taken into account in developing any new definition of a concept. Arguably the views of patients are especially important.

Reliability

When we design a measurement instrument we want to be able to detect the 'true' state of the concept of interest, and we want to be able to detect differences in that concept. These may be differences between people or things (e.g., differences in body weight of different patient groups) or differences over time (e.g., differences in average temperature from year to year).

There are two main reasons why our concepts may differ. If we take the example of weighing scales as an indicator of the concept 'weight over time', the data produced by the scales may differ from day to day because (a) our weight changes from day to day or (b) the weighing scales have a certain amount of random variation, which influences the weight reading over and above any changes in our daily weight. This random variation is an undesirable interference, or 'noise', which reduces our confidence in the accuracy of our data. *Reliability* refers to the extent to which a measure is free from this error.

The term 'reliability' is often used interchangeably with consistency, stability and repeatability, but these are often confusing to those unfamiliar with the true concept of reliability. The term 'stability', for example, seems to suggest that we do not want the data from our measurement instrument to change over time. This is obviously not true: scales would be useless if they told you that you weighed the same every day, even while you are putting on weight!

Reliability may therefore be best thought of as the proportion of differences in measurements due to *true* differences in the concept being measured, having accounted for random variations (errors) in the measurement instrument. The higher the proportion of change in our measurement data that is due to 'true' difference, the more reliable our measurement instrument.

In quantitative research questionnaires can be statistically *tested* for reliability, to make sure that they are not affected by time, by the rater (such as the interviewer) used, or by the setting.

There are two major aspects to testing the reliability of instruments:

- *Test–retest reliability*. This is the extent to which the instrument is stable over time, given that nothing has changed in the concept of interest over that time period. It can be tested by asking respondents to complete the same form at two different times when no change is expected.
- *Inter-rater/observer reliability*. If the questionnaire relies on an interviewer or other (proxy) rater to complete, it can be tested to see that different raters record the same responses in the same way (i.e., that the data produced are not influenced by the rater producing them).

Sometimes the term 'reliability' is also used to refer to the extent to which items in a questionnaire instrument are homogeneous (or consistent with each other). This is tested statistically and Is called *internal consistency*.

Validity

The problem of operationalizing variables was introduced in Chapter 3, and it was noted that choice of indicator often involved a compromise, as concepts in social science are seldom easily measured. *Validity* refers to how well the indicators chosen do actually measure the underlying concept. The validity of the measure depends on the 'fit' between the concept and the indicators chosen. A single indicator will rarely be adequate. Concepts such as 'health' or 'intelligence' are multifaceted, so more faith can be placed in a measurement strategy that uses a variety of indicators, each one operationalizing a different aspect of the concept, than in one that relies on only a single indicator of a concept. Thus, in the WHO definition of health there are three dimensions (physical, mental and social). A set of indicators could be developed to measure each of these dimensions (e.g., questionnaires about physical functioning, mood and/or well-being, and social interaction) and together they would represent the concept of 'health'. To address Huber *et al.*'s (2011) suggestion that measures of health should take account of the individual's ability to adapt and cope, one strategy would be to phrase questions within questionnaires in terms of how *concerned* the patient is about each aspect rather than how well the patient can do each aspect. A patient who has adapted effectively will be less concerned than a patient who is not coping. Thus, the way the concept (i.e., health) is defined has implications for how it is operationalized and measured.

The issue of validity is as important in quantitative work as in qualitative work and it refers to the same general issues: how can the reader have faith in the 'truth' of the researcher's account? In quantitative research, though, there are more formal methods that can help demonstrate validity. Unfortunately, there is never one piece of evidence that can demonstrate conclusively that a measure is valid. Validity cannot be 'proved', but there are ways of improving the credibility of quantitative indicators. These are essential tools not only for researchers who need to reassure themselves that they are using an appropriate instrument but also for readers and users of research who need to consider the validity of indicators chosen.

Types of validity

In your reading, you may encounter different terminology to describe validity across the social science disciplines. However, the underlying principles are the same. The process of ensuring validity of a particular indicator is often described as a process of validity testing (Streiner and Norman 2003). It is more important that you understand the following ideas, rather than remembering the various names for different kinds of validity used by those working in psychometric testing and theory. Taken together, these various sources can strengthen the credibility of the measure used.

Face validity

This is the most straightforward measure of validity, and relies on whether the indicator 'looks like' it is a measure of the variable of interest. Clearly this can never be an adequate measure on its own, as our subjective judgements about measures are likely to be partial and biased. However, using a panel of colleagues, perhaps, to look over an instrument would provide useful information about its face validity.

Content validity

This refers to the representativeness of the range of indicators (questions) chosen to measure a concept. Content validity is high when a questionnaire (or instrument) includes questions (or items) that cover all the elements of the concept it is intended to measure. For example, we would expect a symptom checklist for patients undergoing cancer chemotherapy to include a wide range of symptoms that arise in this situation, and not just to focus on one or two symptoms.

 Activity 10.4

Why would self-reports of disease diagnosis be inadequate in terms of content validity for a survey that was trying to measure health based on the WHO definition?

Feedback

Absence of disease would not be a complete measure of 'health', because the theoretical concept of health also covers other dimensions (physical, mental and social wellbeing) as well as 'absence of disease'.

Criterion validity

This refers to the extent to which the indicator chosen correlates with some other (known to be valid) indicator of the concept. Thus, to know if the questionnaire item 'How many units of alcohol have you drunk today?' was a valid measure of daily alcohol intake, it might be possible to correlate answers with measurements of blood alcohol levels as a 'gold standard' indicator of alcohol intake. Here, 'blood alcohol level' is the *criterion* by which the questionnaire item is being measured. It is important to understand, however, that there are rarely, if ever, true 'gold standard' indicators for the things we are trying to measure; there are just indicators where there is more (or less) agreement on the extent to which they measure what they are supposed to measure.

Construct validity

In the social sciences there is often poor agreement over what constitutes a 'gold standard' indicator, and often there will be agreement that there is nothing approaching a gold standard. Thus it can be difficult to demonstrate criterion validity. In addition (as in the previous example on alcohol intake), it may simply not be possible (for ethical or other reasons) to test it in this way.

An alternative approach is to use construct validation. Here we attempt to measure whether the indicator performs in the way that the underlying theory says it should. To do this we must first generate hypotheses about our concept. Let us use the example of a questionnaire (the indicator) designed to measure the quality of life of people with cancer (the concept). The following are some of the types of hypotheses we might generate about how the questionnaire should perform: known groups differences; convergence with related indicator; lack of convergence with unrelated indicators.

- *Known groups*. We might expect patients with more advanced cancer, or those on treatments with serious side effects, to have lower quality of life scores on the questionnaire than patients with early cancer stages and no treatment side effects.
- *Convergence*. We might expect scores on our questionnaire to correlate positively with related indicators, such as measures of physical or mental health.
- *Lack of convergence (also known as discriminant validity)*. Unless part of our theory, we would not expect women, for example, to have lower scores than men. We would also hope that our questionnaire does not correlate too highly with personality measures, such as the tendency to give socially desirable responses.

One of the main problems with construct validations is the uncertainty over the status of your theoretical assumptions. If, for example, we find that women score lower on our quality of life questionnaire, is this a problem with our questionnaire or our theory?

 Activity 10.5

Read the following summary of a study by Puchot *et al.* (2005) on the development of a psychometric instrument to assess patient satisfaction for people with osteoarthritis in France, and note how they tried to ensure the reliability and validity of their measure. Describe all the types of reliability and validity the researchers were interested in. What types of validity were they unable to establish?

Developing a patient satisfaction questionnaire

Patient satisfaction is thought to be related to patient treatment adherence and outcome. There was no specific medical treatment satisfaction questionnaire available for patients with osteoarthritis (a degenerative disorder which affects the joints). Pouchot *et al.* (2005) therefore aimed to develop a questionnaire to measure patient satisfaction for people with osteoarthritis in clinical trials and observational studies.

The content of the questionnaire was developed from semi-structured interviews with patients and clinicians. Initially a 31-item version of the questionnaire was developed. This was pilot tested with clinicians and patients to ensure that all of the relevant topics had been covered, that there were no redundant items, and that questions and response scales could be easily understood. The time taken to complete the questionnaire was also recorded. As a result of the pilot testing some items were removed. The revised version of the questionnaire consisted of 24 items, later reduced to 18 items based on statistical analysis.

This final version of the questionnaire was administered to 804 people, of whom 137 also completed the questionnaire on a second occasion. Participants were aged between 18 and 80 and all had received treatment for osteoarthritis within the last 3 months. These data were analysed statistically to look for correlations between items indicating that particular items were answered in similar ways and grouped together into 'factors' or dimensions of patient satisfaction. The analysis found that there were four factors, which the researchers named 'treatment advantages', 'satisfaction with physician', 'treatment convenience' and 'treatment confidence'.

Further evaluation of the questionnaire showed that the scores for each of the four factors showed statistically significant differences between groups of different types of patients. For example, all four factors showed significant differences between patients reporting high pain intensity and those reporting low pain intensity. The four factor scores also showed significant differences between patients reporting a high level of knee-related disability and those reporting a low level of knee related disability. In both cases the less severe patients were more satisfied.

Statistical analysis showed that two factors ('treatment advantages' and 'satisfaction with physicians') had internal consistency above the recommended level. Two scales ('treatment convenience' and 'satisfaction with physician') were highly correlated on two occasions where there had been no intervention in between and no change was expected.

Feedback

These are some of the kinds of reliability you may have considered:

- Internal consistency is one way of establishing reliability of an instrument.
- Correlating the factor scores at two time points when no change is expected in between is a way of demonstrating test–retest reliability.
- It was not appropriate for the researchers to evaluate inter-rater reliability as the questionnaire was self-reported.

These are some of the kinds of validity that you may have described:

- Reviewing other work and asking patients about satisfaction with care maximizes content validity, in that the researchers could be fairly confident that there were items covering the major dimensions of their concept.
- Asking colleagues to judge whether the items look reasonable is a way of demonstrating face validity.
- They were not able to look at criterion validity, because there were no 'gold standard' measures currently in use in the UK.
- Instead, construct validity was tested to see if the questionnaire showed lower satisfaction scores for patients with greater severity (e.g., in terms of pain and disability).

 Activity 10.6

Think back to the discussion of different approaches to science in Chapter 2, when different perspectives on social science methodology were discussed. How would you characterize the approach to validity described in the paragraph below?

In the quantitative social sciences, considerations of validity often presuppose that there is one underlying 'truth' about, for instance, health status or satisfaction. Using blood alcohol measures as a test of criterion validity of a questionnaire measure of alcohol intake presupposes, for instance, that blood alcohol readings are a 'true' measure of alcohol intake.

Feedback

It is a positivist approach, because there is an implicit assumption that there is one 'reality' of alcohol intake, and that the proper role of social science methods is to refine our ways of measuring it.

Summary

In quantitative social science research, the aim is to 'measure' concepts such as social and behavioural characteristics, respondents' attitudes and beliefs. Measurement poses problems because the concepts social scientists work with are complex, multidimensional and can be difficult to operationalize. Indicators have to be theoretically informed. The social science discipline of psychometrics provides the scientific methods that enable us to rigorously measure concepts using questionnaires. When using findings from quantitative work, it is necessary to ask whether the researchers have demonstrated the reliability and validity of the indicators they have chosen. In the next chapter, the principles of questionnaire design are outlined.

References

Huber, M., Knottnerus, J.A., Green, L. *et al.* (2011). How should we define health? *British Medical Journal*, 343: d4163.

Pouchot, J., Trudeau, E., Hellot, S.C. *et al.* (2005) Development and psychometric validation of a new patient satisfaction instrument: The osteoARthritis Treatment Satisfaction (ARTS) questionnaire. *Quality of Life Research*, 14: 1387–1399.

Streiner, D.L. and Norman, G.R. (2003) *Health Measurement Scales: A Practical Guide to Their Development and Use* (3rd edn). Oxford: Oxford University Press.

Further reading

Bowling, A. (2005). *Measuring Health: A Review of Quality of Life Measurement Scales* (3rd edn). Maidenhead: Open University Press.

Bowling, A. (2009) *Research Methods in Health: Investigating Health and Health Services.* (3rd edn). Maidenhead: Open University Press

McClure, R.J., Peel, N., Kassulke, D. and Neale, R. (2002) Appropriate indicators for injury control? *Public Health*, 116: 252–256.

McDowell, I. (2006). *Measuring Health: A Guide to Rating Scales and Questionnaires* (3rd edn). Oxford: Oxford University Press.

Medical Outcomes Trust (2002) Assessing health status and quality of life instruments: Attributes and review criteria. *Quality of Life Research*, 11: 193–205.

Finding appropriate indicators for health research is challenging. Bowling (2005, 2009) and McDowell (2006) provide a general review of health measurements issues and specific scales; McClure *et al.* (2002) deals with the problem for one particular area, that of injury control. Medical Outcomes Trust (2002) presents the minimum scientific standards required for a questionnaire where the questions are added up into a score.

Questionnaire design

Overview

There are many pitfalls for the novice questionnaire designer. Designing good, reliable and valid questionnaires is a skilled task and is more difficult than it might look. As a public health practitioner or health services manager, you may need to design simple questionnaires yourself, and you will need some skills in assessing those designed by other researchers. This chapter introduces the principles of questionnaire design.

Learning objectives

After working through this chapter, you will be better able to:

- identify some common problems when designing a questionnaire
- understand the principles of good questionnaire design

Key terms

Closed question: Question which gives the respondent a predetermined choice of responses.

Open question: Question that allows the respondent to give any answer.

Self-reported questionnaire: Questionnaire where the answers are reported by the respondent themselves.

Proxy-reported questionnaire: Questionnaire where answers are reported by someone else on behalf of the respondent.

When should you use a questionnaire?

A questionnaire is a structured schedule used to elicit predominantly quantitative data. There are two main types of questionnaire: a survey questionnaire where questions tend to be analysed individually; and a psychometric instrument where all the items are combined (often added up) to create a score that represents the concept that is being measured. For example, a questionnaire where items are added up to produce a quality of life score would be an example of a psychometric instrument (so long as the final score met the criteria for reliability and validity). Psychometric instruments are sometimes included as part of wider survey questionnaires. Both types of questionnaire are often completed by the respondent themselves (*self-reported*), but it may be necessary for the questionnaire to be administered by an interviewer who reads out each question verbatim to the respondent. In this instance the questionnaire is still self-reported because it is the respondents themselves who provide the answers. Sometimes it is necessary for someone else to complete the questionnaire on behalf of the respondent (e.g., a parent if the respondent is a very young child). This is called *proxy reporting*. Questionnaires have a wide range of uses in health and health services research, including:

- population surveys (see, for example, the Health Survey for England at http://www. hscic.gov.uk/searchcatalogue?q=title%3A%22Health+Survey+for+England%22&area= &size=10&sort=Relevance);
- management evaluations of user experience with services;
- outcomes research, in which psychometric questionnaires are developed to provide patient-based evaluations of constructs such as quality of life.

Like any other method of data collection, questionnaires have a number of advantages and disadvantages.

Advantages

Self-completion questionnaires can be cost-effective, especially when compared to face-to-face interviews. Written questionnaires can be easily sent out by post or given out in context (e.g., in a waiting room). They can also be administered online via the internet. Questionnaires are also easy to analyse provided they address clearly formulated research questions. Data entry and tabulation can be done with computer software packages, which can also reduce the time and money required. Questionnaires are familiar and non-threatening to most people, as nearly everyone has had some experience completing them. Questionnaires also have the potential to reduce researcher bias because each question is presented uniformly (this does not guarantee, however, that questions will be interpreted in a uniform fashion by respondents). Finally, postal or internet-based questionnaires are generally not as time-consuming or intrusive as interviews or focus groups: respondents can complete them when they please, providing they meet the response deadline.

Disadvantages

One major disadvantage of questionnaires that are not administered face-to-face is the lack of control over responses. Response rates can sometimes be as low as 10%, especially if the questionnaire is poorly designed. When this happens the sample may not be representative of the population in question and the results may not therefore be very meaningful. It is even possible that the person completing an anonymous questionnaire may not be the person to whom it was sent. Even if people do send their questionnaires back, it is possible that questions may have been missed or answered in an incorrect fashion (e.g., by ticking more than one box when only one response is allowed). This may be due to poor design but it is also common that some respondents have reading and comprehension difficulties. Another disadvantage of questionnaires is the inflexible nature of such a structured instrument. For example, a questionnaire might reveal that respondents are dissatisfied with their job, but the exact source of that dissatisfaction may be much harder to discover. In an interview we can directly ask what the respondent dislikes about their job, but in a questionnaire we may have to provide a long list of options, which may take a long time to work through and still not capture the exact nature of the problem. By allowing free space for comments one can address this problem, but free text responses are difficult and time-consuming to tabulate, and undermine one of the main advantages of a questionnaire (ease of analysis).

Project design

Most problems with questionnaires can be traced to uncertainty over the goals of the project. You should begin by writing out what you want to discover, and then generate questions that address these issues. One of the best ways to further clarify your study goals is to decide how you intend to analyse each piece of information in your questionnaire. Longer questionnaires tend to have lower response rates, so you should ask only questions that directly address the study goals and avoid the temptation to ask questions because it would be 'interesting to know'. As with any piece of research, you should take time to operationalize carefully the variables under study, as we discussed in Chapter 3.

Generating questions

The first task when generating questions is to choose the variables you want to measure. There are many ways to do this. You may take a purely theoretical approach. Imagine that you are a manager at a hospital where staff absenteeism is considered too high, and you have decided to carry out a questionnaire survey of staff to investigate. You might ask about job satisfaction, worker stress or child care needs in your survey because your theory predicts these are important determinants of absenteeism. It is unlikely, however, that you will anticipate all important issues relevant to your research question on the basis of theory alone. A second useful way to identify important variables to be included is by focus group discussions and/or interviews with key informants. For example, you might ask hospital staff (in a focus group or in one-on-one interviews), why they think people are away from work. A third way of identifying important variables might be a literature review. It is likely that research in other health care settings has already been carried out, and if you are lucky there may be other questionnaires on staff absenteeism that you can use rather than having to design one yourself. However, these will need to be checked carefully to make sure they are appropriate in your setting. At a minimum, even if the instrument is in the language you need, this will include checking that vocabulary is appropriate to the context. For instance, terms such as 'nurse manager' or 'department' are likely to have different meanings in different hospitals.

Once you have chosen the variables to be addressed, you must define these variables in a manner that can be used in a questionnaire. This has implications for both the 'question' and 'response' for each item in our questionnaire. To continue our example, if we want to ask our hospital staff directly about recent absenteeism we must first define 'absenteeism' so that the question is clear. Do we mean absent from work for any reason, absent for all non-health reasons, or absent only for health reasons? What is the time period we are referring to (last month, 3 months, 12 months, . . .)? The choice of this period depends on both our own research question, and what we think is feasible: for instance, if we ask about the last 12 months this might confuse new employees hired within that period or it might be difficult to accurately recall absenteeism over 12 months.

We must then decide how to represent levels of absenteeism in the 'response' part of our question. Should we use an open-ended response format (such as 'How many days have you missed from work for any reason (not including annual leave) in the last 3 months? Please specify number _____'). Or should we use a closed format (such as 'How many days have you missed from work for any reason (not including annual leave) in the last 3 months? Please circle one of the following: 0, 1, 2, 3, 4, 5, 6, more than 6'). If we choose a closed format, should we use numbers as in the previous example, or use non-numerical categories? The latter might be more suited to questions where exact numbers are not appropriate for the variables in question (e.g., 'How would you describe your stress levels at work in the last year: severe, moderate, mild, none?'). In summary, questions and response choices need to be constructed so that respondents can be successful in giving answers that meet the analytic needs of the inquiry.

What makes a good question?

When we ask a question in a questionnaire, we hope that our respondents will answer accurately and honestly. There are a number of psychological processes that can inhibit accuracy and honesty.

Excess mental demands

Streiner and Norman (2003) describe the steps that respondents go through when answering a questionnaire. At each of these steps, accuracy can be impaired because the questionnaire places too much demand on important mental processes. It is imperative, therefore, that we try to minimize the mental demands on our respondents:

* *Misunderstanding the question*. Simple misunderstanding of the intention behind a question is very common. In the next section we describe some ways of minimizing misunderstandings, but some mismatch between questionnaire designer and respondent is always likely to exist.
* *Inability to recall*. If we ask people 'how satisfied have you been with work over the last year?' we are asking them to recall many moods and events over a long period, an extremely difficult task.
* *Guessing*. The answers to many of our questions cannot be recalled with perfect accuracy so our respondents must use a variety of strategies to 'guess' what they consider to be the 'right' answer. Streiner and Norman discuss a number of processes that can lead to errors in these guesses.
* *Mapping the answer onto the response alternative*. Response formats are unlikely to correspond exactly to our respondents' individual mental representations, and the 'true' answer can often become lost in translation. For example, we might provide the response choices 'excellent', 'very good', 'good', 'fair' and 'poor' to a question on subjective health, but our respondents might not consider the discrimination between 'excellent' and 'very good' to be valid for their own health, or they might want the option of describing their health as 'very poor'.

Biased responses

The second main problem for questionnaire designers arises from a variety of biases that occur when answering questions:

- *Satisficing*. This occurs when respondents give what they consider a 'satisfactory' rather than optimal answer. A common example of this is the tendency to select the first response alternative that seems reasonable, rather than considering all options and then choosing.
- *Social desirability and faking good*. Respondents are likely to want their questionnaire answers to present the best version of themselves to the world. This can lead to extreme bias when we ask about, for example, socially undesirable behaviours (such as illegal drug use).
- *Deviation and faking bad*. There are some situations where the respondent may perceive that it is advantageous to appear in as bad a light as possible. For instance, in a survey of adolescents, young men in particular might exaggerate their experiences of alcohol use or smoking, if these are acceptable among their peer groups.
- *Acquiescence*. There is some evidence to suggest that respondents are more likely to agree than disagree with statements in a questionnaire. This is particularly problematic when we are asking about opinions or attitudes.
- *End-avoidance and positive skew*. These problems all arise when respondents are asked to provide an answer on some form of continuous scale. End avoidance occurs because respondents often do not like to choose extreme answers. Positive skew occurs because respondents tend to favour more positive responses, leading to response distributions that do not centre on the middle option.

Individual question tips

Given what we have learned about the psychological processes involved in answering questions, let us now consider some of the qualities of a good question. A good question will:

- have neutral wording. Value-laden questions produce biased responses.
- avoid asking two or more questions at the same time. When a single question is asking about two things we call it a 'double-barrelled' question.
- have a clear time frame (i.e. will be clear about the time period to which the question refers). The choice of time frame should also be appropriate to the question. Sometimes it is helpful to think about the last year, but for other questions respondents might be better able to remember the last week or the last month. In general it is often helpful to have the same time frame for the whole questionnaire and then it can just be stated once at the beginning.
- produce variability in the responses across the sample. When a question produces no variability in responses, we learn little from the question and cannot perform any statistical analyses on the item.
- not make unwarranted assumptions.
- not put the respondent in a position of having to guess (satisfice) the correct answer.
- not imply a desired answer. The wording of a question is extremely important. We are striving for scientific rigour in our questionnaires and, therefore, must be careful not to

lead the respondent into giving the answer we would like to receive. Leading questions are easily spotted because they often use negative phraseology. The exception to this is perhaps where we might expect social desirability to bias responses, and a leading question (implying, for instance, that most respondents did have this experience) may be more likely to generate an honest answer.

- accommodate all possible answers by having comprehensive response options.
- have mutually exclusive response options, so that a single answer cannot fall into more than one category.
- have unambiguous differences between the response choices.

✏ Activity 11.1

Imagine that we have constructed our questionnaire on hospital staff absenteeism. Using the individual question tips above, try to identify the errors present in each of the following questions that we have generated.

1 How would you describe your relationship with your line manager?
  Excellent Very good Good Average Fair Poor Very poor
2 Which type of co-worker do you find it most difficult to work with?
  Nursing staff Medical staff Management Other (please specify)
3 Do you ever miss work for child care or health reasons?
  Yes No
4 Do you feel that you have received enough training in communicating with the relatives of recently deceased patients?
  Yes No
5 Have you ever considered moving to a new job?
  Yes No
6 How many days have you missed from work (for any reason, other than annual leave) in the last 12 months?
  1–5 days 6–10 days 11–15 days 16–20 days
7 Do you often miss work for no good reason?
  Yes No
8 Isn't it true that flexible working hours are likely to improve staff morale?
  Yes No
9 How many times have you felt very tired at work in the last month?
  0 1 2 3 4 5 6 7 8 9 10 more than 10

Feedback

1 Has ambiguous differences between the response choices (e.g., what is the difference between 'average' and 'fair'?). This question also has no time frame. The relationship with the line manager may have changed, so it is helpful to be explicit about the time period we want the respondent to think about.
2 May have response choices that are not mutually exclusive, because in a hospital many of the management may also be nurses or medical professionals.
3 This is a double-barrelled question. It would be better as two questions. We would probably like to be able to separate out poor health and lack of child care as sources of absenteeism.

4 May make unwarranted assumptions. The respondent may not ever have to deal with the relatives of recently deceased patients. One might be tempted to introduce a 'branching' question ('Do you deal with the relatives of recently deceased patients? Yes/No. If yes, please proceed . . .'). However, as a rule, branching in written questionnaires should be avoided because it sometimes confuses respondents. A better alternative might be to simply have the following response alternatives: 'Yes/No/I do not deal with the relatives of recently deceased patients'.

5 Is unlikely to produce a variability of responses. It would be a rare employee who has not thought of moving to a new job.

6 Has broad enough categories that we can feel confident the respondent does not have to guess the answer (although they might find it difficult to be 100% confident about answers around the boundaries of the categories). The main problem is the lack of a zero option, or an option for those who have missed more than 20 days from work.

7 Is value-laden. The phrase 'no good reason' has strong negative connotations and is likely to encourage respondents to 'fake good'. It is also unclear what the term 'often' means.

8 Is leading. The question 'Isn't it true . . .?' seems to encourage the respondent to agree with some conventional wisdom.

9 Imposes high demands on the respondent's memory and is likely to lead to guessing.

Overall questionnaire design tips

Now that you have generated your questions, you should put them together in as attractive and easy-to-use manner as possible. This will help to maximize your response rate and minimize errors in completion. Here are some useful design tips:

- Give your questionnaire a title that is short and meaningful to the respondent.
- State clearly what the purpose of the research is and who is carrying out and funding the research.
- Be sure to state clearly your policy on confidentiality and anonymity, especially if the questionnaire contains potentially sensitive items. A questionnaire should be valid: it should measure what it is supposed to measure. One of the main threats to validity in a questionnaire survey is the possibility of non-truthful responses to sensitive questions.
- Include clear and concise instructions on how to complete the questionnaire.
- Use short sentences and simple, direct language throughout. Avoid abbreviations. Make sure the reading level required is appropriate for your respondents.
- Begin with non-threatening and interesting items. If the first items are too threatening or 'boring', there is little chance that the person will complete the questionnaire.
- Place the most important items in the first half of the questionnaire, as respondents often send back partially completed questionnaires.
- Emphasize crucial words in each item by using bold, italics or underlining.
- Leave adequate space for respondents to provide responses if you are using open questions.
- Give careful consideration to the response options. For survey questionnaires it is sometimes helpful to vary the response format in order to keep the respondents'

attention. However, varying the response options too much can have the opposite effect and become confusing. For psychometric questionnaires (where items are added up into a score) it is usually best to keep the same response options for every item.

- Group questions into coherent categories. It is disconcerting for respondents if questions jump from topic to topic.
- Use professional production methods to maximize the impression that the questionnaire is important and worth completing.
- End the questionnaire in a gentle and friendly manner, expressing gratitude for the respondent's time and effort.
- Make returning the questionnaire as easy as possible (e.g., provide a reply-paid envelope). Print the return address on the questionnaire itself (because questionnaires often become separated from the reply envelopes).

Pre-testing

The final test of a questionnaire is to try it on representatives of the target audience. If there are problems with the questionnaire, they almost always show up here. Pre-testing (or piloting) is an opportunity to identify any questions that are ambiguous, are misunderstood, make respondents feel uncomfortable or where respondents feel they need to say something extra. Piloting can be done in a number of ways, but it is best done face-to-face. During pre-testing respondents can be asked to tell you about any items they find difficult to understand or hard to answer. The pre-testing interviews could be audio-recorded or detailed notes taken so that you can be sure to have the correct information when you come to edit the questionnaire afterwards.

Summary

In designing a questionnaire that is reliable, valid and acceptable to respondents, great care must be taken over wording, response formats and the order of items. Differences in wording can produce very different responses. Items on questionnaires could be factual (e.g., age, gender, number of children), or they may ask about more subjective constructs (e.g., attitudes or quality of life). The researcher must consider whether the item is an appropriate indicator for the kind of information sought. A key consideration is the target population, and the questionnaire designed must be pre-tested with members of the target population before use.

References

Streiner, D.L. and Norman, G.R. (2003) *Health Measurement Scales: A Practical Guide to Their Development and Use* (3rd edn). Oxford: Oxford University Press.

Further reading

Bowden, A. and Fox-Rushby, J.A. (2003) A systematic and critical review of the process of translation an adaptation of generic health-related quality of life measures in Africa, Asia, Eastern Europe, the Middle East, South America. *Social Science & Medicine*, 57: 1289–1306.

Bowling, A. (2005). *Measuring Health: A Review of Quality of Life Measurement Scales* (3rd edn). Maidenhead: Open University Press.

Quality of life scales are a particular kind of questionnaire that have been developed to measure patient-based outcomes of health care. Bowling's book is an excellent introduction to their use.

Bowling, A. (2009) Questionnaire design. In *Research Methods in Health: Investigating Health and Health Services* (3rd edn), pp. 299–337. Maidenhead: Open University Press.

Boynton, P.M. (2004) Hand-on guide to questionnaire research: Administering, analysing and reporting your questionnaire. *British Medical Journal*, 328: 1372–1375.

Boynton, P.M., Wood, G.W. and Greenhalgh, T. (2004) Hands on guide to questionnaire research: Reaching beyond the white middle classes. *British Medical Journal*, 328: 1433–1436.

McDowell, I. (2006) The theoretical and technical foundations of health measurement. In *Measuring Health: A Guide to Rating Scales and Questionnaires* (3rd edn), pp. 10–46. Oxford: Oxford University Press.

Stone, D.H. (1993) How to do it – Design a questionnaire. *British Medical Journal*, 30: 1264–1266.

Ware, J.E. Jr, Keller, S.D., Gandek, B., Brazier, J.E. and Sullivan, M. (1995) Evaluating translations of health status questionnaires: Methods from the IQOLA Project. *International Journal of Technology Assessment in Health Care*, 11: 525–551.

Woodward, C.A. and Chambers, L.W. (1991) *Guide to Questionnaire Construction and Questionnaire Writing*. Ottawa: Canadian Public Health Association.

12 Using surveys in cross-sectional research designs

Overview

This chapter considers the use of surveys in cross-sectional research and how they are designed. It includes sections on issues related to sampling (deciding who to include), different data collection modes, and how to improve survey response rates. The limitations of using surveys are also highlighted.

Learning objectives

After working through this chapter you will be better able to:

- assess the strengths and weaknesses of different sampling strategies
- identify ways of making studies that use surveys more representative

Key terms

Generalizability: The extent to which the results from a sample survey can be applied to the population of interest.

Non-sampling error (or measurement error): The amount of error in the data we have collected that is due to problems with the reliability and validity of our data collection method (as opposed to problems with our sampling of the population).

Probability sample: Each member of the population has a random and known chance of being selected.

Response rate: The proportion of those sampled who responded.

Sample: A group of respondents drawn from a sampling frame to represent the population of interest.

Sampling error: Limitations on how far inferences from a sample can be generalized to the whole population.

Sampling frame: The master list from which the sample is identified.

Purposes of studies that use surveys

In Chapters 3 and 4 the importance of specifying a research question and identifying an appropriate method for investigating it was discussed. Research questions in studies that use surveys are likely to be mainly descriptive. Surveys are a widely used method for answering such questions as:

- How many rural villagers have access to vaccination programmes?
- How satisfied are patients with their hospital services?
- Are young people more likely to smoke if their parents smoke?
- Which sections of the population are lacking in knowledge about HIV infection risks?

Surveys also aid explanation by generating hypotheses, and analysis may also be used not only to test hypotheses but also to expose interesting *associations*. If we want to demonstrate *causality* (e.g., that certain lifestyles *cause* a difference in health status) these associations must be investigated either: (a) under more controlled conditions such as an experiment; or (b) by a cohort design, in which the same respondents are followed up over time so that the researcher can investigate which variables caused later effects. Cohort designs present particular difficulties for survey management. In this chapter, only the design of single, cross-sectional (sometimes called 'snapshot') surveys is considered.

Collecting data

In previous chapters we have used the term 'survey' to refer to a particular type of questionnaire used for data collection. However, the general term 'survey' is also used to describe any study in which the same variables are measured in a standardized way across a *sample* of subjects at a single time point. This is what epidemiologists would call a 'cross-sectional observational study'. The subjects can be individuals, households, health care settings or any other unit. This produces a standard set of data for each subject, which can be analysed statistically to look for patterns within the data, regularities and relationships between the variables measured.

There is a range of ways of collecting measurements in such studies. Some rely purely on observation. If the researcher is interested in how many children cycle to school in various parts of the country, one possible data collection method is to simply count the number of children arriving at the school gates on a bicycle. However, in social science most data collection relies on asking people to report their behaviour, or views, or knowledge (i.e. through a survey questionnaire). Some of the different modes of administration of surveys are described in Table 12.1, with their advantages and disadvantages. Important considerations are cost, response rate, the literacy of the respondents, interviewer bias, whether it is important to probe answers or not, and the need for confidentiality.

How to select the people to be surveyed

Whatever the research question and however the data are to be collected, a key concern is the *generalizability* of a survey. The user of survey results needs to know how far the

Table 12.1 Advantages and disadvantages of different survey administration modes

Mode of administration	Advantages	Disadvantages
Personal (face-to-face) interviews	Longer interaction with respondents possible More flexibility (e.g., opportunity to probe inconsistent or ambiguous responses) More complex questionnaires can be used	More costly Takes longer than telephone or postal surveys Possibility of interviewer bias Possibility that respondents will be less honest about sensitive issues
Telephone surveys	Faster than postal or face-to-face surveys Less costly than postal or face-to-face surveys Respondents may be more honest about sensitive issues	Calling time is limited to a window of 6–9 p.m. if representative samples are sought for most surveys: may inconvenience the interviewee Younger people may be less likely to have landlines (many will only have a mobile phone) Respondents may be less honest if there are people listening
Postal surveys	Less costly than telephone or face-to-face surveys Allow respondent to answer at leisure Eliminate interviewer bias Respondents may be more honest about sensitive issues	Take longer to carry out than telephone surveys but quicker than face-to-face surveys Response rates may be low in populations with lower educational and literacy levels Less control over how the respondent completes the questionnaire (e.g., they may skip questions) Interviewer bias is not a problem
Email surveys (i.e. written version sent to respondent by email)	Less costly than telephone, face-to- face or postal surveys Fast to perform Eliminates interviewer bias Respondents may be more honest about sensitive issues	High resistance to 'spam' means an email survey is only useful with people who have agreed to be contacted by email for surveys People with email may not be representative of the general population (e.g., older people often do not have it)
Internet/intranet surveys (i.e. survey completed interactively online)	Less costly than face-to-face, telephone or postal surveys Fast to perform and analyse Can use features (e.g., question skipping logic) not available to paper-based questionnaires Can be more colourful and attractive to complete Eliminates interviewer bias Respondents may be more honest about sensitive issues Online survey tools are available to make this simpler	People with Internet may not be representative of the general population (e.g., older people often do not have it) Internet use perceived as more 'casual' and optional: interviewees more likely to quit in the middle of a questionnaire May get a low response rate May be difficult to get a probability sample

findings are applicable not only to those surveyed but also to the whole population of interest, whether that is all the citizens of a country, all adolescents, or all potential hospital patients. An obvious way of ensuring that the results of an investigation are completely generalizable is to include the whole population. Occasionally such an exercise is undertaken, for example when a population census is carried out. But such attempts are unwieldy and expensive and so are conducted infrequently. A *sample survey*, if the sample is representative, provides a quicker, more cost-effective, labour-saving way of collecting information about the total population. Results from a smaller sample survey are less unwieldy, and therefore easier to analyse. However, if only a sample is chosen, the researcher needs to consider how representative the respondents are of the whole population. Obviously, we cannot know if a sample is representative of the population if we do not know what the population looks like. Therefore the first task in this process is to clearly define the target population.

Once we have identified the population of interest, we need to identify the *sampling frame*. This is the master list from which the sample is selected. For example, if we wanted to select a representative sample of people living in a certain town then the sampling frame might be a list of all the postcodes and addresses for that area. Sampling methods refer to the way that potential participants are selected from the sampling frame.

Sampling methods are classified as either *probability* or *non-probability*. In probability samples, each member of the population has a known probability of being selected. Probability methods include random sampling, systematic sampling and stratified sampling. In non-probability sampling, members are selected from the population in some non-random manner. These include convenience sampling, judgement sampling, quota sampling, and snowball sampling. The advantage of probability sampling is that *sampling error* can be calculated. Sampling error is the degree to which a sample might differ from the population. When inferring to the population, results are reported plus or minus the sampling error. In non-probability sampling, the degree to which the sample differs from the population remains unknown.

Probability sampling

Simple random sampling is the purest form of probability sampling. Each member of the population has an equal and known chance of being selected. A simple random sample has to be drawn from a record of the population as a whole, known as a *sampling frame*. If the sample is to be free from bias, the sampling frame should be as complete a record as possible of the total population. Typical sampling frames include registers of patients in primary health care, electoral registers, and postcode address files. It quickly becomes clear that such options are more of a reality in highly developed countries than in those that are less well developed and where records are likely to be less complete. Even in countries in which such sources of data are available, in practice no records are perfect, and a trade-off still has to be made between the advantages and disadvantages of each potential data source. All of these contain their own characteristic bias. Electoral registers, for instance, neglect the homeless, the highly mobile, and those who fail to complete forms.

Systematic sampling is often used instead of simple random sampling. After the required sample size has been calculated, and a random starting point selected, every *n*th record is selected from a list of population members. As long as the list does not contain any hidden order, this sampling method is in practice often as good as the random sampling method, although we do need to be aware that there may be 'hidden' biases in ordering of lists such as those of surnames. The advantage of the systematic technique is simplicity. Systematic sampling is often used to select a specified number of records from a computer file.

Stratified sampling is a commonly used probability method that is superior to simple random sampling because it reduces sampling error. A *stratum* is a subset of the population whose members share at least one common characteristic. The researcher first identifies the relevant strata and their actual representation in the population. Random sampling is then used to select subjects from each stratum until the number of subjects in that stratum is proportional to its frequency in the population. Stratified sampling is often used when one or more of the strata in the population have a low incidence relative to the other strata.

Cluster sampling assumes that populations are built up of relevant hierarchies of sampling units. For instance, individuals belong to households, which are clustered in small areas, and then into larger ones. Nurses could be contacted as individuals, or as part of a ward, or of a hospital. Cluster sampling is the sampling of complete groups of units, such as all the households in an area, or all the nurses on a series of wards. Cluster sampling methods offer convenience and often cost savings. It is, for instance, easier to carry out fieldwork for a household survey if covering all (or a subsample of) households in particular clusters than contacting a random sample of individual households spread over a whole country. The disadvantage is that they may increase sampling error.

✎ Activity 12.1

Consider possible sources of bias that might affect the following studies, and the implications for the studies in each case:

1 A postal questionnaire administered to a random sample drawn from a primary health care register of patients.
2 A telephone survey of young people, using a random sample drawn from a telephone directory.

Feedback

1 Registers of patients are often inaccurate. Patients may not inform staff of new addresses, so the survey will under report those who are mobile. Those with no fixed address have little chance of inclusion. If the target population had a low literacy rate, this would also reduce the representativeness of any self-completed questionnaire.
2 As the telephone directory will not list age, a screening question is needed to identify target respondents. Many young people may not have landline telephones, preferring mobiles instead, and so selecting the sample from the telephone directory of landlines will automatically exclude many young people. There may be biases in the willingness of the person who answers the phone to provide information about resident young people. Also, the interviewer may not know whether the respondent is in a room with other people, which may inhibit honest responses.

How large should a probability sample be?

In general, the larger the sample the more closely it will approximate to the characteristics of the target population from which it was drawn, and the greater the likelihood that the results will be reliable. A survey should not be dismissed as unreliable simply because the sample size is small. A relatively modest sample may be large enough to satisfy the aims of the study. The research question is all-important. Obviously cost and time resources are important considerations when choosing a sample size. The following are also important.

Prevalence of target event/behaviour

If your survey is intended to detect something rare then you are likely to need a large sample. Suppose 2% of a population have attended a sexually transmitted disease (STD) clinic in the last year. A sample of 10,000 will yield only about 200 individuals who report having attended an STD clinic. If we want to know more about these people (such as their gender and age) we quickly run into trouble. Analysis by gender would reduce this number by half for each sex, and further analysis by age group might result in only 25 in the subgroup of women aged 16–25. Likewise, if you are interested in minority groups within the population, you would need a larger sample to get sufficient representation in these groups.

Variation in target event/behaviour

Sometimes we are interested in variables that cannot be simply described in yes/no format. Take, for example, a study that includes measurement of how often women visit a family planning service. The majority may be clustered in the middle of the distribution, making two or three visits a year; there may be a further proportion who have made such a visit only once in the past year; and there may be another, equally rare, subgroup who have visited more than three times in a year. If an aim of the survey is to measure a range of behaviours or events, then it must be large enough to capture these extremes.

 Activity 12.2

Rare or diverse behaviours and characteristics can be studied by drawing a random sample from the population, when there is no more appropriate sampling frame. However, to find enough cases for analysis, the sample has to be very large and wastefully collect data about people who are not of interest. Can you think of any alternative sampling strategies for identifying relatively uncommon behaviours? Think about the problems posed by the following two research questions and suggest how a sample could be identified for a survey.

1 How often do injecting drug users share needles?
2 Do urban homeless people have access to primary care services?

Feedback

1 Drug use is illegal in many societies, and those who inject drugs are unlikely to be listed on any 'official' records which could be used as a sampling frame. A whole-population sample may well underestimate numbers, as drug users may be less willing to complete survey questionnaires. Instead, it may be possible to survey users of a relevant clinic, if there is one, by asking patients attending to complete a questionnaire.

2 Any survey that aims to assess 'unmet need' (i.e., those who could benefit from a service but do not receive it) clearly cannot use a register of current service users as a sampling frame. As the homeless are difficult to identify through records, any survey would have to use methods of recruiting respondents where they were, perhaps on the streets or in facilities provided for use by homeless people.

Non-probability sampling

Any sample that is not drawn randomly from a known population is called a non-probability sample. As the two examples above illustrate, there are situations in which it may be necessary to use non-probability sampling, although the disadvantage is that it is impossible to know how representative the survey sample is. Some common methods of non-probability samples are described below.

Purposive sampling involves the deliberate choice of respondents, subjects, or settings to reflect some features or characteristics of interest, for example patients with terminal cancer.

Convenience sampling is where samples are selected because they are conveniently available. This non-probability method is often used during preliminary research efforts to obtain a rough estimate of the results, without incurring the cost or taking the time required to select a random sample.

Snowball samples are collected by networking out from a convenience or purposive sample to reach more covert or inaccessible subjects. Respondents might be asked to introduce the researcher to others who meet the sample criteria. While this technique can dramatically lower search costs, it comes at the expense of introducing bias because the technique itself reduces the likelihood that the sample will represent a good cross-section from the population.

Quota samples are allocated according to proportional distribution of different demographic characteristics, such as gender, age, region, social class. The quota sample has the advantage of being representative in terms of known characteristics, but not necessarily of characteristics which are not controlled by quotas. For example if the age distribution of a population is such that 40% are under age 25, 35% are aged 25–40 and 25% are aged over 40, then the quota sample would be drawn up to represent exactly these proportions. However, quota samples are distinct from stratified samples because the sample within each quota is not randomly selected.

All these non-probability samples present the typical limitations of volunteer samples: that is, they are likely to contain bias related to the variable under study. Suppose the focus of investigation was on health-seeking behaviour relating to stress. The most stressed members of the population might be least likely to agree to take part because of pressure of time.

Activity 12.3

Make a note of possible biases the following situations might present if used in a quota sample survey, and the implications for the study.

1 Administering questionnaires at a mainline railway station in the morning to investigate knowledge of local health care facilities.
2 Carrying out a face-to-face interview with shoppers outside a supermarket during a weekday afternoon to investigate use of alternative health care in one city.

Feedback

1 The sample would be biased towards those who travel in the morning, who may be more likely to be in well-paid jobs. At a mainline station there are also likely to be many respondents from outside the area who would not know about local health care services.
2 This strategy would predominantly identify people with no full-time paid work, and would not be generalizable to the whole population.

How can we tell if the sample is representative or not?

Even when samples are drawn randomly from a reliable sampling frame, the researcher still needs to consider the representativeness of the final achieved sample (those who agreed to take part). There are two main techniques for maximizing representativeness: improving the response rate, and comparing the sample with the population.

Improving the response rate

Response rates are important to a random sample. The higher the response rate, the greater the confidence with which results can be generalized to the population as a whole. Typical response rates for government-instigated surveys tend to be around 70%; for other surveys the response rate may be more typically 50–70%. Low response rates can lead to bias in survey estimates, although this is not always the case. A high response rate gives a good guarantee that there will be little response bias, while a low response rate gives more cause for concern. We cannot know a great deal about those who do not agree to take part, by definition, because if they are not prepared to answer the questions relating to the investigation they are unlikely to answer questions relating to why they did not. All surveys are voluntary, and sample members must not be coerced into taking part.

Activity 12.4

Think of some ways in which you could maximize the response rate to:

1 A postal questionnaire survey of health professionals in your country.
2 A face-to-face interview survey of nurses in one hospital.

Feedback

1 Possible ways to improve response rates might include:

- a letter persuading respondents that the survey was worthwhile;
- reminder letters for those who did not reply;
- assurances of confidentiality and anonymity;
- use of a well-written and well-designed questionnaire;
- monetary incentives.

2 In a face-to-face interview, the calibre of the interviewer is crucial. He or she must be trained to provide information about the study, answer any questions and reassure the respondents that their views will remain confidential. It might be better to use interviewers who are from outside the hospital. Again, information about the need for the research, or how it might be of benefit for the respondents, might help.

In some studies that use surveys, respondents are rewarded in some way for taking part. This is more common in commercial settings than in health care research, but a small payment, in cash or as goods, is sometimes worth considering. The disadvantage (apart from increasing the costs of the survey) is that if it is known that the researcher will be paying for respondents there is then a potential bias towards those who need the reward most. The payment should be small so that it is not interpreted as coercion into taking part.

Many factors, then, may influence the response rate. If the survey is being carried out by a research team with a good reputation, from a credible institution, and if the research questions being asked are important and serious, then respondents are more likely to feel favourably inclined towards taking part in it.

Comparing the sample and the population

The second way of ensuring that a sample is representative is to compare the structure of the achieved sample and the structure of the target population it represents. You can find out whether the study was representative in terms of known variables such as demographic information. In most countries, data are collected in censuses on age, gender, educational level, ethnicity, social class and area of residence. The profile of the achieved sample can be compared with the demographic profile of the population it represents to see how well it 'behaves'. Of course, you can never know how typical the sample was in terms of other variables. People who do not take part are likely to be different from those who do in ways that can be important to the integrity of the study. Some researchers have reported that people who respond to surveys answer questions differently from those who do not. Others have found that late responders answer differently from early responders, and that the differences may be due to the different levels of interest in the subject matter. Demographic characteristics of non-respondents have also been investigated by many researchers. Non-response is sometimes associated with low education, especially for self-completion questionnaires. In some surveys it will be possible to compare to some extent the characteristics of non-responders, if we have some information from the sampling frame about them. This could help in identifying particular kinds of bias.

Limitations of using surveys

In Chapter 10 it was noted that quantitative social science had its roots in the development of 'social statistics' in northern Europe. Although the governments of all countries now use extensive 'fact gathering' about their populations, the acceptability of interviewing and form filling is not universal. Self-completion questionnaires obviously rely on relatively high levels of literacy. In many societies, the notion of an interview itself might be alien, and in others it might be quite threatening. Where, for instance, 'state surveillance' is used to control sections of the population, citizens may be justifiably suspicious of the uses to which survey findings will be put. There may also be a desire on the part of survey respondents to 'tell the interviewer what they want to hear'. This is similar to the 'social desirability' or 'courtesy' bias we discussed in Chapter 11.

For example, one anthropological study using qualitative methods uncovered the severe limitations of previous studies that used surveys (Stone and Campbell 1984). The researchers found that cultural traditions and unfamiliarity with questionnaires had led Nepalese villagers to feign ignorance of abortion and family planning services and to under report their use of contraception and abortion when responding to surveys. These problems are often termed 'non-sampling error', which we shall discuss below.

Sampling error and non-sampling error

So far in this chapter we have only discussed *sampling error*, which is error due to selecting a sample that is not representative of the target population. Sampling error occurs for a number of reasons, including too small a sample size or because we used invalid sampling methods (e.g., sampling only people with access to the Internet when trying to make inferences about the general population). Crucially, sampling error is something that, in theory, we can identify and control.

Non-sampling error is a more profound challenge to cross-sectional studies that use surveys because it introduces biases that undermine the reliability and validity of our findings. Non-sampling error occurs because of problems with our data collection instrument. These problems may be due to poor reliability (too much random noise in our instrument) or poor validity (the instrument systematically 'misses' what it is supposed to measure). One of the main non-sampling errors referred to by Stone and Campbell (1984) is a problem of validity: the survey instruments are influenced heavily by 'social desirability' (the tendency to tell the interviewer what the respondent thinks they want to hear), causing the instrument to systematically miss the concept targeted (such as the 'true' awareness and use of contraceptive devices in Nepal).

How could we have detected this non-sampling error? Qualitative work provides detailed descriptions of cultural values, which could have been used to design questions that were appropriate and to inform researchers of the cultural context. Ethnographic research can therefore complement the findings of survey research.

However, it should also be noted that this may unduly privilege findings from ethnographic work, which are sometimes seen as the 'gold standard' of truth. Stone and Campbell suggest that survey research and more traditional anthropological methods badly need to be guided and supplemented by one another if social science research is genuinely to assist development planning in non-industrialized countries.

Summary

Designing a study that uses surveys involves deciding how to collect the data needed and who to sample to answer the research question. Probability samples should be representative of the whole population of interest, but it may not be possible to achieve this. Non-probability designs may be necessary to identify rare behaviours or hard-to-reach subjects. Whatever the sampling strategy, attention must be paid to how representative the sample is in order to improve the generalizability of the survey.

Surveys are an invaluable method for accessing standardized information across a sample of the population. However, to provide valid and meaningful results they are best used in conjunction with qualitative methods which can aid the development of an appropriate instrument and provide information about the context of findings. Using surveys may present particular problems in developing countries.

References

Stone, L. and Campbell, J.G. (1984) The use and misuse of surveys in international development: An experiment from Nepal. *Human Organisation*, 43(1): 27–37.

Further reading

De Vaus, D.A. (2002) *Surveys in Social Research*. London: Routledge.
This is a good example of the various general books about social research design on the market, which all deal with issues of sampling, design and organization.

Nyandieka, L.N., Bowden, A., Wanjau, J. and Fox-Rushby, J.A. (2002) Managing a household survey: A practical example from the KENQOL survey. *Health Policy and Planning*, 17: 207–212.
This is a useful case study from Kenya on some of the practical issues that have to be dealt with in planning a successful survey on health-related quality of life.

Practical: designing a questionnaire   **13**

Overview

This practical chapter gives you an opportunity to design your own short self-completion questionnaire, which could be used in a survey.

Learning objectives

After working through this chapter you will be better able to

- relate what you have learned about questionnaires and surveys to your own practical experience

Introduction

To complete the chapter to the stage where the questionnaire is finalized, you will need to:

- have to hand any notes you made for Chapter 9, when you carried out a qualitative analysis on your chosen topic;
- review Chapter 11 on the design of questionnaires;
- make about five copies of the questionnaire for use in piloting;
- find five members of the target population who will agree to help you pilot the questionnaire.

✎ Activity 13.1

The qualitative data you produced in Chapter 9 may well have generated some quantitative research questions on the topic you chose. Frame one of these as a research question, which could be answered using a survey. If your data did not raise any appropriate questions, the following are some suggestions for research questions that you could use for this practical chapter.

1 How does patient satisfaction with health care delivery vary between different patient groups? Restrict your question to one health care setting (e.g., a primary care centre or one outpatient department) and choose two groups to sample, such as men and women, or patients with different conditions.

2 How well do professionals understand the roles of other professional groups within your health care organization? Think about aspects of the role of one group that might be uncertain, such as perceptions of what tasks a practice nurse might carry out, or what clinicians' attitude to the role of the hospital administrative staff might be.

3 What proportion of nurses (or people in the community) report using infection control procedures (such as appropriate hand washing)? You might want to consider an infection control policy in force within your organization (if there is one) and whether your respondents are aware of it or its contents.

Construct a short questionnaire (with no more than 12 items and designed for self-completion) to address the research question that you have chosen. Use the notes below to guide you in planning, preparing and piloting your questionnaire. If time permits and you wish to do so, you may then choose to carry out a mini-survey using the questionnaire you have designed.

Guidance notes

When you have framed a research question, decide which population you are interested in (doctors in your hospital, patients of a clinic, all the people who live within the district covered by your health agency). How would you select a representative sample of this population? Would a convenience, or other non-probability, sample be adequate for your needs?

Next, think about relevant indicators for the variables you are interested in. Your questionnaire should contain items that collect some of the following kinds of data:

- demographic information (such as gender, age)
- knowledge
- attitudes
- reports of behaviour.

Check that each item you choose for inclusion has all the desirable characteristics discussed in Chapter 11:

- neutral wording
- avoids asking two or more questions at the same time
- has a clear time frame
- produces variability of responses
- does not make unwarranted assumptions
- does not ask questions where the respondent has to guess (satisfice) the correct answer
- does not imply a desired answer
- accommodates all possible answers by having comprehensive response options
- has mutually exclusive response choices, so that a single answer cannot fall into more than one category
- has unambiguous differences between the response choices

For each item, you will need to decide how the respondents should answer. Will there be a pre-defined set of response options? Or will there be space for free text responses? If there will be pre-defined response options, you should think through all possible responses so that there is an appropriate response for every respondent. If you are asking respondents to agree or disagree with statements to indicate their attitudes, how many responses do you need? Do you need a 'neutral' category? You will also need to think about how you will code responses (i.e. what numerical codes you will assign to each of the responses so that they can be entered into a data analysis package).

If you are looking at reported behaviour, think about how to phrase questions so that they minimize recall and other sources of bias. For instance, asking 'How often did you visit the doctor this month?' may lead to more accurate reporting than asking about 'an average year'. However, you must also take account of the likely frequency of events. In a general population survey, for instance, most people will not have visited the doctor at all in one month.

Also think carefully about phrasing questions about sensitive issues such as sexual behaviour. You need to consider what is 'sensitive' in your setting, as this is culturally specific. In Britain, some women consider 'age' to be sensitive information, for instance.

Next try and design your questionnaire in as attractive and comprehensible a fashion as possible. Check that you have met all the design tips mentioned in Chapter 11:

- Give the questionnaire a short, meaningful title.
- Give clear and concise instructions, including, if appropriate, the time frame to be used for the whole questionnaire (alternatively, this could be different for individual items).
- Include a clear statement of purpose, identifying who is carrying out the survey.
- Include a clear statement of policy on confidentiality.
- Use simple, direct language throughout.
- Begin with non-threatening and interesting items.
- Place the most important items in the first half of the questionnaire.
- Emphasize crucial words in each item by using bold, italics or underlining.
- Leave adequate space for respondents to provide responses.
- Vary the question format.
- Group questions into coherent categories.
- Use professional production methods.
- End the questionnaire in a gentle and friendly manner.
- Print the return address on the questionnaire itself.

Finally, consider how you are going to distribute and collect your questionnaire and, if you are not going to introduce it in person, what kind of introduction and explanation you will enclose with it.

Phrasing good questions for a questionnaire is a more difficult task than it appears. A question for which the meaning seems obvious to you might confuse your colleagues, and some respondents may be offended by a question that appears innocuous to others. There may be valid responses to a question that did not occur to you. This is why you need to pilot your instrument.

Piloting

Give your questionnaire to at least five respondents (ideally choose people from the population your questionnaire is aimed at). Ask them to go through it and give you feedback on how easy it was to complete and whether there were any questions that were difficult or insensitive. Check that they understood questions in the way you intended. If not, how could you improve the wording?

Was the layout clear and inviting, or was it difficult for them to see where they should make their response? Use the feedback from the piloting exercise to review and amend your questionnaire.

 Activity 13.2

Survey (optional)

After making any necessary amendments, you can use your questionnaire in a mini-survey if time permits. The sample size needed to produce statistically significant findings (i.e., findings that we can be confident are not just due to chance) about relationships between variables will depend on your question and the likely variation in the population. However, if you are just interested in descriptive frequencies (such as how many people have a particular attitude or how often they have experienced a particular event) try to get about 30 completed questionnaires.

Reflection

1 If your response rate was low, how could it be improved?
2 Were there questions which did not show good variability in the responses? For instance, if everyone agrees that 'good health care is a priority', this is not really worth asking.
3 Were there any items that were often left blank? Why might this be?
4 What, if any, are the implications for policy or practice in your results?
5 If you were to survey a larger sample, how could you test the reliability of your questionnaire?
6 What kinds of validity would it be important to test?

SECTION 4

Issues in social research

Principles of research ethics in practice 14

Tim Rhodes and Sarah Bernays

Overview

We will all face ethical dilemmas as we proceed through our research. Codes and guidelines, including those upheld by ethical review committees, help, but they do not provide solutions for every eventuality. There is often no clear right or wrong way to deal with an ethical dilemma, especially those emerging when researching in the field. Research ethics is therefore a *process shaped by its contexts*. In this brief chapter, we outline common principles guiding the conduct of ethical research, noting how these are inevitably situated by the settings in which research takes place. We therefore emphasize the need for less 'universalist' and more 'situated' approaches to understanding the principles of ethics in research.

From the outset, then, we see research ethics as *a process of negotiation in context* (Kohler-Riessman 2005). How will you negotiate unforeseen ethical dilemmas when faced with these during or after your fieldwork? How will you negotiate research ethics principles such as informed consent, voluntary participation and confidentiality in different social and cultural settings? While research ethics is a fundamental a priori consideration when designing studies and seeking approval for their implementation, the conduct of ethical research is a journey in the life of a research project and beyond. This chapter illustrates key steps in this journey and provides examples of ethical challenges which can be encountered in health research.

Learning objectives

After working through this chapter, you will be better able to:

- identify the core principles underpinning the ethical conduct of research
- identify some of the practical challenges to applying these core principles

Key terms

Autonomy: Respecting the rights of the individual to self-determination. An individual has the right to decide whether or not to take part in research.

Beneficence: 'Doing good'. Researchers must always act in the best interests of study participants and prioritize their welfare.

Justice: This relates to the fair selection of research participants: avoiding populations which may be coerced into participation (e.g., prisoners) and ensuring that research outcomes are distributed equitably.

> **Non-maleficence:** 'First, do no harm'. Researchers must consider the potential risks involved in taking part in a study and must do their utmost to remove and reduce these harms and ensure that the benefits of participation outweigh the risks.

Values

Our starting point is the reminder that no science or research is value-free (see Chapter 2). Traditionally, scientific approaches rooted in a predominately 'positivist' paradigm posited that researchers should strive to be disinterested in, and detached from, political and social values surrounding their objects of research. The primary role of science in this view is the production of knowledge constituted as objective and credible by virtue of research methods emphasizing the minimization of bias through the removal or distancing of the researcher from the processes of data collection and analysis. In this way, the generation of 'objective' evidence is idealized as being 'free' of values, as untainted by the social or political contexts of its production.

As noted in Chapter 2, this idealized imagination of how research is conducted is naïve to how values pervade the research process, from conception to dissemination. This more 'relativist' position accepts, for example, that the identification of a research problem or question as 'worthy' of investigation from the outset is not a neutral process, free of its context, but instead emerges out of social interactions regarding what is *negotiated* to be of value. This can be especially the case in policy-oriented research, in which expert agencies – such as governments and government-funded research agencies – seek to frame research agendas, sometimes explicitly in specific political directions, for which researchers then compete for funding. Likewise, the processes of data generation, analysis and dissemination in health research are not 'value-neutral' or free of their contexts. Researchers' assumptions, training and broader normative values pervade the practices of questionnaire design, construct development, data analysis, publication and how data are used to lobby for particular causes or changes.

Accepting that research is inevitably framed by values encourages us to consider the social and policy value of our research. Health research is generally conducted for a social purpose, not merely for knowledge generation. When thinking through our research designs, we are therefore asking 'what can we contribute, and to whom?' (Green and Thorogood 2004). Selecting a research question worthy of investigation involves negotiating the balance between research as a resource for *credible* knowledge, and research as a resource for *useful* knowledge. The pertinent question is: who or what is this knowledge for? The answer may be one or a combination of the following: us, our discipline, our research funders, other stakeholders, patients, the general public, or society. Research is a process of balancing the benefits of the generation of useful knowledge against the burden, risks, or harms the generation of this knowledge might create for our participants as well as for others. We are balancing the need for knowledge of a certain value against the rights of individuals and communities involved in research alongside other obligations, such as those to fellow researchers, research sponsors, scientific advancement, policy improvement, and social change. Given how values pervade the research process, and that these may differ according to different settings as well as research approaches, this is a complex path to navigate.

Principles

In the public health field, ethical debate often centres around four equally important principles (autonomy, beneficence, non-maleficence and justice) synthesized in the early 1980s by Tom Beauchamp and Jim Childress (2009). These have shaped the ethics of health care, and have become embraced as core principles framing research ethics reviews in the public health field.

Activity 14.1

1 Considering the principle of 'autonomy', can you think of populations with diminished autonomy for which protections should be put in place when planning and conducting research?
2 Considering the principle of 'justice', can you think of an example of when an injustice occurs in research?

Feedback

1 Those with diminished autonomy include those who may not be in a position to make a fully informed and voluntary decision to participate in research whilst assessing the relative risks and benefits involved, both during and after participation. Examples include: children; people with mental health difficulties; people in prison or detention; and people recruited through gatekeepers who also act as authority figures.
2 Injustice occurs, for example, when the vulnerable or marginalized become overused in research, or when the findings benefit those who can afford them rather than those researched. An example might be a clinical trial in a low-income setting which involves some risk and which develops medicines for use in higher-income settings beyond the accessibility of those in need who acted as research participants.

The 1964 Declaration of Helsinki, which outlines the tenets of ethical research for the World Medical Association, endorses the above four principles in the emphasis it places on informed consent to participate, voluntary participation, confidentiality, and the balancing of risk against benefit. Importantly, the Declaration places the wellbeing of the human subject above all else, including the interests of science and society.

The historical basis for establishing such principles is the documentation of research involving clear ethics and human rights abuses, including harms generated by research in the absence of voluntary or informed participation (Brody 1998). The 1947 Nuremberg Trials of 23 doctors accused of unethical experimentation upon vulnerable groups during World War II led to the establishment the Nuremberg Code for Medical Research. This Code introduced the principles of voluntary participation and informed consent, as well as the need to justify the risks of research participation, disrupting popular assumptions of the time that research was inherently benevolent. Another well-documented example of human rights abuse in research, albeit an extreme one, is the Tuskegee syphilis study (Rockwell *et al.* 1964; Brandt 1978).

The Tuskegee syphilis study

This study took place in Alabama in the USA between 1932 and 1972. A total of 399 impoverished African American men with syphilis and 201 uninfected controls were recruited, and the initial aim was to follow up these participants over 6–9 months to study the natural history of syphilis. However, the study continued for 40 years, becoming what has been described as the longest non-therapeutic experiment on human beings in medical history (Jones 1993). In the 1940s penicillin was validated as an effective cure for syphilis – and yet this was not provided to participants, and worse, was actively withheld, in some cases through acts of deception. Eventually the trial was stopped in 1972 after it was brought to the attention of national media. This study is an extreme reminder of medical research that did harm without benefit to or respect for participants, in the absence of fully informed consent. By the time the study was stopped, only 74 of the original 399 participants were alive.

The Tuskegee study helped spur the *Belmont Report* (National Commission for the Protection of Human Subjects of Biomedical and Behavioral Research 1979) which underlined the key principles of autonomy, beneficence, and justice in all research involving humans, the setting up of the Office for Human Research Protections in the United States, as well as federal requirements for research involving humans to have institutional ethics approval. By the 1980s, most academic and medical research institutions in the West had established committees to help adjudicate on the value and ethics of proposed research.

Principles in practice

The focus on ethical principles and their related operatives of informed consent, voluntary participation, confidentiality, and balancing risk against benefit, provide important guidance, as well as an institutional mechanism through ethics committees, to prevent research from doing harm or injustice. But these seemingly universal principles may be situated differently in practice, depending upon context. There will always be differences in how values are interpreted and ethical dilemmas handled. Researchers will have different stances concerning the funding sources they deem acceptable or the knowledge they feel the public has a right to possess. Enacting the core principles of informed consent and confidentiality is therefore best envisaged as part of an ongoing process of navigating ethics into practice, particularly given the likelihood of unforeseen challenges in the field. While seeking ethical approval or guidance from an appropriate research ethics committee is a necessary step when conducting research involving humans, this is no more than a starting point for reflecting upon research ethics in practice. Catherine Kohler-Riessman and Cheryl Mattingly (2005: 428) have noted that the primary clinical emphasis of most ethics review boards has fostered what they describe as 'the routinization of good intentions' through 'standardised and scripted legalistic informed consent forms designed to handle every contingency, iron-clad guarantees for research participants of confidentiality and anonymity, [and] assumptions of privacy'. Let us consider research ethics in practice through some brief examples regarding informed consent, confidentiality, and managing research relationships in the field.

Informed consent

This comprises participants being 'informed' about all key aspects of the research, including the study rationale, methods, outputs, and potential risks or harms, as well as providing 'consent' for their voluntary participation on the basis of reasoned judgement and without coercion.

 Activity 14.2

What do you consider to be 'best practice' when seeking and obtaining informed consent from participants?

Feedback

Of critical concern is that participants are enabled to make an active choice and informed decision regarding their participation in research. The study information sheet and consent form is but one part of this process. It is important, therefore, to spend time with participants, as well as potential community members, enabling questions and discussion, and to envisage informed consent as a process rather than one-off event. Participants should be informed of: the aims, objectives and purpose of the study; who is funding the study; the voluntary nature of their participation; their right to withdraw at any time, including without reason; what will happen during as well as after the study; how findings will be presented and used; any potential inconvenience or risks linked to participation, against any potential benefits; their role and responsibilities as participants. A study information sheet should be provided to participants, and this should be written in non-technical accessible language in a layout which is easy to navigate, such as in a leaflet format. In research involving repeated data collection, such as in longitudinal designs, consent may be required at each point data is collected. Assessing participant understandings of consent processes before or during the research may also be appropriate.

Whilst informed consent is extremely important, the process of obtaining it can present a number of challenges. In research drawing upon field observations or group interviews, for instance, it may be difficult to secure consent from all involved. In randomized controlled trials it may be unclear how much detail to give regarding study methods without these potentially shaping participant responses and study findings. In some settings, seeking written consent may be problematic. In recruiting some participants, it may be difficult to gauge the degree of gatekeeper persuasion involved. For example, in their reflections on the ethics of doing participation observation in a psychiatric hospital, Oeye *et al.* (2007) note the challenges of applying the principles of informed consent and voluntary participation. First, they question the universal assumption of vulnerability and impaired decision-making capacity in relation to all psychiatric patients. Second, they note that an attempt to secure individual written consent for all they observed on the ward created an 'unnatural' atmosphere of overcaution, even communicating distrust. Third, they question the principle of voluntariness conceived as a matter of individual decision-making, since in the context of observations of a social group or setting, such as a hospital ward, individual participants cannot easily be viewed as free to choose. Whereas the principle of informed consent is rooted in an 'individual-based ethical guideline', they note that participant observation adopts a 'collective approach' to 'observing interaction between participants' (Oeye *et al.* 2007: 2304). They note that despite their best efforts, it was not practically possible to avoid observing participants who likely had impaired decision-making capacity or who had not given their consent to be observed.

 Activity 14.3

In focus groups with young people living with HIV, what do you think might be a particularly important point to emphasize when explaining and obtaining informed consent with potential participants?

Feedback

Potential participants will need to be made aware that by participating in a focus group for patients of a particular condition, for example people living with HIV, they will be deductively disclosing to the others in the focus group that they are living with this condition. Informed consent involves making sure that they are aware of this and that they are voluntarily agreeing to share this information with the other participants. For a more detailed discussion of the risks of disclosure in focus groups, see Theobald *et al.* (2011).

Confidentiality

This comprises all data being unlinked to potentially identifiable personal details, the anonymization of data and the prevention of deductive disclosure when disseminating, and maintaining the security of all data collected. Whereas *confidentiality* means that information revealed by participants to researchers is kept private within certain agreed limits determining what information that can be disclosed to a third party, *anonymity* means that research participants (and potentially organizations and research locations) cannot be linked by name to any information disclosed.

In practice, there are challenges. The protection of individual, organizational or study site identity can be difficult in small and single case studies. Providing participants with pseudonyms might not be enough, and in this respect, anonymity may not constitute confidentiality. For example, in a qualitative study investigating patient and provider perspectives on the dynamics of access to HIV treatment in Serbia and Montenegro (Rhodes *et al.* 2009; Bernays and Rhodes 2009), the researchers were extremely careful in managing how they presented findings emanating from the different clinics, since the HIV treatment clinics and specialists at the time of the study were few in number and thus potentially identifiable. Similarly, the prevention of the deductive disclosure of participants' conditions can be difficult, for instance, when recruiting participants with a particular health condition in the public environment of a clinic or waiting room. Anonymity may also be difficult to ensure should you be conducting a study which relies heavily on gatekeepers to recruit your participants. For instance, if you are relying on doctors to recruit patients in a clinic to your qualitative interview study, how will you ensure that these same doctors are not able to deduce who said what when you come to disseminate the findings?

Any challenges linked to protecting participants' confidentiality need to be considered *at the outset*, before a study commences. When using gatekeepers to recruit participants, for example, you will need to consider how much they need to know about who chooses to participate as well as how to effectively 'anonymize' their data at the writing-up stage.

The principle of confidentiality may also be challenged by the cultural setting. For instance, in reflecting upon her ethnographic research investigating women's infertility in a clinic in south India, Kohler-Riessman notes that she had 'imported assumptions about the privileged nature of conversations between women and their doctors' into a setting where 'there is no privacy'. She notes that 'each woman could hear about the sexual activity of the woman sitting next to her at the table' whilst 'groups of men and women stood behind the table with prying eyes and ears' (2005: 482). She asks: 'Privacy and confidentiality – Do such abstract principles of medical ethics have a place in a clinic burdened with too many patients and too few resources, situated in a sub-continent plagued by over-population?' Kohler-Riessman's approach is to reflect ethnographically on the process of negotiating research ethics principles into practice. She refers to the problems of 'exporting ethics' associated with Western developed ideas of 'ethical universalism' to different cultural contexts without modification or reflection as to their local appropriateness.

 Activity 14.4

Protecting participants' confidentiality is a core principle of ethically conducted research. However, can you think of exceptions where breaching participant confidentiality is warranted? How would you handle this process?

Feedback

There may be exceptions to the rule of confidentiality, with some participants or projects asking to be named, or rare cases when confidentiality may have to be breached to prevent risk or harm to participants occurring. One example of this concerns research with children, where, depending upon the setting, there may also be legal requirements to breach confidentiality to carers in the face of evidence of serious harm or injury potentially occurring to participants, such as in cases of suicide attempt or intention, or in cases of serious physical abuse. This needs to be made clear from the outset as part of informed consent procedures. Even if unlikely in practice, it also requires researchers to plan in advance for how they would deal with a breach of confidentiality situation. Important here is having an understanding of the threshold by which harm is considered sufficiently serious for confidentiality to be breached. Seeking professional local guidance at the point of study design would be appropriate. Also important is planning how to inform and involve the participant, as well as supporting professionals, in the event of information being disclosed which warrants concern.

Managing research relationships

Managing participants' expectations of research, including in relation to its perceived benefits and the nature of the relationships with researchers, is a key responsibility. It is incumbent on researchers to communicate the boundaries of the research relationship to participants clearly. For example, in research investigating fragile treatment delivery – as in the case of people living with HIV coming to terms with interrupted HIV treatment (Rhodes *et al.* 2009; Bernays and Rhodes 2009) – participants may invest hope in the research as a means of providing practical solutions, and in their relationships with researchers as a means of coping. Managing such expectations is an ethical concern, especially if participants invest potential value, benefit or hope in the research beyond its primary purpose or capacity. The possibility that participants derive or seek therapeutic benefit from research relationships may be enhanced in longitudinal and qualitative designs, and when researchers, including fieldworkers and community health workers, are seen to be linked to helping organizations and intervention or funding initiatives. In the context of researchers having built close rapport and strong trust with participants – both important tenets of qualitative and ethnographic research (see Section 2) – the boundaries of research relationships may become especially blurred, for instance, when participants request practical or personal help (Molyneux *et al.* 2013). Taken together, this highlights the ongoing importance of researchers being *reflexive* about how their research is perceived and used in relation to the balancing of situated risks and benefits. This also means it is important to clearly communicate (as well as review) the boundaries of expectation regarding research relationships and the limits these place upon researchers, including the use of research for therapeutic purposes beyond the capacity or expertise of researchers to provide (beyond their capacity to facilitate help through referral).

 Activity 14.5

In a longitudinal qualitative study conducted by the authors in Uganda with children living with HIV, the clinic team noticed the trusting relationships the local qualitative researcher had managed to build with the participants attending their clinic. When the clinic team found out that one of these participants was deliberately not taking their HIV treatment they recommended that she be 'seen' by the qualitative researcher, who they assumed could use her existing relationship with the child to find out the causes of her non-adherence, counsel her and report back their conversations in full to the clinic team. If you were the researcher, what action would you take?

Feedback

Whilst the child might have been in need of additional support, it is not appropriate for the researcher to be expected to fulfil a therapeutic role or to deliberately abuse the child's trust. In this case the researcher reiterated the specific remit of the study, explaining that the research could not be used as a substitute for counselling and that they must at all times, except in the cases of child protection, adhere to their commitment to respect the participant's confidentiality. Having explained this, a clinic counsellor led the therapeutic intervention and any ongoing interviews continued to be treated as solely for the purpose of the research. This highlights the need to ensure that partners involved in research are trained in the role and limits of the particular study. Assuming that everyone already fully understands the boundaries of a study, without any explicit discussion about what it is and is not, risks the research being unwittingly transformed into something beyond its capacity or purpose, which would be unethical and inappropriate.

We noted at the start of this chapter that research is inevitably framed by values, and that this encourages us to consider what the social and policy value of our research is. This means that ethics concerns in health research extend beyond the micro level of interpersonal and clinical relationships as managed through processes of informed consent, voluntary participation and participant confidentiality to include macro-level considerations, which affect whole populations, societies and institutions. This is illustrated, for instance, by recent calls for reflection upon the ethics of transnational research in HIV, malaria, tuberculosis and ill health linked to inequalities, including in relation to the practices of institutions from higher-income settings conducting research in lower-income settings, the dynamics of research collaboration across varied income and cultural settings, and the ethics of locally applying internationally sponsored research (Molyneux and Geissler 2008; Benatar 2002).

Summary

Research ethics principles and codes of ethical research practice provide useful guidance, especially regarding informed consent, voluntary participation, confidentiality and the balancing of risk against benefit. However, the conduct of ethical research is a negotiated process, dependent upon the situations and contexts in which the research is being conducted and the ethical challenges that arise. Challenges concerning the translation of 'universalist' ethics principles into practice may be most accentuated when conducting health research across diverse cultural and income settings, as well as across different research disciplines. Following others (Kohler-Riessman 2005; Molyneux and Geissler 2008), we emphasize a 'situated ethics' approach, which reflects upon how research ethics principles are enacted in different research and cultural settings. A key element of ensuring quality in health research is therefore the capacity for researchers to reflect openly on the ethical dilemmas they face and how they attempt to navigate these.

References

Beauchamp, T. and Childress, J. (2009) *The Principles of Biomedical Ethics* (6th edn). New York: Oxford University Press.

Benatar, S.R. (2002) Reflections and recommendations on research ethics in developing countries. *Social Science & Medicine*, 54: 1131–1141.

Bernays, S. and Rhodes, T. (2009) Experiencing uncertain HIV treatment delivery in a transitional setting: Qualitative study, *AIDS Care*, 21: 315–321.

Brandt, A. M. (1978), Racism and research: The case of the Tuskegee syphilis study. *Hastings Center Report*, 8(6): 21–29.

Brody, B. (1998) *The Ethics of Biomedical Research*. Oxford: Oxford University Press.

Green, J. and Thorogood, N. (2004) *Qualitative Health Research*. London: Sage.

Jones, J. (1993) *Bad Blood: The Tuskegee Syphilis Experiment*. New York: Free Press.

Kohler-Riessman, C. (2005) Exporting ethics: A narrative about narrative research in South India. *Health: An Interdisciplinary Journal for the Social Study of Health, Illness and Medicine*, 9(4): 473–490.

Kohler-Riessman, C. and Mattingly, C. (2005) Introduction: Toward a context-based ethics for social research in health. *Health: An Interdisciplinary Journal for the Social Study of Health, Illness and Medicine*, 9(4): 427–429.

Molyneux, S. and Geissler, P.W. (2008) Ethics and the ethnography of medical research in Africa. *Social Science & Medicine*, 67: 685–695.

Molyneux, S., Kamuya, D., Madiega, P.A., Chantler, T., Angwenyi, V. and Geissler, W. (2013) Fieldworkers at the interface. *Developing World Bioethics*, 13(1): ii–iv.

National Commission for the Protection of Human Subjects of Biomedical and Behavioral Research (1979) *The Belmont Report: Ethical principles and guidelines for the protection of human subjects of research.* Bethesda, MD: The Commission. Available from: http://www.hhs.gov/ohrp/humansubjects/guidance/belmont.html

Oeye, C., Bjelland, A.K. and Skorpen, A. (2007) Doing participant observation in a psychiatric hospital – research ethics resumed. *Social Science & Medicine*, 65: 2296–2306.

Rhodes, T., Bernays, S. and Janković, K. (2009) Medical promise and the recalibration of expectation: Hope and HIV treatment engagement in a transitional setting. *Social Science & Medicine*, 68: 1050–1059.

Rockwell, D.H., Yobs, A. and Moore, M. Jr. (1964) The Tuskegee study of untreated syphilis: The 30th year of observation. *Archives of Internal Medicine*, 114(6): 792–798.

Theobald, S., Nyirenda, L., Tulloch, O. *et al.* (2011), Sharing experiences and dilemmas of conducting focus group discussions on HIV and tuberculosis in resource-poor settings. *International Health*, 3(1): 7–14.

Further reading

American Anthropological Association Statement on Ethics: http://www.aaanet.org/profdev/ethics/

British Sociological Association Statement of Ethical Practice: http://www.britsoc.co.uk/media/27107/StatementofEthicalPractice.pdf

Economic and Social Research Council Ethics Framework: http://www.esrc.ac.uk/about-esrc/information/research-ethics.aspx

Medical Research Council Ethics Guidance: http://www.mrc.ac.uk/Newspublications/Publications/Ethicsandguidance/index.htm

National Research Ethics Service (for UK National Health Service): http://www.nres.nhs.uk/

Office for Human Research Protections, US Department of Health and Human Services: www.hhs.gov/ohrp

Social Research Association Ethical Guidelines: http://the-sra.org.uk/sra_resources/research-ethics/ethics-guidelines/

World Medical Association *Declaration of Helsinki*: http://www.wma.net/en/30publications/10policies/b3/

Documentary approaches

Martin Gorsky

15

Overview

This book has so far been concerned with the collection and analysis of research data generated through direct interaction with people. This chapter turns to projects in which techniques such as the survey, interview or focus group are either impossible or inappropriate. The alternative is the use of documents as primary research material. First the reasons for documentary research are explored and the practicalities are reviewed. Next various methodological issues surrounding the selection and analysis of documentary sources are covered. Throughout the chapter examples drawn from research into smoking and health are used to illustrate the discussion.

Learning objectives

After working through this chapter you will be able to:

- understand which problems in health research are particularly suited to documentary approaches
- describe the practical nature of documentary research, including the range of sources used and their location
- outline issues in the selection and analysis of historical data which can affect validity
- explain the nature and challenges of interpretation in documentary research

Key terms

Archive: A repository, either physical or electronic, where documents are conserved and made available for researchers.

Primary sources: The documents from which original raw data are drawn.

Secondary sources: Books or peer reviewed articles in which findings based on primary data are presented.

Tobacco document research (TDR): Research on the internal documents of the tobacco industry, following their release into the public domain since 1994 due to whistle-blowing and lawsuits.

The nature of documentary research

Primary/secondary distinction

First, there is a distinction to be made between different types of documentary research and the data sources they use. A *primary* source is a document that the researcher treats as raw data, which will be subjected to analysis, just as you would a completed questionnaire or a focus group transcript. A *secondary* source is a book or peer-reviewed article in which the results of such analysis are presented.

Most research projects in the social sciences will begin with a literature review in which secondary sources – published findings by other researchers in the field – are discussed. These can vary from loosely structured discussions of relevant publications, to the highly methodical 'meta-analyses' of controlled trials or health care interventions, such as those carried out by the Cochrane Collaboration. This chapter is not about how to conduct a secondary literature review. Instead the focus is on the use of documents as data sources for research.

 Activity 15.1

Read the two extracts which follow. Which do you think is a primary source, and which secondary, and why?

Extract 1

Is there some miracle cure nobody's told you about?
Sadly no.
There's no foolproof formula for giving up. No easy way.
You might as well face the fact: stopping smoking is often a bit of a battle.
But in a battle you can win if you apply a little psychology . . .
This booklet will help you in two ways:
Firstly it will help make up your mind to actually do something about giving up . . . But remember, no one else can win this battle for you. It's you who must take command.

Source: Health Education Council (1979)

Extract 2

Smoking, as discussed in earlier chapters, had emerged as a public health issue in the 1950s via the route of chronic disease epidemiology. There was no real model of treatment for disease. Let us go back and see how this developed. . . .
. . . smoking treatment remained problematic throughout the 1970s. The dominant mode was the anti-smoking group rather than the clinic, and self-help manuals and programmes proliferated. [These texts] . . . implied a model of self-help and moral purpose free of professional intervention. But there was a professional input, that of psychology – and psychologists were key members of staff in some of the clinics. They contributed to the concept of dependence, which . . . was so important for smoking the 1970s.

Source: Berridge (2007: 249, 252)

Extract 1 is a primary source, an anti-smoking leaflet produced in the UK in 1979, containing the original raw data researchers can use to develop an argument. The author of Extract 2 has used this source and others like it, to do just that. Extract 2 is a secondary source, an academic monograph on the history of smoking and public health in which documents like Extract 1 are used in an analysis of the development of treatment approaches.

Why use documentary approaches in social science health research?

At the most general level, all social scientists are likely to conduct some primary documentary research at one time or another. Most research projects begin with discussion of the context (what is known already) and the rationale (why further study is important). You may well have had experience of this already, perhaps citing data on morbidity or mortality gathered by a national government, or a report from the World Health Organization (WHO) or the World Bank about a particular aspect of health policy, to justify and set the scene for your study.

Another general reason is to avoid 'reinventing the wheel'. If, for example, a UK researcher wanted to examine long-term trends in cigarette smoking amongst school children, to learn about prevalence and attitudes, she would not need to start from scratch. Instead she could turn to a survey regularly undertaken since 1988, *Smoking, Drinking and Drug Use among Young People in England* (e.g., Health and Social Care Information Centre 2004–2011), which would provide her the validated and reliable primary data she needed. Such options may also be attractive to researchers who do not enjoy the day-to-day interactions with people that other styles of data collection involve – not everybody does!

There are, however, three more specific reasons why you might adopt a documentary approach:

- *Adversarial research*. Health research often enters sensitive or adversarial areas. Industries whose products shape health behaviours that you consider negative are a case in point, for they may have no incentive to provide you with direct research data. In these projects documentary sources offer an alternative source of information. The best-known recent example is tobacco document research (TDR), which followed litigation in the US against several tobacco companies for conspiring to cover up the hazards of smoking, stifling development of safer cigarettes and targeting the young as customers. In the ensuing settlement they were compelled to place millions of business documents in the public domain, and these have provided a gold mine for researchers. As one TDR academic put it: 'few single events in the history of public health have had as dramatic an effect' (Hurt *et al.* 2009: 454). Hundreds of articles have been written analysing subjects such as the companies' marketing and sales techniques, their methods of lobbying and influencing politicians and their global trade strategy. This in turn has allowed the public health community to develop counter-strategies such as combating branding or sports sponsorship, and has also galvanized support for the WHO's Framework Convention on Tobacco Control (WHO 2003).

- *Historical research*. In historical research, you self-evidently cannot go back in time and conduct a survey or convene a focus group to answer your research question. Even so, there are good reasons why studying the past can be relevant to public health policy. History is our collective memory, helping us understand our present circumstances by illuminating the long processes of change that have led to today. As we plan for the future, it makes sense to examine recurring dilemmas, the solutions that have been tried before and their outcomes.

  History is one of the oldest academic disciplines, long pre-dating sociology or epidemiology, and is concerned with understanding change in time. Although it initially focused on matters such as high politics, 'great men' and military affairs, in the twentieth century it broadened its concerns to embrace social life, economic change and cultural experience. A critical history of medicine and health (as opposed to a celebration of heroic doctors) dates back to the work of pioneers such as George Rosen, whose 1958 publication, *A History of Public Health*, was a key milestone (see Rosen 1993).

  History's contribution lies in three main areas. First, it helps us understand trends in population health, and in particular the long-run demographic transitions, which have seen life expectation rise in many countries. Second, it allows us to trace the development of health systems and public health policy. Third, it illuminates the social construction of disease over time. Just as anthropologists explore diverse understandings of sickness across different cultures, so the historian examines different periods. Often this reveals that medicine has been deeply intermeshed with social and political currents, rather than a stately progress of scientific knowledge.

- *Health communication*. In research on health promotion you might want to analyse different media through which messages related to health behaviours are communicated. Academic work in health promotion tends to focus either on identifying the groups and behaviours which merit intervention, or on evaluating those interventions to see if behaviour change took place. However, the ability to analyse different sorts of media in which health messages are projected is also important if we are to understand how attitudes are constructed. This might involve the study of how scientific work is translated by television, newspapers or websites into popular understanding. For instance, Hellman's (2009) analysis of how the concept of addiction is portrayed in newspaper journalism reveals that the messages reaching the public tend to depict it as an individual rather than a social problem. Or it might consider the production and content of visual material like posters or films. Johnny and Mitchell's (2006) critical evaluation of how posters used in the UN's recent World AIDS Campaign might send confusing messages depending on cultural context is a good example.

✎ Activity 15.2

Study the documentary source shown in Figure 15.1. Write down what you think it is. How might it be useful to: (a) a tobacco document researcher?; (b) a historian of public health?; (c) a health promotion researcher?

Figure 15.1 'A young woman smoking, with silver coins representing the expense of buying cigarettes'. Colour lithograph, size 75 x 49.6 cm, by Reginald Mount, London: Central Office of Information, 1965. Wellcome Library, London

Feedback

This is an anti-smoking image designed to persuade its audience to give up by high-lighting the expense of cigarettes. Judging by the size and publication detail, it appears to be a poster prepared by a communications agency (in fact the Central Office of Information was a branch of the UK government). TDR investigators may be interested in how the industry priced its products to sustain consumer demand, and how it responded to campaigns like this, challenging tobacco on grounds of cost. Historians might be interested in charting the emergence of an anti-smoking lobby in the UK in a period when consumption was higher than today, in exploring how some groups – here, younger adult women – became the targets of their interventions, and in asking why an economic rather than a health-based message was chosen at this time. Health promotion researchers may be interested in how visual media such as this can affect behaviour: does the image and accompanying text have an accessible, unambiguous message, and what are its strengths and weaknesses as a communication tool?

The range of primary documentary sources

There are various different categories of documentary sources used in these types of research, each serving different purposes.

* *Records of national or regional governments*. These include official publications, such as laws, commissions of inquiry, proceedings of legislatures and records of health ministries, which we use to examine how policies are made, as well as quantitative materials such as censuses and the registration of births, marriages and deaths which allow us to track demographic trends, and social surveys which tell us about knowledge, attitudes and practice. We can also use unpublished records of politicians and bureaucrats, such as internal memos, letters, speeches and now emails to understand individual motivation.
* *Business and institutional records*. These may include, as in TDR, the internal records of industries whose activities in some way affect public health, or those of non-governmental organizations (NGOs), such as medical charities or not-for-profit hospitals. For example, a hospital's archive might contain committee minutes, financial accounts, records of staff and buildings, patient admission and discharge registers, and clinical case notes.
* *Grey literature*. This related term refers to printed documents that are not published commercially and not generally available, such as publications by agencies of government, businesses, charities or academic institutions. It covers items such as commissioned reports, working papers, newsletters, bulletins, fact sheets and conference proceedings. 'Grey' signifies literature which, because it is ephemeral and peripheral, is harder to obtain than through the 'black and white' channels of libraries and publications databases (Farace and Schöpfel 2010: 2–7). Note that grey literature may also include material useful for literature reviews of secondary sources.
* *Books and journals*. These can be treated as primary sources, for example in the history of public health, where we may wish to know about past therapies and understandings of disease. So while we might treat a contemporary article in a peer-reviewed journal as a secondary source, we could use an earlier one as raw data to investigate

how scientists thought at the time. Some medical journals date back many years: in the US the *New England Journal of Medicine* began in 1812, in Britain *The Lancet* dates back to 1823, and in Asia the *Indian Journal of Medical Research* was launched in 1913. From 1879 a comprehensive record of every publication related to medicine, the *Index Medicus*, was compiled by the US Surgeon General's Library, though this has now been superseded digitally by Medline.

- *Personal papers.* Sources such as letters, diaries or personal memorabilia, which were not originally intended to be in the public domain, can provide researchers with access to private opinions and intimate feelings.
- *Oral history recordings or transcripts.* In studies of contemporary history (the recent past) it may be possible to conduct interviews with surviving individuals, whether elites, if the focus is on policy, or ordinary people, if the concern is with social beliefs and practices.
- *Visual material.* The term 'document' also signifies different kinds of visual objects. These can range from posters, cartoons and film, to photographs, maps and plans which provide a spatial dimension to research, and physical artefacts such as buildings, uniforms and medical instruments.
- *Internet websites.* Following the launch of the World Wide Web in the early 1990s, many formerly paper-based records are now created electronically. Organizations typically represent themselves both internally and externally through their websites, while individual attitudes are captured in personal web pages, blogs and social media sites.

Locating documentary sources

Researchers using documents, at least until recently, typically found their sources by going to repositories where they were held. There are various different types of library and archive.

- *National and regional collections.* The practice of archiving printed works began with the state's need for an official record of law- and policy-making. Over time local archives have broadened their terms to collect non-governmental records too. Many states have also established national libraries, sometimes backed by legal deposit rules, which apply to all published work from that country. In Britain, for example, a Public Record Office was opened in 1838 to preserve the papers of government ministries, while in India an Imperial Record Department (now National Archives of India) was set up in 1891. The British Library began in 1753, as the printed books department of the British Museum, while the National Library of India opened as the Calcutta Public Library in 1836.
- *Specialist libraries.* Public health researchers may also draw on various dedicated medical libraries. Examples include the US National Library of Medicine in Washington and London's Wellcome Library.
- *Institutional archives.* It is also common for businesses, universities, NGOs and health services institutions to retain their own records, though there may not be formal arrangements to allow researchers access.
- *Family and individual papers.* Similarly personal archives may be still in private hands.

Increasingly, documentary sources are archived electronically. Again these fall into different categories.

- *Scanned and searchable document collections.* These might include dedicated collections such as the archives used in TDR. For example, the Legacy Tobacco Documents

Library site created by University of California at San Francisco has copied and published more than 14 million documents released by tobacco companies under the legal settlement. In addition, many national agencies and libraries have begun to digitize their collections. In the US, for instance, the National Library of Medicine has digitized material from key subject areas, ranging from nineteenth-century cholera texts to Chinese public health posters.

- *Digital books and e-journals.* Since 2004 Google Books has been constructing an online database, which aims ultimately to contain all the world's books. According to an affidavit filed in 2010, it had by then scanned over 12 million books, some available in full, others in limited preview or by 'snippet'. Many journals are available in digital format, such as through the digital library JSTOR (short for 'Journal Storage'), which licenses and provides access to over 1400 journals, and PubMed Central, a free biomedical archive, which, for example, includes research articles from the *British Medical Journal* going back to 1840.
- *Web archiving.* Since 1996 the Internet Archive (which also conserves books and music) has been periodically trawling the web to capture over 240 billion web pages, which can be viewed through its Wayback Machine. National libraries are now following suit, though copyright issues currently (2013) restrict search and access facilities. There are also dedicated collections providing open access to captured websites on particular themes, such as those in the British Library's Web Archive.

Working with documents

As you saw in Chapter 4, documentary studies do not adopt the experimental or observational designs common to public health research. Indeed, it would be rare in a history research report to find an explicit statement of 'research design' of the sort you would expect in an epidemiological study. Broadly there are three characteristic approaches:

- *Qualitative interpretive analysis.* This is where a qualitative data set of documents is selected, recorded and subjected to analysis. Berridge's (2007) historical study of smoking and public health in the UK (see Extract 2 in Activity 15.1) typifies this approach. In her research, she first collects a wide variety of different sources, spanning government publications, scientific articles, grey literature, NGO artefacts, business records and oral history, and then develops an interpretation based on deep critical reading of these texts.
- *Quantitative reconstruction and analysis.* Alternatively some research questions might necessitate the collection and analysis of historical statistics. For instance, Hansell *et al.* (2003) wanted to determine the relative importance of air pollution legislation and tobacco consumption to lowering trends in chronic obstructive pulmonary disease. They collected mortality data on lung cancer and chronic bronchitis for different places between 1950 and 1999, and subjected these to an age–period–cohort analysis to discover the answer (which was that strong controls on smoke pollution did lead to health gains!).
- *Content analysis.* This is where a quantitative data set based on qualitative sources is constructed and analysed, using a systematic coding frame to record content in a particular communication medium. This could mean, for example, counting the frequency of newspaper reports on a given issue and classifying their features according to a small number of categories. A characteristic example from TDR is content analysis of media such as movies or websites to examine exposure to smoking imagery (e.g., see Anderson *et al.* 2010).

Selection issues: the archives

Just as questions of representativeness and validity figure in planning survey work or interviewing, they also inform documentary research. At the outset, some different types of selection bias need to be considered.

- *Survival: selection processes.* Researchers cannot assume that the documents preserved in archives are either comprehensive or representative. Instead, deposit follows a process of prior selection that reflects a particular set of conditions. In the case of the millions of pages of tobacco company documents, researchers cannot be certain that all the material needed to illuminate their questions is now made public. Despite legally mandated deposit requirements some key documents have been destroyed, withheld or discarded (Carter 2005: 368). Similarly, national and local governments simply cannot physically store everything they generate, so all require some selection criteria. The UK's National Archives, for instance, advises that government departments should preserve records on 'the formulation and interpretation of policy and legislation', but only 'more selectively, its implementation' (National Archives 2006: 6). Survival of family or private institutional records is even less assured, and many historians have horror stories of precious records destroyed. Yet they must also acknowledge 'the relentless drive for space economies within the public health sector and the periodic relocation of health facilities into new buildings' (Melling 2001: 162–164).
- *Survival: unplanned destruction.* Sometimes more tragic losses can occur. Spurr (2008: 276) documents that in April 2003, during the Iraq War, arsonists and looters attacked the country's national library, destroying about 25% of its books and 60% of its manuscripts, including rare archives of the Ottoman Empire and of Islam's past. His account suggests that Saddam Hussein ordered this arson to ensure that records of his regime, and with them its history, would be lost.
- *Access and censorship.* Even where records are deposited there may be limits to researcher access. Patient records or case notes may be subject to an embargo for a given time period to protect confidentiality. Sometimes this can also apply to political records. In the UK, for example, despite Freedom of Information laws, documents can be 'redacted' (i.e., censored or withdrawn) under some circumstances. These include not just issues such as national security, but also where their availability prejudices 'the effective conduct of public affairs': the theory is that policy-makers may not have 'free and frank' discussions if these might attract bad publicity in the future (Ministry of Justice 2008).

All of these selection issues mean that researchers need to bear in mind that available documents may not be comprehensive or representative. To a greater or lesser degree, there are likely to be gaps and silences in the record, particularly in distant historical periods, and these may affect the robustness of your conclusions.

Selection issues: the researcher

Having said this, the chances are that you will succeed in finding a wide range of potential documents to draw on and the challenge will be to narrow it down. Here are some general considerations:

- *Time frame?* An initial selection decision, particularly in historical studies, concerns the period from which you will draw your documents. This needs to be specific and justified. For example, Berridge's (2007) history of smoking focused on the years 1945–2000, which she argued was a distinct phase for UK public health.
- *Quantitative or qualitative?* Selection will then depend on whether you want to build a quantitative data set, perhaps for content analysis, or a set of qualitative research notes for interpretive analysis. Suppose, for example, you wanted to investigate the public understanding of the risks of smoking in contemporary history. One approach might be a content analysis of the press using a digital newspaper archive to quantify and categorize all reports about smoking in a given period. An alternative might be to select a few reports of scientific bodies and analyse in detail their texts and reception.
- *Deductive or inductive?* A second question is whether you begin with a specific theory that provides you with a hypothesis you want to test. Or are you starting with a more general research question, with the intention of building theoretical explanation from the source? If the former, you may be able to narrow your selection of documents just as in an interview study you would narrow your schedule of questions and your analytic strategy.
- *Researcher reflexivity.* Self-awareness about your own role in the research process also needs consideration. As in all scientific work, strict objectivity should be your goal, yet public health researchers often enter the field with an advocacy agenda and a strong political commitment. How can these two demands be reconciled? This is a common problem for historians, especially those who work on subjects on which moral detachment is impossible, such as the Nazi genocide of European Jews in the 1940s. Here is one viewpoint:

> None of this means that historical judgement has to be neutral. But it does mean that the historian has to develop a detached mode of cognition, a faculty of self-criticism and an ability to understand another person's point of view. This applies as much to politically committed history as it does to a history that believes itself to be politically neutral. Politically committed history only damages itself if it distorts, manipulates or obscures historical fact in the interest of the cause it claims to represent.
>
> (Evans 1997: 252)

In other words, you need to be conscious and critical of your own theoretical assumptions or political standpoints, both in the selection phase and beyond.

Using documents: some practicalities

Preparation: secondary reading

The historian Christopher Cheney famously said that documents 'only speak when they are spoken to, and they do not talk to strangers' (Cheney 1956: 11). He meant by this that before entering the archive for primary research, you should prepare by reading as widely as possible in the secondary literature. That way you will have a better grasp of the context of a particular source, the language through which it presents the social world and its potential importance to your research.

Data gathering

An iterative process of selection and analysis runs through all aspects of documentary data gathering. Your goal is to come out with a collection of research notes which you can then interpret. So, having identified from the catalogue (say) a group of files that you think will be relevant, how should you proceed?

- *Confirm authenticity*. Is the source really what it purports to be? This may seem an odd point to make, but very occasionally fakes do surface. An extreme example from 1983 was the forged Hitler diaries, which temporarily fooled experts.
- *Check and record provenance*. Clarify the date, author, origin and purpose of the document – this is the first step to establishing context and evaluating significance. Ask yourself: when, who, where, why?
- *Preliminary reading*. Now read quickly through the surface content, to establish which elements of the data are useful. Which can you discard? Which should you come back to for more detailed critical analysis?
- *Create your research notes or data set*. Having identified which material you need to record, now go ahead and do so. Your notes may take the form of digital photographs of original pages, or of a spreadsheet, or of extracts from the sources, either transcribed verbatim or summarized in your own words; these in turn may be typed into your notebook or even (depending on the facilities and rules of the archive) written out longhand in pencil.
- *Record the references*. When written up, documentary analysis needs to be supported by detailed references, using the archive or library's catalogue number, so that future researchers can check and validate your findings. Accurate referencing is therefore vital throughout data collection.

Qualitative textual analysis: From 'conduit' to 'constructor'

The critical analysis of documentary texts begins in the archive as you select and record your data, and it continues when you return to your desk to make sense of your research notes. What does it involve?

A helpful description of the process is given by Stacy Carter in her interpretive study of TDR based on a review of 173 peer-reviewed articles written since 1995. She argued that the earliest examples of TDR were often poorly carried out, because researchers were naïve and uncritical in their use of sources, though now this was improving. She used the metaphors of 'conduit' and 'constructor' to describe these changing approaches:

> When the researcher was positioned as a passive conduit, documents were used as straightforward nuggets of general truth, . . . with one quote purporting to prove an expansive contention . . . with no source, searching, analysis, or researcher information . . . When the researcher was positioned as an active constructor, documents were treated as problematic, complex sources of specific information that needed a context to be understood, and readers were made aware of the way in which the researcher had constructed their account of the past.
>
> (Carter 2005: 373)

In addition to being transparent about your methodology, then, what techniques should you follow to ensure that you are an 'active constructor' in documentary analysis?

- *Context of production*. Situate the source within the historical or policy context in which it was produced. Who was the author, what was the intended audience, and what does this tell you about the motives for production? If generated within a business, government or institution, what are the conventions of language and discourse that shape its content? Do they impose any self-censorship on the author?
- *Authorial position*. With that in mind, what do you conclude of the intent, biases, politics or ideological agenda of the author? All these issues of context and intent bear on the relationship between the language of the text and the underlying social reality that it mediates.
- *Witting and unwitting evidence*. Try to distinguish the surface information in the source – that which the author intends the reader to understand – from the 'unwitting' evidence about how the author constructs the social world. Look back, for example, to the anti-smoking poster in Figure 15.1. The 'witting' evidence, as we have already seen, tells us that in the UK in the mid–1960s a government campaign tried to persuade young women to abstain from cigarettes on economic grounds. The caption and image, though, suggest some 'unwitting' evidence of assumptions during this period about gender and motivation. The artist assumes that fashionable clothes and dating are such priorities for young women that they might effect behaviour change.
- *Triangulation with other sources*. Once you have begun to develop an interpretation from one source or group of sources, it is important to check whether other, different sources confirm or refute your idea(s). In the social sciences this process of corroboration is known as triangulation, suggesting that if more than two different methods or data sets point towards the same conclusion then it is more robust. Recall, for example, Extract 2 in Activity 15.1, on treatment for smoking in the 1970s. Here Berridge is arguing that this took the form of self-help manuals premised on new psychological theories about dependence on tobacco. In addition to checking that this was indeed a common theme in surviving manuals (like Extract 1), she might have corroborated this by looking at the scientific literature on addiction, and on the records of commissioning agencies.

Documentary analysis: advanced theory and technique

Finally, though beyond the scope of this chapter, it is worth noting that some public health researchers now draw on theory and techniques developed in the academic study of literature and the media.

- *Discourse analysis*. So far in the discussion the assumption has been that documentary texts reflect an underlying social reality. However, recall now the relativist, social constructionist position outlined in Chapter 2. Some researchers argue that rather than *describing* social experience, language actually *constitutes* it, shaping our consciousness of the material world. Discourse analysis is the method by which they explore features of texts to examine how linguistic statements structure social understanding, and to consider the interplay between language, power and ideology (see Lupton 1992).
- *Semiotics*. Again deriving originally from linguistics, semiotics is the study of how words or images convey meaning. It assumes a distinction between what words or images *denote* (the surface meaning) and what they *connote* (the more complex layers of meaning which may be attributed to them). Thus a picture of a bunch of red roses signifies not just flowers of a particular colour, but also (in some cultures at least) a token of love and admiration. If semiotic analysis is applied, for example, to tobacco

advertising, researchers might study visual imagery to explore how smoking has been infused with cultural meanings, such as glamour or independence (see Anderson *et al.* 2006).

- *Text analytics software.* New digital technologies are now starting to be used in both interpretive and content analysis. 'Data-mining' software can analyse large bodies of electronic text to detect patterns in the use of words and terms. This is not simply to measure the frequency of an individual word, as a Google Ngrams graph, or a Word Cloud on a website, will do. Programs can also detect co-occurrence of groups of words, and thus automatically identify key concepts and subsidiary themes running through a text. These range from those that can be freely downloaded, such as AntConc, to sophisticated commercial packages such as Leximancer. Also, drawing on the marketing technique of 'sentiment analysis', researchers can assess the values attached to a particular concept.

The provisional nature of interpretation

The idea of the documentary researcher as 'active constructor' leads to one last point. When your analysis is complete and the findings are written up, the results cannot be considered a definitive 'truth' about the world. Instead your conclusions are always provisional and hypothetical, open to others to challenge and test. The problem lies partly in the nature of documentary sources, which can never fully capture an external reality, but are always selected, and always fragmentary. And partly, as noted above, our interpretations are shaped by ourselves as researchers, with our theoretical assumptions and our political or moral standpoints. Activity 15.3 illustrates this through two very different interpretations of the same issue.

 Activity 15.3 Contradictory interpretations

The extracts that follow are by two contemporary historians of tobacco control in the UK. They are both analysing the same subject, the reluctance of the government to adopt a strong anti-smoking policy following the 'breakthrough' epidemiological study by Richard Doll and Austin Bradford Hill in 1950, which demonstrated the smoking/lung cancer link. Read both extracts and then:

1 List the main differences in the interpretation the two authors advance.
2 Suggest reasons for the differences.

> **Extract 1**
>
> The record speaks for itself. Fourteen years after Hill and Doll were 'satisfied that the case against smoking as such is proven' . . . seven years after the Medical Research Council told the Government that 'the evidence now available is stronger than that which, in comparable matters, is commonly taken as the basis for definite action' and two years after the Royal College of Physicians in exasperation produced a popular summary of the evidence with specific policy recommendations, the Government was still equivocal about taking effective action against this egregious cause of disease and premature death.

Of course, one must make allowances. . . . Government was . . . less ready to intervene in people's everyday lives. The tobacco industry was of enormously greater importance to the Treasury than it is now. . . .

Nevertheless, the precedents and evidence were there for those with eyes to see. Government did conduct mass health campaigns directed at combating diphtheria or promoting immunisation. Ministers and civil servants did not have to cow-tow [sic] to the potentates of the industry to the extent they did. But the prevailing ethic was one of doing the bare minimum to protect the Government from criticism for doing nothing while avoiding creating any effect for which one might have to answer.

Source: David Pollock (1999: Epilogue). (Pollock was director of the anti-smoking pressure group Action on Smoking and Health between 1991 and 1994 and subsequently sat on its Advisory Council.)

Extract 2

In the post-war history of smoking . . . a one-dimensional 'heroes and villains' analysis has tended to dominate . . . 'Denial and delay' does not seem adequate as an explanation of the responses to smoking in the 1950s. Economic interests and the role of the industry were important; but the industry was an important post-war ally of government at this stage, no different from other such interests. There were other political considerations, like air pollution and health education's funding and role. The scientific evidence was indeterminate and cultural normality was centre stage: there was no interest group or 'policy community' round the issue. Apart from key individuals . . . no significant lobby was pushing the anti-smoking case, nor indeed was there any consistent policy position. Nor were the researchers themselves activists, another significant difference from later developments. Although Bradford Hill had worked within government during the War, he had advised Doll that it was best to steer clear of the political dimensions of the research.

Source: Berridge (2007: 5, 48). (Berridge is Professor of History at the London School of Hygiene & Tropical Medicine.)

Feedback

1 Pollock's interpretation is that the UK government could and should have done more in the face of compelling scientific evidence. Instead, it 'denied and delayed' taking action because it was under the influence of the tobacco industry, and afraid of attracting popular criticism. Berridge argues instead that the government's inaction was understandable, not only because the science was not yet clear-cut, but also because of the broad cultural acceptance of smoking and the lack of a coherent opposition.

2 As a prominent anti-smoking campaigner, Pollock's assessment may be coloured by his own experience and beliefs about governmental responsibility. Possibly he intends his historical writing as a vehicle for advocacy, a call to action. Berridge is an academic historian, who, as her comment about 'heroes and villains' suggests, is aiming for a 'detached mode of cognition' in her work. Notice, too, that Pollock's title indicates the limited selection criteria applied to his sources, which draw

on official records in the state archive; Berridge, meanwhile, uses a wider range of sources and archives in reaching her conclusions. It may also be that both interpretations are coloured by prior theoretical assumptions. Berridge's remarks about lobbying and activism suggest a view of health politics as essentially pluralistic, where democratic decisions are reached through debate between different interest groups within a policy community. Pollock's position though is that states are vulnerable to capture by one particular lobby, that of big business. None of this automatically means one explanation is better or more 'true' than the other. It is up to the reader to decide whether the interpretation in a secondary source represents a compelling critical analysis of an appropriate selection of primary documents.

Summary

Primary documentary studies offer a valuable approach to social research in public health, for example in adversarial areas, historical analysis and work on health communication. An eclectic range of documentary sources exists, though the nature of archiving and survival raises issues of selection and representativeness. Documentary sources are complex and fragmentary, and the analytical process should be thought of as 'active construction', involving careful contextualization, critical assessment and triangulation. Finally, it is good to remember that the excitement of documentary research lies in the constant possibility of revision, as new documents, new methods and different perspectives are brought to bear.

References

Anderson, S.J., Dewhirst, T. and Ling, P.M. (2006) Every document and picture tells a story: Using internal corporate document reviews, semiotics, and content analysis to assess tobacco advertising. *Tobacco Control*, 15: 254–261.

Anderson, S.J., Millett, C., Polansky, J.R. and Glantz, S.A. (2010) Exposure to smoking in movies among British adolescents 2001–2006. *Tobacco Control*, 19: 197–200.

Berridge, V. (2007) *Marketing Health. Smoking and the Discourse of Public Health in Britain, 1945–2000.* Oxford: Oxford University Press.

Carter, S.M. (2005) Tobacco document research reporting. *Tobacco Control*, 14: 368–376.

Cheney, C.R. (1956) *The Records of Medieval England: An Inaugural Lecture*. Cambridge: Cambridge University Press.

Evans, R. (1997) *In Defence of History*. London: Granta.

Farace, D. and Schöpfel, J. (2010) Introduction grey literature. In D. Farace and J. Schöpfel (eds) *Grey Literature in Library and Information Studies*. Berlin: De Gruyter.

Hansell, A., Knorr-Held, L., Best, N., Schmid, V. and Aylin, P. (2003) COPD mortality trends 1950–1999 in England & Wales – Did the 1956 Clean Air Act make a detectable difference? *Epidemiology*, 14(5): S55.

Health Education Council (1979) *The Smoker's Guide to Non-Smoking*. London: HEC.

Hellman, M. (2009) Designation practices and perceptions of addiction – a diachronic analysis of Finnish press material from 1968–2006. *Nordic Studies on Alcohol and Drugs*, 26: 355–372.

Health and Social Care Information Centre (2004–2011) *Smoking, Drinking and Drug Use Among Young People in England*. http://bit.ly/1kHfzZN

Hurt, R.D., Ebbert, J.O., Muggli, M.E., Lockhart, J. and Robertson, C.R. (2009) Open doorway to truth: Legacy of the Minnesota tobacco trial. *Mayo Clinic Proceedings*, 84(5): 446–456.

Johnny, L. and Mitchell, C. (2006) 'Live and let live': An analysis of HIV/AIDS-related stigma and discrimination in international campaign posters. *Journal of Health Communication*, 11(8): 755–767.

Lupton, D. (1992) Discourse analysis: A new methodology for understanding the ideologies of health and illness. *Australian Journal of Public Health*, 16(2): 145–150.

Melling, J. (2001) A healthy future for medical records? A view from south-west England. *Health Information & Libraries Journal*, 18(3): 162–164.

Ministry of Justice (2008) *Freedom of information guidance. Exemptions guidance: Section 36 – Prejudice to effective conduct of public affairs.* Crown copyright. http://www.justice.gov.uk/downloads/information-access-rights/foi/foi-exemption-s36.pdf

National Archives (2006) *General guidelines for the selection of records.* Crown copyright.

Pollock, D. (1999) *Denial & Delay: The Political History of Smoking and Health, 1951–1964: Scientists, Government and Industry as seen in the papers at the Public Records Office.* London: Action on Smoking and Health.

Rosen, G. (1993) *A History of Public Health*. Baltimore, MD: Johns Hopkins University Press.

Spurr, J. (2008) Iraqi libraries and archives in peril. In P. Stone and J.F. Bajjaly (eds) *The Destruction of Cultural Heritage in Iraq*, pp. 273–282, 276. Woodbridge: Boydell.

World Health Organization (2003) *WHO Framework Convention on Tobacco Control*. Geneva: WHO.

Useful websites (all accessed November 2013)

British Library UK Web Archive: http://www.webarchive.org.uk/ukwa/

Legacy Tobacco Documents Library: http://legacy.library.ucsf.edu/

Tobacco Documents Online: http://tobaccodocuments.org/us

US National Library of Medicine, Digital Projects: http://www.nlm.nih.gov/digitalprojects.html

Further reading

Green, J. and Thorogood, N. (2013) Physical and virtual documentary sources. In J. Green and N. Thorogood, *Qualitative Methods for Health Research* (3rd edn). London: Sage.

James, M. (1994) Historical research methods. In K. McConway (ed.) *Studying Health and Disease*. Milton Keynes: Open University Press.

Mixed method and multidisciplinary approaches

16

Tim Rhodes, Andy Guise and Judith Green

Overview

Why mix research methods? How might this be done? There is growing consensus, especially in applied public health research, that mixed method research approaches are a good thing. Different methods of data generation and analysis both reveal and conceal different aspects of the phenomena under study. By mixing methods, it is argued, a more 'complete' picture can be generated. Moreover, research questions in public health are often complex. They tend not to comprise a single question answerable by a single method or data source, but rather generate a series of linked and complementary questions, which require different forms of data combined with different types of research method to address.

Take, for example, the question of why a socially marginalized population may fail to access health services from which they may benefit. Surveys can indicate the extent and distribution of health service access, but may tell us little about why service uptake appears so low. Treatment records can likewise indicate trends in the extent and nature of service use, but may tell us little about what factors shape service engagement or adherence. We might then turn to qualitative individual interviews in an attempt to capture, from participant perspectives, the factors which shape their understandings of health service need and the accessibility and acceptability of the health services on offer. Group interviews may tell us specifically how different social groups may perceive their health needs and access to services differently. Interviews with service providers may capture how the dynamics of patient–provider communications make a difference. Observations undertaken at particular services may help unpack the dynamics of service delivery and how various systemic and administrative factors mediate access. Different methods and data sources help to evidence different elements of the topic under study.

When addressing a research question, we may therefore ask: What forms of data are required to build as complete a picture as possible? To what multiple sources of data might I turn? Which multiple methods of data generation and analysis might I use? And how am I going to integrate these together into a single research design? These are some of the questions addressed by this final chapter. We will consider approaches to studying health that draw on *more than one* method of data generation and analysis. We will address the questions of *why, whether* and *how* research methods can be mixed. We will tackle these questions in light of the *theoretical* as well as *practical* challenges they generate, including in light of research which seeks to work across different disciplinary approaches.

Learning objectives

After studying this chapter, you will be able to:

- appreciate the complementary roles of different methods in health research
- appreciate the benefits as well as potential challenges of working across different disciplinary approaches
- explain the possibilities and limitations of 'triangulation'

Key terms

Mixed methods: Combining two or more different methods into a single study.

Multidisciplinary approaches: Working across multiple research disciplines and methodological approaches in a single study.

Triangulation: Using different data sets, methods or approaches to improve the validity of findings and deepen the quality of analysis.

Why mix methods and disciplines?

We are used to talking about quantitative and qualitative methods of data generation and analysis as being distinct from one another. This book similarly distinguishes between social science methods that are quantitative and those that are qualitative. The notion of *mixed methods* research generally refers to the mixing of quantitative with qualitative methods rather than mixing between different qualitative methods (e.g., interviews and ethnographic observations), or between different quantitative methods (e.g., surveys and treatment records). Mixing between qualitative methods and between quantitative methods is both possible and often desirable, but our primary focus here is on mixing qualitative with quantitative methods. Mixed methods investigations are therefore often defined as those 'integrating quantitative and qualitative data collection and analysis in a single study or programme of inquiry' (Creswell 2003: 7).

Why might study designs seek to integrate or mix quantitative with qualitative methods? Our short answer is twofold. First, public health questions are sufficiently nuanced that they cannot easily or reliably be addressed by drawing upon a single data source or research method. Second, all methods inevitably have their weaknesses and strengths, at once concealing and revealing different aspects of the topic being investigated. From this perspective, mixing methods is *pragmatic*. It is based on the acceptance that multiple methods are needed to build up a picture that is as 'complete' as possible (Creswell 2003). This implies that we need to think from the outset, at the design stage, what the scope and limits of certain proposed methods might be, given our research question, in order to build a design which prevents an overly partial view on our topic, and which uses different methods and data sources to substantiate the findings generated.

We are probably familiar with this pragmatic logic. We can easily see, for instance, how quantitative measures of outcome in an intervention trial seek to generate data of a different form and for a different purpose than qualitative interviews with participants engaged in the intervention being trialled. In the former, data may be generated to assess *output* and *impact*, whereas in the latter, data may be generated to explore *process* and *context*. With one or other, a partial view is produced; with both, used in combination, it might become possible to appreciate how process shapes outcome, which is altogether more practically useful for future intervention development. There are many examples of mixed method intervention trials, where methods are mixed before and during as well as after interventions are trialled (Lewin *et al.* 2009). Similarly, we can appreciate how a cohort or epidemiological study investigating the incidence of an infection will generate data of a different form and utility than ethnographic observations of transmission risk practices, but that both are needed to understand how the incidence of infection occurs, and how infection risk might be prevented, in a given context.

So far, and in keeping with most writing about mixed methods, we have talked about mixing the quantitative with the qualitative. Table 16.1 lists some of the often mentioned strengths and weaknesses of each. In general, whereas quantitative methods tend to test and validate existing hypotheses about the relationships between variables (e.g., between diseases and populations), qualitative methods tend to generate understanding as well as new concepts and ideas for future study. Whereas quantitative methods usually seek to generalize numerical findings to a representative sample, qualitative methods seek to authenticate non-numerical data in relation to particular social practices, situations and contexts. Whereas quantitative methods may purport to generate findings relatively independent of the researcher and claim to minimize bias as a consequence, qualitative methods enable greater reflexivity about the dynamics of relationships between researchers and research subjects and how these can shape the data produced. Whilst we are exaggerating the differences – for it is not always helpful to think of qualitative and quantitative methods as 'divided' in this way (see below) – we can nonetheless see how methods might be used differently within research designs, as well as how they might complement (and sometimes work in tension with) each other.

In addition to methods of data generation and analysis, research projects may involve researchers working from multiple *disciplinary* perspectives. Public health professionals utilize research from a range of different perspectives when planning and delivering health care: from basic medical sciences, epidemiology and economics as well as the social science disciplines that have been introduced in this book. Increasingly, we need skills in both understanding research findings from diverse disciplinary perspectives, and thinking broadly about the most appropriate combinations of methods to use in any one project. In practice, public health research often involves a range of disciplines and methods working together.

Table 16.1 The strengths and weaknesses of quantitative and qualitative methods

	Quantitative methods	*Qualitative methods*
Hypothesis testing	Strength	Weakness
Concept generating	Weakness	Strength
Generalizability of findings	Strength	Weakness
Participant understandings and meanings	Weakness	Strength
Extent and range of phenomena	Strength	Weakness
Accessing complexity, detail and hidden areas of social life	Weakness	Strength
Credibility to policy-makers	Strength	Weakness
Role of context	Weakness	Strength

What are the benefits of mixing methods?

Let us consider the potential benefits of mixing methods (we will consider issues specific to working across disciplines later). If we begin by thinking broadly about the combination of quantitative and qualitative methods within research programmes, there are a number of apparent benefits, including the following:

- Using qualitative data to *inform* quantitative measures and studies. For instance, when developing a quality of life outcome instrument, or a survey questionnaire, it is necessary to undertake detailed qualitative work to identify the main domains that are salient for the target group, and to explore the kind of concepts and language they use to describe them. Qualitative research, such as a combination of focus groups, interviews and observations, may also be used to inform the development of quantitative sampling and recruitment methods, for instance, when planning surveys among hard-to-reach populations.
- Using qualitative data to add *depth* of understanding to quantitative data. For instance, qualitative research can generate the data useful to help make sense of difficult-to-interpret associations between variables generated through survey analyses, as well as helping to build explanations for why particular quantitative variables appear related. For instance, a survey of 81 mothers caring for their children with disabilities suggested that social issues related to care were often more burdensome than the emotional distress experienced (Green 2007). Follow-up qualitative work generated more depth of understanding by revealing how the logistics of health care organization as well as financial concerns were felt as primary concerns. Sometimes the findings of qualitative research may *question* the findings generated from quantitative studies, including regarding their relevance to a particular local context. Qualitative research may also help translate the findings of quantitative studies into recommendations for intervention. See also the case study in the box below.
- Using quantitative work (such as a survey) to test the *generalizability* of qualitative research. Qualitative studies tend to produce in-depth accounts in relation to particular situations or contexts, as well as generate new concepts or hypotheses, which can be taken forward for testing by quantitative studies.
- Using quantitative and qualitative work in tandem to add *strength* to interpretations and to help *validate* findings. This is where the strengths of one method of data generation and analysis help offset the weaknesses of another. In Chapter 12, for instance, we noted how Stone and Campbell (1984) used ethnographic methods to estimate non-sampling error in survey work in Nepal. Work by Lopez *et al.* (2013) illustrates how using multiple methods can enhance the strength of interpretations generated in HIV prevention research. 'Triangulation' is a strategy through which researchers can combine methods to enhance the strength of their interpretations and validate their findings (see the next section).

Case study: Adding depth of understanding

In a 2005 cohort study investigating the incidence of hepatitis C among 428 people who inject drugs in London, high levels of incidence (41.8 cases per 100 person-years) and prevalence (44%) were found (Judd *et al.* 2005). This pointed to the public health urgency of developing interventions to prevent hepatitis C, especially among those new to injecting drugs, where the risk of infection acquisition was high. In parallel with the cohort study, the researchers also undertook qualitative research to investigate the social conditions giving rise to such high levels of hepatitis C virus transmission risk (Rhodes *et al.* 2004). The qualitative study showed that hepatitis C was commonly perceived as ubiquitous, inevitable, less important than HIV, as well as uncertain and misunderstood. Taken together, these factors contributed to a social context in which hepatitis C was presented as 'beyond prevention' (Davis *et al.* 2004). By combining cohort and qualitative data, a deeper understanding was generated, which was also useful for making recommendations for health promotion. While surveys can describe the 'big picture' (breadth), qualitative methods can focus on understanding it, especially in specific local contexts (depth).

What is triangulation and how is it used?

One common justification for using different data sets, methods or approaches within a study is to increase the validity of the findings, or our confidence in their credibility. This is called *triangulation* (Denzin 1989). Triangulation is built on the assumption that using two or more different 'readings' of one phenomenon will improve accuracy. Denzin (1989) describes four types of triangulation:

* *method triangulation* – comparing data produced by different methods;
* *data triangulation* – comparing data in different settings, at different points in time or place;
* *investigator triangulation* – comparing multiple researcher perspectives within a team;
* *theory triangulation* – approaching data using different explanatory models or from different disciplinary perspectives.

An example of the use of different designs in tandem for increasing validity comes from Brent Wolff *et al.* (1993), who were interested in the relationship between family size and socioeconomic wellbeing in rural Thailand. Specifically, they wanted to explore the relationship between completed family size and outcomes such as the educational attainment of children, material wealth of the household and women's economic activity. They decided to run focus groups and a survey concurrently in order to generate two sets of data on the same phenomena. The focus groups enabled the researchers to explore perceptions of family size and wellbeing, whereas the survey aimed to gather objective measures of family composition and economic activity. In order to enhance the comparability of the findings from the two data sets, the researchers chose focus group participants from the survey respondents. There are a number of ways, claim Wolff *et al.*, that the two sets of data can be used to strengthen the credibility of the findings of the research overall. First, where focus group findings and survey findings confirm each other, we can have increased faith that we have valid data. One example the researchers gave in this case was data on who paid for children's education. Both survey results and focus group discussions suggested that this was exclusively the responsibility of the parents. Second, the focus group discussions help validate the survey when they provide contextual data to explain apparent anomalies. Third, the survey can provide detailed data on individual birth and work histories that allow statistical analysis, which could not be provided by focus groups. Using qualitative approaches thus strengthens our faith in the contextual detail provided, whereas the quantitative approach strengthens representativeness and offsets the limits to generalizability typical in small-scale qualitative studies. As Wolff *et al.* (1993: 133) conclude:

When surveys and focus groups point to the same conclusions, the results of independent analyses tend to confirm each other. When analysis of either one appears to be internally inconsistent or contradictory, the other source of data may help to elaborate or clarify the underlying mechanisms that produce these inconsistencies.

Cross-checking the data from different methods is helpful not only when it corroborates, but also when it shows difference or inconsistency. If data sources disagree then this helps draw attention to what might explain the difference. Traditionally, triangulation is posited as a way of maximizing 'validity'. Yet, if two or more methods verify a particular finding, does this mean that it is necessarily 'correct' or 'true'? If data methods produce inconsistent findings, how are we to judge between the accounts? Do we add particular weight to one method over another? For example, if people more readily report smoking during their individual qualitative interviews than in their questionnaire administered surveys, how are we to interpret this? Do we assume that surveys are more 'accurate' than interviews, or vice versa? Crucially, this draws attention to how *particular methods*, as well as the *contexts in which data are produced*, can generate their findings differently. We therefore use the occurrence of contradiction generated through triangulation to ask further questions as to what it is about the research methods and context that might produce different accounts of the same phenomena. This might lead to us asking what is it about smoking which might make it difficult to measure or discuss, and how different research formats might shape its measurement and discussion differently. Inconsistency and contradiction in triangulation can be useful, for it *deepens* the layers of investigation and generates an *iterative* approach, in which negative or difficult-to-interpret cases are investigated further.

Different methods produce different data

Hilary Graham's (1987) mixed method study of smoking provides such an example of a nuanced approach to triangulation. When accounting for inconsistency, Graham uses different data sets not to dismiss one over another, but to identify complexity and avenues for further exploration. Her work shows how different methods produce different data, thus cautioning against an overly simplistic approach to triangulation. In light of survey data linking women's smoking in the UK with low income, Graham was interested to explore why women of low income continued to smoke. She used diaries (completed over 24 hours to collect data on daily routines), in-depth interviews (to describe women's perspectives and experiences), and data from a self-administered questionnaire (designed to measure subjective health status).

All these methods have their limitations. However, they cannot 'validate' each other in any simplistic way, as they address different aspects of Graham's research question. The questionnaire data could be used to compare the self-rated health of smokers and non-smokers in the sample, and those on low and higher incomes, while the interviews and diaries could be used to provide detailed data on the everyday experiences of women. While the surveys measured health status, the interviews and diaries provided rich data on the meaning of everyday smoking practices. But Graham (1987: 52) also noted differences in the data produced by diaries and interviews: 'Compared to statements made in interviews about smoking behaviour, there was a significant under-reporting of smoking in the dairies of those who smoked. Unless smoking was reported as the "main" activity, it tended not to be reported.' This inconsistency does not invalidate the data from diaries. Rather, it provided Graham with a clue to the meaning of her data. She noted that smoking is intricately tied to the routines of everyday life: the cigarettes that are 'noticed' and therefore recorded in the diary are those that mark the breaks in the routines of housework and child care. Similarly, the interview data did not 'invalidate' the diaries: it provided data on a rather different aspect of the research question, and enabled Graham to explore the meaning women attached to their smoking as a coping strategy in the context of poverty.

Taken together, triangulation is not as simple as comparing data produced by different methods around a 'single point of truth', but is a way of exploring how different methods shape the data they produce differently and of deepening the investigation when contradictions are observed.

How do different disciplinary perspectives shape mixed methods research?

The theoretical assumptions researchers bring to their topic will frame how their research is designed, the methods they use, the data they generate, and the conclusions they draw. This is the case whether research is primarily quantitative, qualitative, or mixed methods. As we have noted, there is a tendency to position quantitative and qualitative methods as representing distinct paradigms in the approach to research, each of which make different *epistemological assumptions* about what constitutes evidence and how it should be generated. Quantitative research is often linked with the philosophical assumptions of positivism, which represents reality as stable and 'out there'. Here, there is a single 'truth', and the object of science is to uncover this truth, describing it as objectively as possible (see Chapter 2). In the contrasting view, qualitative research is often linked with interpretivism, which envisages reality not as stable and simply 'out there' waiting to be discovered but as produced by context-based understandings. Here, there are potentially multiple interpretations of 'accepted truths', and the aim is to understand how actors come to make the interpretations they do in given social contexts. An extreme (and now less commonly voiced) position, therefore, is that quantitative and qualitative methods are framed by research paradigms which offer *competing* ways of knowing the world, which makes them incompatible.

In contrast, evidence-based approaches to public health research tend to emphasize mixing methods as a question of pragmatics (Creswell 2003). Here, methods are selected according to 'need', given the specifics of the research question. We have, then, two potential extremes to consider – the incompatibility of mixing methods because they represent competing approaches to generating evidence; and a toolbox of methods that are mixed according to need irrespective of any underlying epistemological association. Where do you sit in relation to these extremes? To what extent do you think methods are simply techniques of data collection and analysis, rather than also linked to different theoretical or disciplinary paradigms? If the approach of the anthropologist to evidence is different than that of the epidemiologist, how might they resolve their disciplinary differences when conducting mixed method research?

In considering these questions, you may have noticed that we are suggesting a distinction between *methods* (i.e., techniques of data generation and analysis) and *methodologies* (i.e., overarching epistemological or disciplinary approaches). We advocate an approach to mixing methods which encourages *critical reflection* regarding how researchers' epistemological assumptions shape their methodological choices and evidence interpretations. We accept that there are competing epistemological approaches to research, and that these map differently across the disciplines engaged in public health research. It is our view that these differences do not simply 'disappear' when adopting a 'pragmatic' approach to mixing methods. Rather, choices are made (and negotiated in research teams) as to how research is theoretically positioned. This accepts that mixing methods across disciplines can, and does, get messy, sometimes giving rise to differences of interpretation. Look, for example, at the published dialogue between Philippe Bourgois (anthropologist) and Andrew Moss (epidemiologist) reflecting on the challenges of their multidisciplinary collaborations in the field of HIV prevention research (Bourgois 2002; Moss 2003).

Making a distinction between methods and methodologies also highlights that it is overly simplistic to assume that the quantitative and qualitative represent a clear-cut epistemological or paradigmatic divide. Quantitative methods can be applied in a relativist approach, just as qualitative methods can be applied in a positivist one. Methods do not have clear-cut epistemological membership, though researchers and the disciplines they represent often do. How researchers apply their methods, and how they mix them, will depend upon their methodology. We therefore cannot ignore how our theoretical assumptions shape our approaches to mixed method research.

✎ Activity 16.1

Mixed method and multidisciplinary approaches are now commonplace in public health. Public health research teams may include epidemiologists, statisticians, economists, sociologists and anthropologists, all working together on the same research question. What barriers do you think there might be to effective multidisciplinary working in health research?

Feedback

Those trained in one discipline may find it difficult to present their work in ways that those from another discipline will understand. Some methodological starting points may appear incompatible, such as a strong relativist and a positivist position. Additionally, some research designs are more widely accepted by policy-makers and funders than others. Chapter 2 introduced some of these epistemological differences: these can be real barriers to multidisciplinary work, and most researchers find that building trust and mutual understanding takes considerable time and resources.

How can methods be mixed in a research design?

Two key questions in designing a mixed methods study are the *ordering* of the different methods used, and the *priority* they are given (Creswell 2003). Methods can be ordered either sequentially or concurrently, depending on the purpose. Qualitative data can be used *to inform* quantitative studies, or vice versa; this is a sequential ordering. The most common instance of this is when qualitative research is used to help develop the design, methods or measures of quantitative research. Qualitative approaches can also explore the findings of quantitative studies. For instance, a trial of an evidence-based foetal health surveillance guideline showed that the success of its introduction varied between settings. A qualitative study using interviews and focus groups with health care professionals explored the reasons for this, finding issues of staff concerns, leadership and institutional agendas affected success (Graham *et al.* 2004). A study using different methods concurrently would have multiple methods implemented at the same time. For

Table 16.2 The ordering and priority of methods

	Concurrent	Sequential
Equal emphasis	qualitative + quantitative	qualitative → quantitative quantitative → qualitative
Dominant emphasis	*quantitative* + qualitative *qualitative* + quantitative	*qualitative* → quantitative qualitative → *quantitative*
		quantitative → qualitative quantitative → *qualitative*

instance, a study might involve repeated qualitative interviews at particular stages of a longitudinal study linked with an intervention so as to capture transitions over time.

Priority refers to the relative emphasis given to a particular method or approach. Different methods can have equal importance to the overall study question, but often researchers tend to give priority to one particular approach or set of methods. Often, as in the case of randomized controlled trials, the quantitative components of research take precedence in public health research (Lewin *et al.* 2009), with qualitative methods used as an adjunct, either before a trial to inform the development of quantitative measures or after a trial as a means of interpreting and responding to its results. While the combination of ordering and priority thus gives rise to different mixed method designs (see Table 16.2), it is also the case that mixed method studies proceed in the absence of a priori design, often organically and in response to need. The contribution of mixed method designs is enhanced when different methods are properly *integrated*, including via joint analyses (e.g., using triangulation), rather than used simply in parallel to one another.

Activity 16.2

What mixed method research design would you propose to explore the acceptability and efficacy of a new vaccine?

Feedback

Randomized controlled trials are commonly used to test the effectiveness of vaccines. Alongside this, qualitative work could be used sequentially as a precursor to inform study design or after a trial to explore experiences and acceptability, and concurrently to explore the process of implementing the new vaccine. This could include interviews to explore beliefs, focus groups to understand how beliefs and norms are discussed and constructed, and observations of natural settings to see how new interventions are actually implemented in practice. Mixing methods could therefore work to explore different aspects of the phenomena under trial (e.g., questions of acceptability alongside questions of impact), or data analysis could be triangulated to highlight and explore inconsistencies (e.g., observation of trial sites may generate more hidden accounts from participants indicating the vaccine under trial is not being implemented as intended and so casting doubt on any claims of efficacy). This insight could lead to both reassessing quantitative data analysis and further exploration of the meaning and social context for the vaccine to understand implementation processes.

What are the challenges of mixing methods?

In addition to developing research designs which seek to fully integrate the use of mixed methods throughout data generation and analyses, including through the use of strategies of triangulation, our discussion above has identified multidisciplinary working to be a key challenge of mixed methods research.

A first challenge is that in combining methods the particular strengths of any one method or approach may be limited by the constraints of others. For example, the time constraints, or at least fixed structure, of some quantitative approaches may impose limits on the more open-ended and emergent nature of some qualitative approaches which are less predictable in how they develop. The imposition of a particular research paradigm may also impede the insights from one discipline. For example, epidemiological studies may simply see 'culture' as one variable influencing the success of an intervention, whereas anthropologists and sociologists would view culture holistically as the context within which the intervention is taking place and with myriad roles in an intervention. Such a perspective can be neglected if one approach takes priority. Hence, research leaders need to foster open and mutually supportive communication to ensure that research team members demonstrate cross-disciplinary respect and appreciate the value of adopting a mixed method approach.

A related challenge is communication amongst researchers. In practice it can be difficult to work in multidisciplinary teams, or even to communicate findings effectively across disciplines. Public health researchers are often skilled at disseminating findings to those within their own discipline but may be less skilled at presenting findings to those who are unused to the particular vocabularies, theoretical models or favoured methods of that discipline. In a classic study, Scrimshaw and Hurtado (1988) had to consider how to disseminate their anthropological findings in appropriate ways to those from other disciplines and so reflected on these issues of communication. The Central American Diarrheal Disease Control Project they were involved in included a number of different disciplines and research methods, including basic research on pathogens that caused diarrhoeal disease, development of effective rehydration therapies, and monitoring of child health in the area, as well as anthropological research on folk health beliefs. Scrimshaw and Hurtado argue that, to be useful, the findings of anthropologists need to be presented in ways that health care planners and providers can use. In their study, they collated a detailed knowledge of local health beliefs, culture and language for effective health interventions – in this case the introduction of oral rehydration therapy to treat diarrhoeal disease. Although it is vital to know local terms for different kinds of diarrhoea in order to target health promotion effectively, and to understand local health beliefs about both the causes and potential cures, the kind of anthropological research that produces this knowledge may not be accessible for health planners not familiar with anthropological writing. The research team collated information on 'ethnoclassifications', or folk taxonomies. These proved to be complex. One classification, from a highland community in Guatemala, identified eight different kinds of diarrhoea, distinguished by their primary cause: the mother, food, tooth eruption, fallen fontanel or stomach, evil eye, stomach worms, cold or dysentery. These primary classifications were further subdivided, and different therapies were deemed appropriate for different causes. One example was diarrhoea caused by the mother being 'overheated' (from pregnancy or being out on a hot day), which might spoil her milk. In this case, the folk remedy would be to abstain from breastfeeding, or to wean the baby. The only type of diarrhoea that was seen as appropriate to take to the clinic was that of dysentery, while others were seen as amenable to home cures and various traditional healers.

These kinds of findings have significant implications for project planners. To be effective, health promotion has to reflect the different kinds of diarrhoea in the local folk classifications and terminology, and make it clear that rehydration is still needed for forms of diarrhoea that are seen as less serious than dysentery. Scrimshaw and Hurtado (1988) stress the need to present anthropological findings in ways that workers from other disciplines can understand. They used a number of strategies that aided the utilization of ethnographic findings. First, the researchers trained fieldworkers to carry out similar projects to map the folk taxonomies of the communities they worked with, and in one area clinic workers were trained to carry out rapid assessment of community beliefs. A newsletter to the wider project team regularly carries findings from the ethnographic projects. Joint workshops with clinicians and health educators were used to look at ways of integrating the findings. Rather than expecting project staff from other disciplines to read lengthy anthropological monographs, the researchers summarized the ethnoclassifications briefly as taxonomies, with diagrams if possible. These were presented at meetings wherever possible, with time to discuss them.

 Activity 16.3

1 In the case of the Scrimshaw and Hurtado study (see above), how did anthropological fieldwork inform the disease control project?
2 What factors did the authors think contributed to their influence on other professionals involved with this project?

Feedback

1 Anthropologists found that the way in which people classified diarrhoeal diseases was more complex than planners predicted, and only some causes were seen as reason to visit the primary health care post. Their findings informed the delivery of care and influenced the form of a survey; they also had an impact on training in the countries within the project.
2 The authors attributed their relative success in this multidisciplinary setting to several factors, including: meetings and workshops that included those from other disciplines; and the researchers' willingness to present findings in a clear and useful way.

An extension of this challenge of communicating across disciplines and methods is reflecting on the 'political economy' of public health research. Research agendas, as well as what kind of research is funded, are often shaped by institutions and actors other than social scientists themselves. Social scientists may have to 'defend' the utility and validity of their approaches in relation to a context which gives more capital to particular forms of data and approach. They may have little opportunity to shape the research questions driving research funding or policy agendas. Moreover, an increasing emphasis on multidisciplinary work and the promotion of mixed methods as a 'pragmatic' approach in public health research may work against approaches which are more theoretically nuanced or critical, and which help to reflect on some of the tensions generated through mixed method research.

Summary

Health practices are complex, and influenced by multiple factors. Public health research questions can rarely be addressed adequately by a single research method or data source. Using different methods of data generation and analysis, and drawing on the perspectives of different disciplines, can add to our understanding of the relationships between the multiple factors which shape health and the effects of health interventions. A fundamental challenge when conducting mixed method and multidisciplinary research is finding ways to integrate not only the findings but also the theoretical perspectives of different approaches.

References

Bourgois, P. (2002) Anthropology and epidemiology on drugs: The challenges of cross-methodological and theoretical dialogue. *International Journal of Drug Policy*, 13: 259–269.

Creswell, J.W. (2003) *Research Design. Qualitative, Quantitative and Mixed Methods Approaches.* Thousand Oaks, CA: Sage.

Davis, M., Rhodes, T. and Martin, A. (2004) Preventing hepatitis C: 'Common sense', 'the bug' and other perspectives from the risk narratives of people who inject drugs. *Social Science & Medicine*, 59: 1807–1818.

Denzin, N.K. (1989) *The Research Act: A Theoretical Introduction to Sociological Methods* (3rd edn). Englewood Cliffs, NJ: Prentice Hall.

Graham, H. (1987) Women's smoking and family health. *Social Science & Medicine*, 25: 47–56.

Graham, I.D., Logan, J., Davies, B. and Nimrod, C. (2004) Changing the use of electronic fetal monitoring and labor support: A case study of barriers and facilitators. *Birth*, 31: 293–301.

Green, S.E. (2007) 'We're tired, not sad': Benefits and burdens of mothering a child with a disability. *Social Science & Medicine*, 64: 150–163.

Judd, A., Hickman, M., Jones, S., McDonald, T., Parry, J.V., Stimson, G.V. and Hall, A.J. (2005). Incidence of hepatitis C virus and HIV among new injecting drug users in London: Prospective cohort study. *British Medical Journal*, 330: 24–25.

Lewin, S., Glenton, C. and Oxman, A.D. (2009) Use of qualitative methods alongside randomized controlled trials of complex healthcare interventions: Methodological study. *British Medical Journal*, 339: b3496.

Lopez, A.M., Bourgois, P., Wenger, L.D., Lorvick, J., Martinez, A.N. and Kral, A.H. (2013) Interdisciplinary mixed methods research with structurally vulnerable populations: Case studies of injection drug users in San Francisco. *International Journal of Drug Policy*, 24(2): 101–109.

Moss, A. (2003) Put down that shield and war rattle: Response to Philippe Bourgois. *International Journal of Drug Policy*, 14: 105–109.

Rhodes, T., Davis, M. and Judd, A. (2004) Hepatitis C and its risk management: Renewing harm reduction in the context of uncertainty. *Addiction*, 99(5): 621–633.

Scrimshaw, S. and Hurtado, E. (1988) Anthropological involvement in the central American diarrheal disease control project. *Social Science & Medicine*, 27: 97–105.

Stone, L. and Campbell, J.G. (1984) The use and misuse of surveys in international development: An experiment from Nepal. *Human Organisation*, 43(1): 27–37.

Wolff, B., Knodel, J. and Sittitrai, W. (1993) Focus groups and surveys as complementary research methods. In D.L. Morgan (ed.) *Successful Focus Groups: Advancing the State of the Art*. Newbury Park, CA: Sage.

Further reading

Mason, J. (2006) Six strategies for mixing methods and linking data in social science research. Working paper, University of Manchester. Available at http://eprints.ncrm.ac.uk/482/1/0406_six%2520strategies%2520for%2520mixing%2520methods.pdf

Saks, M. and Allsop, J. (eds) (2007) *Researching Health: Qualitative, Quantitative and Mixed Methods*. Los Angeles: Sage.

Tashakkori, A. and Teddlie, C. (eds) (2010) *Sage Handbook of Mixed Methods in Social and Behavioral Research*. Los Angeles: Sage.

Glossary

Archive A repository, either physical or electronic, where documents are conserved and made available for researchers.

Autonomy Respecting the rights of the individual to self-determination. An individual has the right to decide whether or not to take part in research.

Beneficence 'Doing good'. Researchers must always act in the best interests of study participants and prioritize their welfare.

Closed question A question on a questionnaire or interview schedule that gives the respondent a predetermined choice of responses.

Coding In qualitative analysis, the process by which data extracts are labelled as indicators of a concept.

Concepts The phenomena that the researcher is interested in (such as 'inequalities in health' or 'social status'), which are not directly observable but which are assumed to exist because they give rise to measurable phenomena.

Controlled experiment A research design in which outcomes in the experimental group are compared to those in a control group.

Cross-sectional design Aims to collect the same data from each member of a study sample at one particular point in time.

Deliberative methods Those that enable the participants to develop their own views as part of the process.

Documentary sources All sources of information that are written or printed. They may be verbal or visual.

Focus groups Groups of people brought together to discuss a topic, with one or more facilitators who introduce and guide the discussion and record it in some way.

Generalizability In survey research, the extent to which the results from a sample survey can be applied to the whole population.

Hypothesis A provisional explanation for the phenomenon being studied.

In-depth interviews The interviewer uses a topic list, but respondents' priorities influence the final range of questions covered.

Indicators The empirical attributes of variables that can be observed and measured (such as 'blood pressure' or 'monthly wage').

Interaction Communication between people.

Interpretive approaches Approaches that focus on understanding human behaviour from the perspective of those being studied.

Justice This relates to the fair selection of research participants, avoiding populations which may be coerced into participation (e.g. prisoners) and ensuring that research outcomes are distributed equitably.

Measurement scale The level of measurement used (nominal, ordinal, ratio, interval).

Method A set of strategies for asking useful questions, designing a study, collecting data and analysing data.

Methodology The study of the principles of investigation, including the philosophical foundations of choice of methods.

Multidisciplinary Combining two or more different disciplines.

Natural groups Groups which occur 'naturally', such as workmates or household members.

Naturalism Studying social behaviour in the context in which it 'naturally' occurs.

Non-maleficence 'First, do no harm'. Researchers must consider the potential risks involved in taking part in a study and must do their utmost to remove and reduce these harms and ensure that the benefits of participation outweigh the risks.

Non-sampling error The amount of error in the data we have collected that is due to problems with the reliability and validity of our data collection instrument (as opposed to problems with our sampling of the population).

Observational designs Aim to record, describe and understand the meaning of what is happening in a particular setting.

Open question A question on a questionnaire or interview schedule that allows the respondent to give any answer.

Operationalization The process of identifying the appropriate variables from concepts or constructs and finding adequate and specific indicators of variables.

Oral history Interview-based recollection of events in the past.

Paradigm A set of beliefs and practices shared by a scientific community at a particular point in time.

Phenomena Objects of people's perceptions, or situations that are observed to exist or happen, whose cause or explanation may be in question.

Positivism A philosophy of science that assumes that reality is stable and can be researched by measuring observable indicators.

Primary sources The documents from which original, raw data are drawn.

Probability sample Each member of the population has a random and known chance of being selected.

Qualitative Pertaining to the nature of phenomena: how they are classified.

Quantitative Pertaining to the measurement of phenomena.

Rapport Relaxed, natural communication between interviewer and respondent.

Reflexivity Self-awareness about your role in the research process, and how your personal and professional values, assumptions and experiences can influence this process.

Relativism An alternative to positivism, which assumes that reality can change depending on who is observing it and from what perspective.

Reliability The extent to which an instrument is free from error.

Response rate The proportion of those sampled who responded.

Sample Group of respondents drawn from a population to represent the whole.

Sampling error Limitations on how far inferences from a sample can be generalized to the whole population.

Secondary sources Books or peer-reviewed articles in which findings based on primary data are presented.

Semi-structured interviews The interviewer uses a guide in which set questions are covered, but can prompt for more information.

Structured interviews The interviewer uses a schedule in which questions are read out in a predetermined order.

Triangulation Using different data sets, methods or approaches to improve the validity of findings.

Validity The extent to which an indicator measures what it purports to measure.

Variables Aspects of phenomena that change (such as 'disease severity' or 'income').

Index

Note: Glossary terms are in **bold** type.